Online Chinese Learning

Online Chinese Learning aims to investigate the types of language learning strategies (LLSs) that online Chinese learners use across asynchronous and synchronous learning environments in different learning contexts.

This book examines how the use of language learning strategies by online Chinese learners is influenced by the interactants; the characteristics of the specific learning context; and selected individual learner characteristics. This book will provide: (1) new and detailed information about students' LLS use in online Chinese learning; (2) insights into how individual students adopt LLSs and technological tools to solve learning problems in various learning contexts; (3) an exploration of factors influencing LLS use; and (4) recommendations regarding LLS adoption, use, and training.

This book will be a valuable resource for university instructors in languages, language teaching methods, and second language acquisition, as well as researchers in languages, linguistics, and language learning and teaching.

Lijuan Chen gained her PhD from the School of Humanities, Languages and Social Science at Griffith University, Australia. Her research interests include technology-enhanced language teaching and learning, and in particular, language-learning-strategy adoption in online and distance learning, Chinese as a foreign language, and foreign language learners' educational experiences. She has taught Chinese in China and Singapore, and teaches both Chinese and English in Australia.

Routledge Studies in Chinese as a Foreign Language
Series Editor: Chris Shei, Swansea University, UK
and Der-lin Chao, New York University, USA

The series will strive to produce not only scholarly books investigating aspects of Chinese language learning such as pedagogy, policy, materials and curriculum, assessment, psychology and cognition, aptitude and motivation, culture and society, media and technology and so on, but also textbooks drawing from results of this research and compiled following the pedagogical models suggested by these studies and taking into consideration the individual and social factors related to Chinese language learning uncovered by this series of research. The two strands of books published within this series complement and strengthen each other in their academic achievement and practical implication.

Teaching and Researching Chinese Second Language Listening
Wei Cai

Teaching Chinese by Culture and TV Drama
Lingfen Zhang

Reading in Chinese as an Additional Language
Learners' Development, Instruction, and Assessment
Edited by Liu Li and Dongbo Zhang

Online Chinese Learning
Exploring Effective Language Learning Strategies
Lijuan Chen

For more information about this series, please visit: www.routledge.com/Routledge-Studies-in-Chinese-as-a-Foreign-Language/book-series/RSCFL

Online Chinese Learning
Exploring Effective Language Learning Strategies

Lijuan Chen

LONDON AND NEW YORK

Designed cover image: nazar_ab via Getty Images

First published 2024
by Routledge
4 Park Square, Milton Park, Abingdon, Oxon OX14 4RN

and by Routledge
605 Third Avenue, New York, NY 10158

Routledge is an imprint of the Taylor & Francis Group, an informa business

© 2024 Lijuan Chen

The right of Lijuan Chen to be identified as author of this work has been asserted in accordance with sections 77 and 78 of the Copyright, Designs and Patents Act 1988.

All rights reserved. No part of this book may be reprinted or reproduced or utilised in any form or by any electronic, mechanical, or other means, now known or hereafter invented, including photocopying and recording, or in any information storage or retrieval system, without permission in writing from the publishers.

Trademark notice: Product or corporate names may be trademarks or registered trademarks, and are used only for identification and explanation without intent to infringe.

British Library Cataloguing-in-Publication Data
A catalogue record for this book is available from the British Library

Library of Congress Cataloging-in-Publication Data
Names: Chen, Lijuan (Chinese teacher), author.
Title: Online Chinese learning : exploring effective language learning strategies / Lijuan Chen.
Description: Abingdon, Oxon ; New York, NY : Routledge, 2024. | Series: Routledge studies in Chinese as a foreign language | Includes bibliographical references and index.
Identifiers: LCCN 2023037800 (print) | LCCN 2023037801 (ebook) | ISBN 9781032479149 (hardback) | ISBN 9781032479125 (paperback) | ISBN 9781003386513 (ebook)
Subjects: LCSH: Chinese language—Study and teaching—Foreign speakers. | Chinese language—Computer-assisted instruction for foreign speakers. | Web-based instruction.
Classification: LCC PL1065 .C5628 2024 (print) | LCC PL1065 (ebook) | DDC 495.180078/5—dc23/eng/20231026
LC record available at https://lccn.loc.gov/2023037800
LC ebook record available at https://lccn.loc.gov/2023037801

ISBN: 978-1-032-47914-9 (hbk)
ISBN: 978-1-032-47912-5 (pbk)
ISBN: 978-1-003-38651-3 (ebk)

DOI: 10.4324/9781003386513

Typeset in Times New Roman
by codeMantra

Contents

Preface   *xi*

1 **Introduction**   1
   1.1 Chinese language learning around the world 2
   1.2 Learning challenges and this book 5
   1.3 The online Chinese programme and the research project 7
      1.3.1 The online Chinese programme for this research project 7
      1.3.2 Participants 12
      1.3.3 In-depth individual student studies 14
      1.3.4 Data collection and research instruments 14
   1.4 Organisation of this book 16
   1.5 Audience 16
   1.6 How this book is different 16

2 **Review of related study fields**   21
   2.1 Online learning and TELL 21
      2.1.1 Online learning 21
      2.1.2 TELL 22
   2.2 Chinese as a particularly difficult language for English speakers to learn 24
   2.3 LLSs and LLS research 25
      2.3.1 Definition of LLS 25
      2.3.2 LLS research 26
      2.3.3 TELL task types and LLS adoption 27
      2.3.4 LLS training 28
   2.4 LLS research in online language learning 28
      2.4.1 Affective strategies 29
      2.4.2 Cognitive strategies 29
      2.4.3 Social strategies 30

    2.4.4 Memory strategies 33
    2.4.5 Compensation strategies 33
    2.4.6 Metacognitive strategies 34
    2.4.7 LLSs specific to online learning 35
    2.4.8 Summary of LLS research in online language learning 36
2.5 An overview of Chinese LLS research 36
    2.5.1 LLS adoption in Chinese language learning 37
    2.5.2 Chinese-character-learning strategy use 38
    2.5.3 LLS use in Chinese speaking 39
    2.5.4 LLS use in Chinese essay writing 39
    2.5.5 Chinese LLS use in TELL 40
2.6 Different variables that influence LLS adoption 40
    2.6.1 Individual differences 41
    2.6.2 Motivation 41
    2.6.3 Language proficiency 42
    2.6.4 Learner autonomy 43
    2.6.5 Age 44
2.7 Summary 45

3 The repertoire of LLSs in online Chinese learning   54

3.1 Introduction 54
3.2 LLSs obtained from the self-reported data 66
    3.2.1 LLS use by category 66
    3.2.2 Affective strategies 67
    3.2.3 Cognitive strategies 71
    3.2.4 Social strategies 76
    3.2.5 Memory strategies 81
    3.2.6 Compensation strategies 85
    3.2.7 Metacognitive strategies 86
3.3 LLSs obtained from the observed data 90
    3.3.1 LLS adoption observed in the asynchronous learning environment 91
    3.3.2 LLS adoption observed in the synchronous learning environment 98
3.4 Summary 104

4 Factors influencing LLS adoption   107

4.1 Introduction 107
4.2 The impact of the learning contexts and interactants on the participants' LLS use 107

4.2.1 The impact of the asynchronous and synchronous
environments on the participants' LLS use 108
4.2.2 The impact of the interactants on the participants'
LLS use 115
4.3 The impact of individual-learner characteristics on the
participants' LLS use 121
4.3.1 Motives for learning Chinese and LLS use 122
4.3.2 Learning goals and LLS use 127
4.3.3 Age and LLS use 133
4.3.4 Length of prior learning of Chinese and LLS use 138
4.4 Summary 141

5 Individual LLS reports on the interviewees 143
5.1 Student 5 (S5) 143
5.1.1 Background information, learning motives, goals,
difficulties, and strengths 143
5.1.2 The key LLSs used by S5 and the tools used for these
LLSs 144
5.1.3 Summary of S5's LLS report 147
5.2 Student 18 (S18) 148
5.2.1 Background information, learning motives, goals,
difficulties, and strengths 148
5.2.2 The key LLSs used by S18 and the tools used for these
LLSs 149
5.2.3 Summary of S18's LLS report 151
5.3 Student 8 (S8) 152
5.3.1 Background information, learning motives, goals,
difficulties, and strengths 152
5.3.2 The key LLSs used by S8 and the tools used for these LLSs 153
5.3.3 Summary of S8's LLS report 157
5.4 Student 9 (S9) 157
5.4.1 Background information, learning motives, goals,
difficulties, and strengths 157
5.4.2 The key LLSs used by S9 and the tools used for these
LLSs 158
5.4.3 Summary of S9's LLS report 161
5.5 Student 10 (S10) 161
5.5.1 Background information, learning motives, goals,
difficulties, and strengths 161
5.5.2 The key LLSs used by S10 and the tools used for these
LLSs 162

viii Contents

      5.5.3 Summary of S10's LLS report 164
   5.6 Student 12 (S12) 165
      5.6.1 Background information, learning motives, goals, difficulties, and strengths 165
      5.6.2 The key LLSs used by S12 and the tools used for these LLSs 166
      5.6.3 Summary of S12's LLS report 169
   5.7 Student 13 (S13) 169
      5.7.1 Background information, learning motives, goals, difficulties, and strengths 169
      5.7.2 The key LLSs used by S13 and the tools used for these LLSs 170
      5.7.3 Summary of S13's LLS report 172
   5.8 Student 14 (S14) 172
      5.8.1 Background information, learning motives, goals, difficulties, and strengths 172
      5.8.2 The key LLSs used by S14 and the tools used for these LLSs 173
      5.8.3 Summary of S14's LLS report 176
   5.9 Student 15 (S15) 176
      5.9.1 Background information, learning motives, goals, difficulties, and strengths 176
      5.9.2 The key LLSs used by S15 and the tools used for these LLSs 177
      5.9.3 Summary of S15's LLS report 180
   5.10 Student 17 (S17) 180
      5.10.1 Background information, learning motives, goals, difficulties, and strengths 180
      5.10.2 The key LLSs used by S17 and the tools used for these LLSs 181
      5.10.3 Summary of S17's LLS report 185

6 Discussion and recommendations for online Chinese learning   **186**
   6.1 Introduction 186
   6.2 Key findings and recommendations in regard to LLS use in self-directed learning outside online classes 186
      6.2.1 Affective strategies 186
      6.2.2 Cognitive strategies 192
      6.2.3 Social strategies 196
      6.2.4 Memory strategies 198

6.2.5 Metacognitive strategies 202
6.2.6 Summary 204
6.3 Key findings and recommendations in regard to LLS use in assessment-task completion 205
  6.3.1 Cognitive strategies 205
  6.3.2 Social strategies 207
  6.3.3 Compensation strategies 210
  6.3.4 Summary 211
6.4 Key findings and recommendations in regard to LLS use in online class participation 212
  6.4.1 Cognitive strategies 212
  6.4.2 Social strategies 214
  6.4.3 Summary 217
6.5 Two important observations from this research project 218
  6.5.1 The importance of technology in LLS use 218
  6.5.2 The complexity of LLS classification 219
6.6 Summary 220

7 Conclusion 229
7.1 Introduction 229
7.2 Contributions of this book 229
7.3 Implications for online language teaching and learning 231
7.4 Limitations of this research project 233
7.5 Recommendations for future research 233

Appendix I: Survey questionnaire	235
Appendix II: Interview questions	240
Index	243

Preface

Language learning strategies (LLSs) are 'complex, dynamic thoughts and actions, selected and used by learners with some degree of consciousness in specific contexts in order to regulate multiple aspects of themselves (such as cognitive, emotional, and social) for the purpose of 1) accomplishing language tasks; 2) improving language performance or use; and/or 3) enhancing long-term proficiency' (Oxford, 2017, p. 48). Considerable research into LLSs has demonstrated their significance in making learning more effective and enjoyable, and has contributed to advancements in pedagogy as well as language learning theory.

Online language learning has become an integral part of 21st-century education. This newer form of learning has presented specific challenges which require language learners to adopt particular LLSs and develop new LLSs to effectively manage their learning. However, existing LLS studies have largely been concerned with on-campus students. Furthermore, there has been a lack of context-specific LLS research in online language learning, that is, research that distinguishes between synchronous and asynchronous environments.

With the popularity of the Chinese language increasing globally over recent decades, this book aims to investigate the types of LLSs that online Chinese learners use across asynchronous and synchronous learning environments in the contexts of self-directed learning, assessment task completion, and online class participation. It also examines how online Chinese learners' use of LLSs is influenced by the interactants, the characteristics of the specific learning context, and selected individual-learner characteristics.

This research project employed a mixed-methods approach to investigate online Chinese language learners' LLS use. Four research instruments were utilised: an online survey questionnaire adapted from the Strategy Inventory for Language Learning (SILL) (Oxford, 1990), online interviews, observations of online classes, and tracking of learner activity online.

The investigation of online Chinese students' LLS use in this book is of significance in four areas. It has provided: (1) new and detailed information about students' LLS use in online Chinese learning; (2) insights into how individual students adopt both LLSs and technological tools to solve learning problems in various learning contexts; (3) an exploration of factors influencing LLS use – on one hand, the characteristics of language-learning contexts (asynchronous or synchronous environments, and interactants) and, on the other, individual learner characteristics (motives, learning goals, age, and length of prior learning of Chinese); and (4) recommendations regarding LLS adoption, use, and training.

This book would not be in its current shape without the guidance and support of Associate Professor Yuping Wang, Dr Claire Kennedy, and Dr Claire Rodway, all at Griffith University, Australia. The author would also like to extend her gratitude to the series editor, Associate Professor Chris Shei, for his encouragement with regard to getting this work published. A special thank you goes out to the participants who generously volunteered their time to take part in this research.

References

Oxford, R. (1990). *Language learning strategies: What every teacher should know*. Boston, UK: Newbury House.
Oxford, R. (2017). *Teaching and researching language learning strategies: Self-regulation in context* (2nd ed.). New York, NY: Routledge.

1 Introduction

Give a man a fish and he eats for a day. Show him how to fish and he eats for a lifetime.
授人以鱼，不如授人以渔。

Ancient Chinese Proverb

Online language courses, along with the increasingly popular massive open online courses (MOOCs), have begun to be offered by many universities over the past decade. The recent COVID-19 pandemic further sped up the adoption of online learning in language courses by universities around the world. However, as a relatively new form of learning, online learning has its own features and challenges. There is, therefore, an urgent need to update our understanding of online students' language-learning-strategy (LLS) use in order to help them learn more effectively and autonomously. LLSs have been defined as

> complex, dynamic thoughts and actions, selected and used by learners with some degree of consciousness in specific contexts in order to regulate multiple aspects of themselves for the purpose of a) accomplishing language tasks; b) improving language performance or use; and/or c) enhancing long-term proficiency.
>
> (Oxford, 2017, p. 48)

This book explores the types of LLSs that online Chinese learners use across asynchronous and synchronous learning environments in the contexts of self-directed learning, assessment task completion, and online class participation. It also examines how online Chinese learners' use of LLSs is influenced by the interactants, the characteristics of the specific learning context, and selected individual learner characteristics. Appropriate LLS use is particularly important in online language learning, as LLSs can assist students in coping with various learning tasks enjoyably and effectively. Conversely, poor LLS selection can inhibit the students' learning and lead to loss of motivation and increased frustration. The book is based on research conducted among students enrolled in the online Chinese courses offered by Griffith University through the Open Universities Australia (OUA).

DOI: 10.4324/9781003386513-1

1.1 Chinese language learning around the world

The Chinese language discussed in this book is Modern Standard Chinese (also known as Mandarin and Putonghua), which is the official language of the People's Republic of China (PRC). The language is written in Chinese characters, which are referred to here using simplified Chinese characters. Pinyin, or Hanyu Pinyin, refers to the official phonetic system developed in 1958 by the Chinese government for transcribing the Mandarin pronunciation of Chinese characters into the Latin alphabet (B. Zhang, 2002). The Pinyin system reproduces the sounds to assist language learners who are familiar with the Roman alphabet. Pinyin can also be used as an input method for typing Chinese characters on computers or handheld devices.

Globally, the popularity of the Chinese language has been gradually increasing over recent decades. For example, Chinese was ranked the second most essential business language behind English in the 2011 Bloomberg Rankings (Wang, 2012). In the USA, there were over 500 schools and universities offering Chinese language programmes in 2011 (Liu & Wang, 2018), whilst in the United Kingdom (UK), an online Chinese course has been offered by the Open University since 2009 (Stickler & Shi, 2013). This increasing interest in learning Chinese is evidenced by the number of candidates enrolling in Chinese language proficiency tests. In 2013, there were 56 test centres in mainland China and 800 overseas, and over 370,000 international test-takers took the New Hànyǔ Shuǐpíng Kǎoshì (HSK, a test of Chinese language proficiency) in that year alone (D. Zhang & Lin, 2017).

In Australia, Chinese has also attracted much attention because of the strong political, investment, and trade relationships between China and Australia, as well as factors such as educational exchanges and research and development in science and technology (ACARA, 2015; Wang, 2012). Over time, Australian governments have tried various initiatives to encourage students to learn Chinese as a foreign language. For example, in the late 1980s and early 1990s, the Hawke government tried to promote the teaching of Asian languages and studies through the National Asian Languages and Studies in Australian Schools (NALSAS) Program (Harrington, 2012).

Despite such initiatives, the enthusiasm of students for learning Chinese has remained low (Sturak & Naughten, 2010). This led the current Australian government to develop a target that by the end of 2020, 12% of Year 12 students will be fluent in one of four key Asian languages (Chinese, Japanese, Korean, and Indonesian) (Sturak & Naughten, 2010). However, whilst the NALSAS Program appears to have been successful in promoting proficiency in Japanese, this has not been the case with Chinese. Orton's report, *Chinese Language Education in Australian Schools*, provided three reasons for the current situation – that is, the slow rate of progress in Chinese learning – namely: (1) the difficulty of learning the language, (2) the lack of qualified Chinese teachers familiar with learner-centred classrooms, and (3) students' learning behaviour in Australia (Orton, 2016).

As of 2022, most Australian universities offer students Chinese language programmes and courses on campuses, and some offer online Chinese language courses (e.g., Deakin University, the University of New England, and the University of Queensland). It is clear, therefore, that there is an acknowledged understanding of the importance of learning Chinese, despite the limited success in achieving this at the school level.

In parallel, distance language learning has developed rapidly in recent decades with constant improvements in delivery modes. Before the 21st century, distance language learning mainly relied on broadcasting and TV, with printed materials delivered from the universities to the language learners (Stickler & Shi, 2013) through postal services. As a result, distance language learners had limited opportunities to communicate with their peers or proficient speakers in the target language. In the 21st century, however, both asynchronous and synchronous tools have been introduced to support distance language learning (Stickler & Shi, 2013). The asynchronous tools, such as discussion forums, text chat, and email, enable language learners to interact with their teachers and peers online anywhere and anytime. The synchronous tools, such as Skype, Elluminate, FlashMeeting, WebCT, Zoom, Blackboard Collaborate, and DimDim, allow communication online simultaneously, but from a distance.

In such distance learning modes, language learners can study at their own pace by themselves or interact with other students and language teachers synchronously or asynchronously through group work, discussions, and peer feedback. This means online students need to learn how to learn in order to be effective, and they have to take responsibility for using appropriate LLSs and developing new ones to adapt to online learning. They also need to apply LLSs to evaluate their own learning outcomes through a combination of study, discussion, investigation, and practice. However, how distance language learners can learn most effectively in an online environment still remains a challenging issue (Bezuidenhout, 2018). Understanding the importance of LLSs, and how best to apply them in language learning is clearly important in providing an effective means whereby online students can learn a foreign language. Just as the ancient Chinese proverb at the beginning of this chapter suggests, helping students to develop methods and strategies for learning is of greater benefit to them in the long term than a one-off handout.

LLS research is a product of research interest in what explains individual variations in language learning achievement (Ellis, 2008, 2012), and is very much related to the development of psychology theories, initially influenced by behaviourism, and later by constructivism. Behaviourism, which dominated psychology over a long period, sees learning as the product of teaching (De Bot et al., 2005). In 1957, Skinner published a landmark book called *Verbal Behaviour* in which he suggested that, from a behaviourist perspective, only observable and measurable learning behaviour is worthy of study, and that, as a rule, language learners are best equipped to solve learning problems when they are assisted by instructors and a small group of upper-level students (Livengood et al., 2012).

At that time, the grammar-translation method dominated language teaching (Griffiths, 2004). The grammar-translation method highlights the teaching of grammar and practising translating from the first language to the target language. It also focuses more on reading and writing than listening and speaking. As a consequence,

LLSs were rarely mentioned in the literature of that time, and there is now a general assumption that LLS use is limited by this teaching approach (Griffiths, 2004).

However, this situation changed as cognitive theories began to be developed in psychology in the 1960s (Ellis, 2012; Griffiths, 2004). In cognitive psychology, learning is seen as a constructive process in which learners focus on the construction of meaning rather than knowledge and skill acquisition (Bruning, 2004). Constructivism as a learning theory in the field of education builds on theories of cognitive and social constructivism (Kaufman, 2004), and is influenced by cognitive theory. With the introduction of these theories, language educational research switched its focus to learners and their second language acquisition (O'Malley & Chamot, 1990). Second language learning and teaching research gradually shifted its emphasis from a teacher-centred to a learner-centred approach (Livengood et al., 2012; Nunan, 1992). A learner-centred approach highlights the learner's role as a decision-maker and responsibility taker. It considers learners' interests, enthusiasm, and aspirations in the learning process first (Brown, 2007).

Constructivism is concerned with two areas in the language-learning process: social interactions in building a linguistic system, and learners' language acquisition, which focuses on obtaining meaning out of existent linguistic input (Brown, 2007; Bruning, 2004). LLS research has been influenced by two types of constructivist theories: cognitive constructivism and social constructivism. In LLS research that was founded on cognitive constructivism (e.g., O'Malley & Chamot, 1990; Oxford, 1990; Oxford & Nyikos, 1989), learning was seen as consisting of mental processes as part of a cognitive activity. LLSs could be understood as 'special ways of processing information that enhance comprehension, learning, or retention of the information' (p. 1) and 'strategic processes' (p. 12) (O'Malley & Chamot, 1990). Later, social constructivists emphasised the role of social context and culture in the language-learning process. LLS researchers concentrated on learners' language-learning experiences in specific contexts, and the cultural backgrounds which, in turn, shape their behaviour patterns through their previous learning experiences (e.g., Gao, 2006, 2008, 2010; Norton & Toohey, 2001; Wenden, 1998).

The literature on LLSs presented in previous research has led to the development of various LLS classification systems. Rubin (1975) first explored the features of a good language learner, and later O'Malley and Chamot (1990) and Oxford (1990) developed two widely accepted LLS classification systems to present an explicit description and classification of LLSs. More recently, scholars have suggested different LLS classifications, such as Cohen, Oxford, and Chi's (2002) LLS classification, which corresponded to the four macro skills (listening, speaking, reading, and writing), and Dörnyei's (2014) suggestion of a four-component LLS classification. In 2011, Oxford updated her LLS classification and introduced the Strategic Self-Regulation (S^2R) framework and discussed the strategic role of self-regulation in LLS use (Oxford, 2011). Recently, Oxford (2017) focused on LLS use in diverse contexts and provided an intensive discussion of self-regulation and related factors as the core of LLSs.

LLS research has developed quickly and constantly, but the emphasis on understanding students' use of LLSs in various learning contexts has not been taken up by research into online students, especially their LLS use in synchronous environments (i.e., online class participation). On the other hand, a number of studies (Akiyama & Saito, 2016; Altunay, 2014; Hadwin et al., 2018; Hauck & Hampel, 2008; Huang et al., 2009; Lai et al., 2022; Rasheed, Kamsin, & Abdullah, 2021; Solak & Cakir, 2015) have paid special attention to LLS use by online students in the learning contexts related to asynchronous environments. However, there is an ongoing shift of LLS use in terms of the increasing use of synchronous technologies. As Xu (2010) explained, in response to what has been discovered about the way in which the human brain works, a different online learning environment that stimulates the senses in various ways is emerging with more and more varied input clues (e.g., those associated with colour, shape, distance, name, and size) via technologies. In other words, in comparison with asynchronous learning, the synchronous learning environment presents learners with different kinds of challenges that call for the use of different LLSs. Nevertheless, research into LLS use in online Chinese learning remains scant. Therefore, given all the above, we can see the importance of investigating and improving LLS use in online language learning, and especially in online Chinese learning.

1.2 Learning challenges and this book

It is commonly acknowledged that learning a foreign language is a challenge for adult learners in a non-target-language-speaking country, such as English speakers learning Chinese in English-speaking countries. Furthermore, for English speakers, the character-based Chinese language is generally seen as a more time-consuming and difficult language to learn than alphabetic languages such as Spanish and Italian (Bureau of Human Resources, 2016). Such a perception can be attributed to features of the Chinese language itself, such as its orthography (Kan & McCormick, 2014; Shen, 2005; Shen & Xu, 2015), or pronunciation and tones (Kan & McCormick, 2014). For learners who choose to study Chinese language as part of a distance education programme, these difficulties are compounded.

One of the major challenges for distance language learners who study online is their lack of knowledge of strategies for that learning environment (Efriana, 2021; Reinders & Hubbard, 2013). Learning how to learn in this setting means that the learners reflect on their language learning and LLS use whilst simultaneously learning the target language. Sharples et al. (2014) explained that this involves 'double-loop thinking' which is more complex than 'single-loop thinking'. In double-loop thinking, students need to adapt to the learning environment, solve learning problems, and adjust their learning behaviours in order to achieve their learning goals. Language teachers in online courses can facilitate student learning by applying double-loop thinking and incorporating LLS training into their course design and delivery, so as to guide learners to acquire and practise LLSs.

In order to understand how languages can be effectively learnt online, it is important to investigate what LLSs students use, and what LLSs they need to develop in a fully online learning environment. Tracking online students' strategy adoption and changes in their strategy use during the learning process can, therefore, be expected to extend our understanding of which LLSs are effective in improving language learning outcomes and which are not. For example, it is important to comprehend how LLSs that are classified as 'social strategies' could be used effectively in collaborating with a language partner in completing a written assignment.

Therefore, this present book was inspired by online Chinese learners and their LLS use in an asynchronous environment (i.e., self-directed learning outside online classes and assessment task completion outside online classes in a synchronous environment, i.e., online class participation). It also concerns how online Chinese learners' LLS use is influenced by the interactants and the characteristics of the specific learning context (i.e., self-directed learning outside online classes, assessment task completion outside online classes, and online class participation), and individual learner characteristics.

In this book, Oxford's (1990) taxonomy for traditional language learning was used as the basic tool to explore LLS use, in the expectation that it could be extended to produce an appropriate classification scheme for the online learning environment and could potentially lead to the discovery of some LLSs specific to Chinese learning. Oxford's (1990) classification comprises two categories of strategies: direct (cognitive, memory, compensation strategies) and indirect (affective, social, metacognitive strategies).

In Chinese-language learning online, students can be expected to adopt three kinds of LLSs: (1) LLSs that are used in language learning generally and are not specific to online learning or Chinese, (2) LLSs that are specific to synchronous and asynchronous environments in online learning, and (3) LLSs specific to Chinese learning.

This book also focuses on the technological tools (language-learning tools, Collaborate Classroom functions, and communication tools) that support learners' LLS use. The online Chinese courses in this book contain two main learning environments: a synchronous environment and an asynchronous environment. The synchronous environment refers to the online classes, which are conducted in Blackboard Collaborate. This allows students to communicate with their teachers and peers online simultaneously from a distance. The asynchronous environment consists of a web-based discussion board, wikis, online quizzes, email, and WeChat.

This book provides a picture of the process of LLS decision-making by studying a particular group of online Chinese language learners. It focuses on students who enrolled in the online Chinese courses provided by Griffith University through OUA. This online Chinese programme is offered at beginning, intermediate, and advanced levels. Both asynchronous and synchronous tools are used in the courses.

In the study, which relied on a mixed-methods design, students in the online Chinese courses reported their LLS adoption through taking part in a survey questionnaire and an interview. Ten of the survey respondents participated in the interview in order to provide further evidence to verify the data collected from the survey. An individual student report was then compiled for each interviewee, which was also used to inform my analysis of individual learner characteristics as an influencing factor in LLS adoption. With the students' consent, I also observed their learning behaviour in online classes and tracked their learning activities online through Blackboard Collaborate. Students' emails and instant messages (such as those from the messaging app WeChat) related to their collaborative learning were also collected on a voluntary basis in order to enrich the data.

1.3 The online Chinese programme and the research project

1.3.1 *The online Chinese programme for this research project*

The Chinese courses reported in this book contain Chinese-language-learning resources, assessment items, and the asynchronous and synchronous environments that were provided by Griffith University. The unit Modern Standard Chinese (Mandarin) 1A (CHN11) is used in this section as an example to introduce the learning design of the course, including its instructional approaches and assessment task design, and the learning environments and the technologies used in this programme to support student learning.

Overview of the Chinese programme

Increasing demand for language learning through distance education encouraged OUA to introduce the online Chinese programme for distance language learners, which was provided by Griffith University from 2010. This is a fully online Chinese programme consisting of six courses (or 'units' in the OUA system): CHN11 and CHN12 at the beginning level, CHN221 and CHN222 at the intermediate level, and CHN31 and CHN32 at the advanced level (Wang, 2014). The following description of the basic features of this online programme is based on the information contained in the CHN11 Study Guide (Wang, 2014). The information on the learning design used in the online Chinese programme was discussed in Wang and Chen (2013).

Learning design

The learning design highlighted a learner-centred teaching and learning process, which took into account students' characteristics, such as students' knowledge of educational technology. Three learning and teaching approaches were adopted: collaborating, scaffolding, and a flipped classroom. Each course was delivered through a mix of synchronous online classes and asynchronous interactions. The synchronous online classes (two hours for the beginners' course CHN11, one hour for other courses) were conducted in Blackboard Collaborate, a 'cyber face-to-face classroom' (Wang & Chen, 2012, p. 314), on a weekly basis. The asynchronous environment consisted of a web-based discussion board, wikis, journals, announcements, mini-lecture videos on basic grammatical knowledge, online quizzes, and emails. Each study period had a duration of 13 weeks, covering 10 lessons in the core textbook, titled *Short-Term Spoken Chinese* (Ma, 2005). There were about 10 students attending each online class. Students learnt using both paper-based resources, such as textbooks and Chinese-character tracing sheets, and digital resources, such as character-learning apps (e.g., Quizlet), audio materials, mini-lecture videos, lecture recordings of the online classes, and digital sound files accompanying the textbook. They practised Chinese and interacted with the teacher and other classmates through collaborative learning in both the online classes and the various collaborative assessment tasks.

Learners in these courses mainly rely on self-directed learning, along with the weekly online classes (Wang & Chen, 2013). Therefore, a flipped-classroom approach was adopted to meet the needs of the learners (Wang, 2014). In short, this approach required students to master the basic contents such as grammar and vocabulary before attending the online classes. In such mastery-based learning, they needed to watch the prerecorded mini-lecture videos on grammar, learn all the new vocabulary, go through the texts in the textbook, and complete various exercises and online quizzes for each lesson. In class, instead of explaining new grammar and vocabulary, the teacher and the students focused on practising the new vocabulary, and understanding the associated linguistic features, grammar, and usage, through collaboration in task completion. Thus, students were encouraged to fully prepare for each lesson before the class within an asynchronous environment, and then engage in learning activities in the synchronous environment. If the students did not master the basic content in advance and were always absent from the online classes, they would find it extremely difficult to achieve the desired learning outcomes.

Assessment-tasks design

LLS adoption by students is significantly influenced by the language-learning tasks they are set (Oxford, 1990). In the Chinese programme under investigation, the assessment tasks formed the core tasks for each course and were designed as an ongoing evaluation to reflect and assess students' learning progress (Wang & Chen, 2013). For example, students who enrolled in CHN11, CHN222, or CHN32 were required to progressively complete five assessment tasks in the 13-week study period, as summarised in Table 1.1.

Table 1.1 reflects two important aspects of assessment design that were present in all the online Chinese courses within this OUA programme at Griffith University. Firstly, the design was aimed at improving students' four macro skills through completion of various assessment tasks which focus on Chinese reading, listening, speaking, and writing. Nine types of language-learning tasks were involved: (1) exercises for each lesson; (2) practising writing Chinese words; (3) online quizzes; (4) translation exercises; (5) lecture-notes submission; (6) group wiki writing; (7) role play; (8) preparation for a written test; and (9) preparation for an oral test. Secondly, the design required students to complete the tasks in both synchronous and asynchronous environments, and both individually and collaboratively.

The framework for this online assessment design comprised three related dimensions: interaction, collaboration, and reflection (Wang & Chen, 2013). The interaction dimension highlighted the communications between and among

Table 1.1 Assessment tasks and modes of interaction for the courses at the three proficiency levels

Tasks	Modern Standard Chinese 1A (CHN11, Beginning)	Modern Standard Chinese 2B (CHN222, Intermediate)	Modern Standard Chinese 3B (CHN32, Advanced)	Mode
Weekly activities	Completing all the exercises for each lesson in the textbook and recording these exercises with a language partner in Collaborate; practising writing all the new words	Completing all the exercises for each lesson in the textbook and recording these exercises with a language partner in Collaborate; translating 10 sentences from English to Chinese	Completing all the exercises for each lesson in the textbook and recording these exercises with a language partner in Collaborate; translating 10 sentences from English to Chinese	Asynchronous, individual; synchronous, paired
	Watching mini-lecture videos and completing online quizzes Submitting lecture notes	Watching mini-lecture videos and completing online quizzes Submitting lecture notes	Watching mini-lecture videos and completing online quizzes Submitting lecture notes	Asynchronous, individual Asynchronous, individual
Speaking assignment	Role-playing a 1–2-minute interview in pairs in Collaborate	Role-playing in pairs in Collaborate: 4 scenes	Presenting a 2-minute talk in Chinese on a given topic	Synchronous, paired
Written assignment	Designing a group webpage using a wiki in both Chinese and English	Transcribing lecture recordings	Designing two editions of a Chinese newspaper on the wiki in collaboration with a language partner	Asynchronous, individual; collaborative
Written test	None	Translating sentences and paragraphs from English into Chinese	Answering grammar questions; completing reading-comprehension questions	Synchronous, individual;
Final oral test	Presenting a 1.5-minute talk and answering questions from the assessor	Playing the role of a guest to attend a 10-minute interview with the assessor; telling a 2–3-minute story	Playing the role of a Chinese language teacher and teaching for 10 minutes	Synchronous, individual, paired

students and teachers. The collaboration dimension focused on co-constructing knowledge in a learning community, such as in role play or wiki writing. The reflection dimension referred to the individual reflection on language learning to develop students' metacognitive strategies, such as the use of ongoing weekly reading-comprehension quizzes (online). Students were expected to gain benefits from collaborating with peers and groups, which included the promotion of deep learning, critical thinking skills, shared understanding, and high levels of participation, achievement, and self-esteem (Wang & Chen, 2013).

The asynchronous and synchronous environments

In a well-designed language-learning course that specifically focuses on online language learners, both asynchronous and synchronous functionalities should be provided in order to build an interactive and a collaborative learning environment (Wang & Chen, 2009). The main purpose of using both asynchronous and synchronous functionalities is to increase the interactions among teachers and students in an effort to overcome 'the Achilles heel of distance education', that is, the lack of interaction in language learning (Kan & McCormick, 2014).

The asynchronous environment in the course (CHN11) contained the course website, the Discussion Board (The CAFE), wikis, online quizzes, and journals, accessed via Blackboard Learn 9.1, a Learning Management System (LMS). The students also used WeChat, a messaging app, to interact with each other for collaborative learning.

The course website on Blackboard Learn played a central role in the online Chinese programme (see Figure 1.1). Blackboard Learn provided hyperlinks to online language-learning resources, unit information, unit content, online classrooms, assessment information, the course profile, and staff information. It also guided students through their weeks of study and provided them with announcements, technical help, a weekly study plan, online language learning resources, study tips, and a discussion board (The CAFE).

The *Discussion Board (The CAFE)* was an open forum for students to socialise with one another. Students were able to post course-related questions, suggestions, and recommendations to others (e.g., how to study Chinese or which books, dictionaries, tools, or online resources were thought to be useful). This forum was not monitored by the course teachers. In parallel, student support came from the course team, from services provided by the university administration such as technical help, and also from students themselves via the Discussion Board (The CAFE).

Wikis were a shared online space in which students could create written content to practise their writing skills. The written task design required the students to work in collaboration on wikis regularly throughout the study period. The students could start by finding the information needed individually and sharing it on their group wiki page. This was followed by rounds of discussions with each other and commenting on each other's writing before submitting the final version for marking.

Online quizzes could be listening or reading quizzes. Students might answer questions to check their understanding of the prerecorded mini-lecture videos.

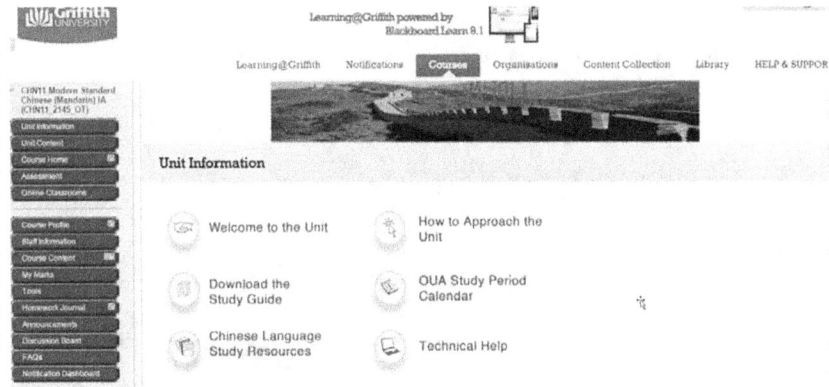

Figure 1.1 A screenshot of the CHN11 course site (as accessed by students in the 2015 academic year)

After their submissions, the system provided answers and explanations for students' self-checking.

The online classes were conducted through Blackboard Collaborate in Blackboard Learn 9.1. Blackboard Collaborate is a virtual classroom designed to provide teachers and learners with a synchronous learning environment for online virtual classes or meetings (see Figure 1.2). Students and teachers could communicate using audio, video, and text chat during online classes. Language-learning activities, such as role play, presentations, and discussions with their language partners could also be achieved in this synchronous environment. All the language-learning activities could be recorded by Blackboard Collaborate for students' further review.

Figure 1.2 shows the user interface in an online classroom in Blackboard Collaborate. This interface consisted of four main panels: an audio and video panel, a panel identifying current participants, a chat panel, and an onscreen whiteboard. All the sizes and locations of panels on the screen can be adjusted by the users for their convenience.

The Audio and Video panel showed the names of the speakers, or the speaker's video once the participant had pressed the talk or the video icon. The audio and video Collaborate Classroom functions were core components in online classrooms. Once students accessed an online class, they would interact with other students and the teachers in a situation similar to face-to-face classes. The maximum number of simultaneous speakers was six, and the same number applied to the video cameras.

The Participants panel showed all participants' names and photos as a list. There were four icons above the student list. Students could express their feelings via the first icon, such as a smiley face, LOL, applause, confusion, approval, disapproval, slower, faster, and so on. The second icon was used to indicate participant's unavailability, whilst the third icon signalled a request to speak. Students could use the last icon to vote Yes or No to questions from teachers or other students.

12 *Introduction*

Figure 1.2 User interface of Blackboard Collaborate

The Chat panel could be used by students to type texts in Chinese characters, English, and Pinyin. They could use emoticons to express feelings, such as a smiley face, an unhappy face, a rainbow, or a broken heart.

The onscreen whiteboard could be used by teachers to present PowerPoint (PPT) slides, draw/write on the whiteboard, and show pictures. During online classes, teachers and students could also use the whiteboard to communicate in writing, practise writing Chinese characters, and use various cartoon stickers to express their feelings and attract others' attention.

Another important tool used in the Chinese programmes was WeChat, one of the most popular instant messaging applications in China (Figure 1.3). It is owned by Chinese technology company Tencent and according to company data, had more than 1 billion daily active users in March 2018 (G. Wang et al., 2019). Students in this research project used WeChat as a tool to support their learning in two ways: (1) to directly interact with their teachers and peers individually or in a group, via texts, sound files, images, emojis, and audio and video conferencing calls; and (2) to share course-related information by posting texts, website links, photos, and video clips in the class WeChat groups or in a private friend circle via 'WeChat moments'.

1.3.2 Participants

The participants in this project were adult learners enrolled in online Chinese courses (CHN11, CHN12, CHN222 and CHN32) with OUA at Griffith University. There were a mix of beginning-level, intermediate-level, and advanced-level Chinese students. A total of 63 students agreed to participate in the research project and allowed me to record and observe their language learning in their online

Figure 1.3 Sample screenshots of the WeChat interface

Chinese courses. Twenty-three of the 63 participants provided valid responses to the online survey questionnaire; 10 of these 23 respondents attended the online interviews. Most of the 23 survey respondents (82.6%) studied in the beginning-level classes, 13.0% in an intermediate-level class, and 4.3% in an advanced-level class. In presenting the results, each participant was identified by the letter 'S' and a number (e.g., S5 = student 5). The participants were numbered according to the sequence in which they appeared in the online class recordings, from beginning-level classes to advanced-level classes.

The ten interviewees were S5, S8, S9, S10, S12, S13, S14, S15, S17, and S18. When studying the online courses, six were living in English-speaking countries (Australia and the UK), three in countries where Chinese is spoken (China and Malaysia), and one in South Korea. Six interviewees' first language was English. However, all ten interviewees spoke English fluently and could learn Chinese and other subjects through English instruction at university level. Of these students, two were enrolled in the lower-beginning-level course CHN11, five were in the higher-beginning-level course CHN12, and three were in the intermediate-level course CHN222.

14 *Introduction*

1.3.3 In-depth individual student studies

The purpose of using individual studies as a research strategy was mainly in order to obtain an in-depth insight into how the interviewed students used LLSs and the influencing factors in their LLS use. This research design involved the 10 interviewed students.

Individual studies were used as a research strategy for two important reasons. Firstly, using individual studies provided deep and rich data with which to understand the interviewed students' learning behaviour and how they use LLSs effectively to complete various language-learning tasks, especially in the tasks that required collaborative learning. Research has established that task requirements can help students determine LLS decisions (Oxford, 1990). In the present project, the assessment tasks in the online Chinese courses required students to collaborate with others. The LLSs used in collaborative exercises were identified not only from the interview data, but also from the interviewees' emails and instant messages. These data reflected how effective the LLSs were for completing different language tasks in collaboration. This research strategy helped to reveal these invisible data and provided a pathway to explore Chinese language learners' LLS in an online Chinese learning process.

The second reason for using this strategy was that individual learner characteristics (e.g., learning goals, learning motives, age) were expected to be a significant influencing factor in respect of the students' LLS use. Researchers have already identified that individual learner characteristics are a factor in relation to different LLS use and learning outcomes (Arispe & Blake, 2012; Martinez, 2001), and my research was designed to investigate this aspect. Some of the issues relating to individual learner characteristics are discussed in Section 2.6, but the relatively small size of my research project meant that it could not reflect all learner characteristics. Therefore, I have only reported those showing significant relationships with LLS use according to preliminary data analyses of the survey responses, and then used individual student examples to support or refute the survey results.

1.3.4 Data collection and research instruments

This project adopted a convergent mixed-methods approach and collected data from various sources. These included an online survey questionnaire adapted from the Strategy Inventory for Language Learning (SILL) (Oxford, 1990), interviews, and class observation. Table 1.2 summarises the data sources, provides brief explanations of them, and highlights the abbreviations used in this thesis for these data sources.

When reporting the results for the survey questionnaire (for which a five-point Likert scale was used, and the scale percentages were often reported in quintuplets), median (Mdn) and mean (M) were frequently used. The 'key to understand the averages' for language-learning-strategy (LLS) use in Oxford (1990, p. 291) was adopted to facilitate the description of LLS use in terms of high-, medium-, or low-frequency range of use (abbreviated as H, M, L when no confusion could be caused by this). The median, mean, and LLS usage range were often reported as a triplet of 'median, mean, LLS usage' in tables in order to save space. For example,

Table 1.2 Data sources, their explanations and abbreviations used in this book

Abbreviation	Data source	Explanation
Reported data Specifically:		Participants' self-reported data
SI	Survey questionnaire part I	Data from the first part of the survey questionnaire which includes eight questions: (1) name, (2) age, (3) heritage, (4) proficiency level, (5) study years, (6) learning motives, (7) study hours, and (8) learning goals
SII	Survey questionnaire part II	Data from the 45 LLS-specific items in the survey questionnaire on a five-point Likert scale: 1 = Never or almost never true of me; 2 = Generally not true of me; 3 = Somewhat true of me; 4 = Generally true of me; 5 = Always or almost always true of me
SIII	Survey questionnaire part III	Data from three open-ended questions in the survey questionnaire: 1) the most difficult aspect of working with a language partner; 2) the most effective LLSs; 3) actions the student takes to support their Chinese learning
I	Interview	Data from the online interviews with participants
Observed data Specifically:		My observed data
OI	Observation part I	Data from conversations in online classes
OII	Observation part II	Data from Discussion Board posts; students' marks and the content of their assignments
T	Tracking	Blackboard tracking data
AD	Additional data	Data from additional material provided by the students, e.g., personal emails between students, WeChat messages between students, and writing drafts shared between students via Google Drive

if a strategy item was reported to have the triplet of '4, 3.95, H', it meant that the strategy item was reported to have a median of 4 and a mean of 3.95, and was used with a high-frequency range.

Pearson's r correlation analysis was employed as well. The analysis results were interpreted using the suggestions from Evans (1996). More specifically, the correlations were interpreted as:

.00–.19 'very weak';
.20–.39 'weak';
.40–.59 'moderate';
.60–.79 'strong'; and
.80–1.0 'very strong'.

16   *Introduction*

1.4 Organisation of this book

This book consists of seven chapters. Following this introductory chapter, Chapter 2 deals with the essential concepts of terminology and provides a review of relevant existing literature on LLSs. It focuses on LLS research in online language learning, and considers a number of individual learner characteristics (such as language-learning experience, motivation, age, and learner autonomy) as potential factors influencing learners' LLS use.

The data collected from this research are mainly presented in Chapters 3 to 5. Specifically, Chapter 3 reports the repertoire of LLSs adopted by the participants in online Chinese learning. Chapter 4 investigates the impact of the learning contexts and the individual learner characteristics on LLS use. Chapter 5 presents the individual student LLS reports for the 10 interviewees in this project.

Chapter 6 synthesises and further discusses the key findings. It focuses on interpreting the results relating to the most significant and unique aspects of LLS use in online language learning in general, and online Chinese-language learning in particular. Finally, Chapter 7 summarises the research project and discusses its limitations, and recommends areas for further research.

1.5 Audience

A vast number of readers may find this book valuable, including:

- Researchers in languages and linguistics, as well as those who investigate language learning and teaching. In addition, the data collection and analyses could inspire future research.
- Teachers of university students in areas such as languages, language teaching methods, second language acquisition, LLSs, and related subjects.
- Language teachers of online students, adult students, university students, distance students, and so on.
- Chinese-language-course designers (especially at the beginning and the intermediate levels) in various institutions such as universities, colleges, and technical and further educational institutions.
- Chinese-language learners might find the LLSs reported in this book helpful for their language learning, and the student learning cases inspiring.
- This book will also provide all language-teaching professionals interested in strategy-based research a current perspective on online language learning and research ideas for the use of LLSs in both synchronous and asynchronous environments.

1.6 How this book is different

The results in this book fill a number of gaps in the literature: LLS adoption by tertiary-level students engaged in online Chinese learning, LLS adoption in collaborative learning, LLS use within a flipped-classroom approach, and different LLS use in different learning contexts, such as self-directed language learning outside online classes, assessment task completion, and online class participation.

Secondly, this book provides insights into LLS adoption by individual language learners. Those students who were interviewed were able to provide detailed information on how they engaged with language-learning activities, such as Chinese-character learning, role plays and wiki writing (writing assignments which ask students to collaboratively work on wiki pages) with language partners, and how they adopted and developed LLSs with the support of technological tools to solve learning problems during task completion in both individual and collaborative learning.

Thirdly, this book also provides recommendations on LLS training for language teachers and instructors to incorporate in their online language courses. These teachers and instructors have an essential role in helping learners learn how to learn. By facilitating strategy training, teachers and instructors may empower learners with active self-directed learning skills which encourage them to tackle learning difficulties in online environments and adjust their learning behaviour towards successful online language learning. The LLSs discussed in this book may also help teachers better understand online students' needs, including the necessity of equipping them with the right technological tools for online language learning.

References

ACARA. (2015). *The Australian curriculum: Chinese.* Retrieved from https://www.australiancurriculum.edu.au/f-10-curriculum/languages/chinese/

Akiyama, Y., & Saito, K. (2016). Development of comprehensibility and its linguistic correlates: A longitudinal study of video-mediated telecollaboration. *The Modern Language Journal, 100*(3), 585–609. https://doi.org/10.1111/modl.12338

Altunay, D. (2014). Language learning strategies used by distance learners of English: A study with a group of Turkish distance learners of EFL. *Turkish Online Journal of Distance Education, 15*(3), 291–305. https://doi.org/10.17718/tojde.30083

Arispe, K., & Blake, R. J. (2012). Individual factors and successful learning in a hybrid course. *System, 40*(4), 449–465.

Bezuidenhout, A. (2018). Analysing the importance-competence gap of distance educators with the increased utilisation of online learning strategies in a developing world context. *International Review of Research in Open and Distance Learning, 19*(3), 263.

Brown, H. D. (2007). *Teaching by principles: An interactive approach to language pedagogy* (3rd ed.). White Plains, NY: Pearson Education.

Bruning, R. H. (2004). *Cognitive psychology and instruction* (4th ed.). Upper Saddle River, NJ: Pearson/Merrill/Prentice Hall.

Bureau of Human Resources. (2016). *Five year workforce and leadership succession plan: Fiscal years 2016–2020.* Washington, DC: US Department of State.

Cohen, A. D., Oxford, R., & Chi, J. C. (2002). Language strategy use survey. In A. D. Cohen & S. J. Weaver (Eds.), *Style and strategies based instruction: A teachers' guide* (pp. 68–74). Minneapolis, MN: University of Minnesota Center for Advanced Research on Language Acquisition.

De Bot, K., Lowie, W., & Verspoor, M. (2005). *Second language acquisition: An advanced resource book.* New York, NY: Routledge.

Dörnyei, Z. (2014). Language learning strategies and student self-regulation. In Z. Dörnyei (Ed.), *The psychology of the language learner: Individual differences in second language acquisition* (pp. 162–194). New York, NY: Routledge.

Efriana, L. (2021). Problems of online learning during Covid-19 pandemic in EFL classroom and the solution. *Journal of English Language Teaching and Literature*, *2*(1), 38–47.

Ellis, R. (2008). *The study of second language acquisition* (2nd ed.). Oxford, UK: Oxford University Press.

Ellis, R. (2012). *Language teaching research and language pedagogy* (1st ed.). Malden, MA: John Wiley & Sons Inc.

Evans, J. D. (1996). *Straightforward statistics for the behavioral sciences*. Pacific Grove, CA: Brooks/Cole Pub.

Gao, X. (2006). Understanding changes in Chinese students' uses of learning strategies in China and Britain: A socio-cultural re-interpretation. *System*, *34*(1), 55–67. https://doi.org/10.1016/j.system.2005.04.003

Gao, X. (2008). You had to work hard 'cause you didn't know whether you were going to wear shoes or straw sandals! *Journal of Language, Identity & Education*, *7*(3–4), 169–187. https://doi.org/10.1080/15348450802237798

Gao, X. (2010). Autonomous language learning against all odds. *System*, *38*(4), 580–590. https://doi.org/10.1016/j.system.2010.09.011

Griffiths, C. (2004). *Language learning strategies: Theory and research* [Doctoral thesis, Auckland University, New Zealand].

Hadwin, A. F., Bakhtiar, A., & Miller, M. (2018). Challenges in online collaboration: effects of scripting shared task perceptions. *International Journal of Computer-Supported Collaborative Learning*, *13*(3), 301–329. https://doi.org/https://doi.org/10.1007/s11412-018-9279-9

Harrington, M. (2012). *Australia in the Asian century: Asian studies in schools*. Retrieved from https://www.aph.gov.au/About_Parliament/Parliamentary_Departments/Parliamentary_Library/FlagPost/2012/November/Australia_in_the_Asian_Century_Asian_studies_in_schools

Hauck, M., & Hampel, R. (2008). Strategies for online learning environments. In S. Hurd & T. Lewis (Eds.), *Language learning strategies in independent settings* (pp. 283–302). Bristol, UK: Multilingual Matters.

Huang, H.-c., Chern, C.-l., & Lin, C.-c. (2009). EFL learners' use of online reading strategies and comprehension of texts: An exploratory study. *Computers & Education*, *52*(1), 13–26. https://doi.org/10.1016/j.compedu.2008.06.003

Kan, Q., & McCormick, R. (2014). Building course cohesion: The use of online forums in distance Chinese language learning. *Computer Assisted Language Learning*, *27*(1), 44–69. https://doi.org/10.1080/09588221.2012.695739

Kaufman, D. (2004). Constructivist issues in language learning and teaching. *Annual Review of Applied Linguistics*, *24*, 303.

Lai, Y., Saab, N., & Admiraal, W. (2022). Learning strategies in self-directed language learning using mobile technology in higher education: a systematic scoping review. *Education and Information Technologies*, *27*(6), 7749–7780.

Liu, S., & Wang, F. (2018). A qualitative study on learning trajectories of non-native Chinese instructors as successful Chinese language learners. *Asian-Pacific Journal of Second and Foreign Language Education*, *3*(1), 1–21. https://doi.org/10.1186/s40862-018-0043-5

Livengood, K., Lewallen, D. W., Leatherman, J., & Maxwell, J. L. (2012). The use and evaluation of scaffolding, student centered-learning, behaviorism, and constructivism to teach nuclear magnetic resonance and IR spectroscopy in a two-semester organic chemistry course. *Journal of Chemical Education*, *89*(8), 1001–1006. https://doi.org/10.1021/ed200638g

Ma, J. (2005). *Short-term spoken Chinese: Volume 1. Threshold* (2nd ed.). Beijing, China: Beijing Language and Culture University Press.
Martinez, M. (2001). Mass customization: Designing for successful learning. *International Journal of Educational Technology, 2*(2).
Norton, B., & Toohey, K. (2001). Changing perspectives on good language learners. *TESOL Quarterly, 35*(2), 307–322. https://doi.org/10.2307/3587650
Nunan, D. (1992). *Research methods in language learning.* Cambridge, UK: Cambridge University Press.
O'Malley, M., & Chamot, A. U. (1990). *Learning strategies in second language acquisition.* Cambridge, UK: Cambridge University Press.
Orton, J. (2016). Issues in Chinese language teaching in Australian schools. *Chinese Education & Society, 49*(6), 369–375. https://doi.org/10.1080/10611932.2016.1283929
Oxford, R. (1990). *Language learning strategies: What every teacher should know.* Boston, UK: Newbury House.
Oxford, R. (2011). *Teaching and researching: Language learning strategies.* London, UK: Routledge.
Oxford, R. (2017). *Teaching and researching language learning strategies: Self-regulation in context* (2nd ed.). New York, NY: Routledge.
Oxford, R., & Nyikos, M. (1989). Variables affecting choice of language learning strategies by university students. *The Modern Language Journal, 73*(3), 291–300. https://doi.org/10.1111/j.1540-4781.1989.tb06367.x
Rasheed, R. A., Kamsin, A., & Abdullah, N. A. (2021). An approach for scaffolding students peer-learning self-regulation strategy in the online component of blended learning. *IEEE Access, 9*, 30721–30738.
Reinders, H., & Hubbard, P. (2013). CALL and learner autonomy: Affordances and constraints. In M. Thomas, H. Reinders, & M. Warschauer (Eds.), *Contemporary computer-assisted language learning* (pp. 359–375). London, UK: Bloomsbury Academic.
Rubin, J. (1975). What the 'good language learner' can teach us. *TESOL Quarterly, 9*(1), 41–51. https://doi.org/10.2307/3586011
Sharples, M., Adams, A., Ferguson, R., Gaved, M., McAndrew, P., Rienties, B., . . . Whitelock, D. (2014). *Innovating pedagogy 2014: Open University innovation report 3.* Retrieved from http://www.openuniversity.edu/sites/www.openuniversity.edu/files/The_Open_University_Innovating_Pedagogy_2014_0.pdf
Shen, H. H. (2005). An investigation of Chinese-character learning strategies among non-native speakers of Chinese. *System, 33*(1), 49–68. https://doi.org/10.1016/j.system.2004.11.001
Shen, H. H., & Xu, W. (2015). Active learning: Qualitative inquiries into vocabulary instruction in Chinese L2 classrooms. *Foreign Language Annals, 48*(1), 82–99. https://doi.org/10.1111/flan.12137
Solak, E., & Cakir, R. (2015). Language learning strategies of language e-learners in Turkey. *E-Learning and Digital Media, 12*(1), 107–120. https://doi.org/10.1177/2042753014558384
Stickler, U., & Shi, L. (2013). Supporting Chinese speaking skills online. *System, 41*(1), 50–69. https://doi.org/10.1016/j.system.2012.12.001
Sturak, K., & Naughten, Z. (Eds.). (2010). *The current state of Chinese, Indonesian, Japanese and Korean language education in Australian schools: Four languages, four stories.* Carlton South, Victoria, Australia: Education Services Australia Ltd. Retrieved from https://www.asiaeducation.edu.au/docs/default-source/Research-reports/overarchingreport.pdf.

Wang, G., Zhang, W., & Zeng, R. (2019). WeChat use intensity and social support: The moderating effect of motivators for WeChat use. *Computers in Human Behavior, 91*, 244–251. https://doi.org/10.1016/j.chb.2018.10.010

Wang, Y. (2012). Teaching Chinese as a foreign language to beginners in an Australian university context. *The Internet Journal of Language* (35), 68–75.

Wang, Y. (2014). *Study guide: CHN11 Modern Standard Chinese (Mandarin) 1A*. Nathan, Queensland, Australia: School of Languages and Linguistics, Griffith University.

Wang, Y., & Chen, N.-S. (2009). Criteria for evaluating synchronous learning management systems: Arguments from the distance language classroom. *Computer Assisted Language Learning, 22*(1), 1–18. https://doi.org/10.1080/09588220802613773

Wang, Y., & Chen, N.-S. (2012). The collaborative language learning attributes of cyber face-to-face interaction: The perspectives of the learner. *Interactive Learning Environments, 20*(4), 311–330. https://doi.org/10.1080/10494821003769081

Wang, Y., & Chen, N.-S. (2013). Engendering interaction, collaboration, and reflection in the design of online assessment in language learning: A reflection from the course designers. In *Computer-Assisted Foreign Language Teaching and Learning: Technological Advances (1st ed.)* (pp. 16–39). Hershey, PA: IGI Global.

Wenden, A. L. (1998). Metacognitive knowledge and language learning. *Applied Linguistics, 19*(4), 515–537. https://doi.org/10.1093/applin/19.4.515

Xu, Z. (2010). *Chinese as foreign language research: Cognitive model and strategy (*汉语作为外语的学习研究：认知模式与策略*)* Beijing, China: Peking University Press.

Zhang, B. (2002). *The new modern Chinese* 现代汉语. Shanghai, China: Fudan University Press.

Zhang, D., & Lin, C.-H. (2017). *Chinese as a second language assessment*. Singapore: Springer.

2 Review of related study fields

2.1 Online learning and TELL

The emergence of online learning has presented new challenges and difficulties for distance learners. These challenges need to be examined in the context of online learning environments and technology-enhanced language learning (TELL). This section reviews the related literature of online learning and TELL.

2.1.1 Online learning

As noted by Moore et al. (2011), the term *online learning* is defined by most scholars as access to learning experiences via the use of technology, whilst other scholars' definitions have emphasised its features, such as connectivity, flexibility, and an ability to promote interactions. Online learning facilitates the development of online courses that include not only content, but also instructional methods that are designed to help students learn (Clark & Mayer, 2016, p. 30). The emergence of massive open online courses (MOOCs) has had a great impact on the development of online learning in higher education since the first MOOC was created in 2008 (Liyanagunawardena et al., 2013).

Of the many learning theories, behaviourism, cognitivism, and constructivism have all had an influence on online teaching and learning. Behaviourism is a teacher-centred theory which posits that teachers should design the teaching process in order to encourage positive and prevent unwanted behaviour by students (Anderson, 2008). Cognitivism is another teacher-centred approach; cognitivists see learning as a process of obtaining, processing, and storing information (Bruning, 2004). By contrast, constructivism is a learner-centred theory, and constructivists believe that learners construct their knowledge through their own experiences and interactions with the real world (Bruning, 2004). Thus, teachers should design collaborative and cooperative activities in online learning to enable students to facilitate constructivist learning.

However, Siemens (2005) has noted the limitation of these three theories and argue that connectivism is also an important aspect of learning with technologies in a digital age. Connectivists emphasise a process in which individual learners study in an online environment, and through this obtain and critique information from connections before making decisions (Siemens, 2005). Hence, connectivists recommend that teachers design the same collaborative and cooperative activities as proposed by social constructivists, but that those teachers should play an active role in informing and evaluating the activities for learners in online learning, as opposed to an advising and facilitating role, as suggested by constructivists (Anderson, 2008; Siemens, 2008).

When delivering online content to students, collaborative and flipped learning approaches are often used. Influenced by learner-centred theories, such as constructivism and connectivism, and also by Vygotsky's 'zone of proximal development' (ZPD), collaborative approaches are seen as key in online course design for effective online learning (Devlin & Trad, 2014; Jacobs, 2013; R. Liang & Chen, 2012). The effectiveness of online learning is measured in terms of students' satisfaction with their collaborations and interactions with other students and teachers in online environments (Jacobs, 2013). Collaborative learning was implemented in the online Chinese courses in this research project.

The flipped learning approach is an instructional model which can also be applied to online learning. This approach was labelled 'classroom flip' by J. Wesley Baker in a conference paper in 2000 (Baker, 2000). The concept was applied in American K12 schools in 2007 and has since been continuously employed as a teaching and learning approach in education, including tertiary education (O'Flaherty & Phillips, 2015; Y. Wang & Qi, 2018). The flipped approach can be understood as a blended learning method which reverses the traditional learning environment. Such an approach delivers instructional learning content, often in an asynchronous environment, although it can also be used to organise learning activities in a synchronous environment (Brame, 2013; Sales, 2013). The asynchronous environment allows students flexibility in arranging their self-paced learning, whilst the synchronous environment provides them with opportunities to participate in various collaborative learning activities.

However, some tertiary-level students may find the flipped classroom more difficult to adapt to, despite its potential advantages for student learning. This is evidenced by the work of a group of researchers who surveyed 563 tertiary students enrolled in flipped courses in Australia (McNally et al., 2017). Their results indicated that half of the participants resisted the flipped approach. The challenges of the flipped classroom are largely related to aspects of self-directed learning outside classes, such as issues with the task design (McDonald & Smith, 2013), inadequate student preparation before class, and the students' need for guidance when undertaking self-directed learning (ibid.). If students do not take adequate time to study, they may not perform well when participating in in-class learning, and consequently the advantages of the flipped classroom approach diminish (Akçayır & Akçayır, 2018). There remains a lack of research which investigates how students employ LLSs to cope with the requirements of the flipped classroom approach.

2.1.2 TELL

Technically, TELL was first referred to as computer-assisted language learning (CALL), but both alternatives refer to the same language-learning approach (Bush & Terry, 1997). The acronym TELL, rather than CALL, is used in this book for two reasons. The first is that this approach can involve various technology devices, such as a computer, a tablet, or a mobile device, and TELL is therefore a more inclusive term than CALL. The other reason is that TELL highlights the 'impact' of technology on foreign-language learning, and therefore is a more accurate term than CALL for this research project.

TELL has developed rapidly since the 1970s (Levy & Stockwell, 2006), and this directly relates to the fast-paced development of computer systems, the now-widespread use of the internet, and improvements in wireless technologies (Lambropoulos, Christopoulou, & Vlachos, 2006). These technologies, both singly and in combination, have become more and more capable and sophisticated, and have all facilitated changes in TELL over the last 40 years.

The most often highlighted form of interaction in TELL is computer-mediated communication (CMC). CMC engages language learners in active learning, negotiation, seeking information, and error correction in the target language (Levy, 1997). CMC involves two types of communication between teachers and learners: synchronous computer-mediated communication (SCMC) and asynchronous computer-mediated communication (ACMC) (Beatty, 2003; Levy, 1997). SCMC is supported by software, such as text chat, Skype, Elluminate, FlashMeeting, WebCT, NetMeeting, and DimDim, all of which can provide audio- or video-conferencing environments (Stickler & Shi, 2013). With the support of such software, SCMC can facilitate instantaneous communication and information exchange between the language learner and the teacher in the forms of reading, listening, speaking, and responding (Stickler & Shi, 2013). On the other side, ACMC allows delayed online interactions to take place, for example through email, bulletin boards, and blog discussions.

A review of existing literature evidences that learning with a single technology in an online environment may cause disadvantages to language learners, such as the limiting of language output (Antoniou, 2022; Barnes, 2000; Golonka et al., 2014; Kan & McCormick, 2014). However, contemporary distance learners are not constrained by one single technology, and the limitations of using single technologies in online environments can therefore be overcome by adopting multiple technologies in both synchronous and asynchronous environments – nonetheless, this means that distance learners now have to cope with various technologies in online learning environments. As a result, they face new challenges in online language learning, such as learning specific technical skills, using unfamiliar learning devices, and observing netiquette (i.e., guidelines for communication over the internet, see Hauck & Hampel, 2008; Larry & Gary, 1997). These challenges therefore need to be overcome by language learners by using appropriate LLSs in online learning.

Another drawback of using most TELL technologies is the lack of language output and communication. For instance, a recent study by Antoniou (2022) stressed that continuous technological developments had influenced the students' learning effectiveness for the worse. In an asynchronous environment, some language learners can even choose not to respond to messages and hide offline, which is called the 'lurker' phenomenon (Barnes, 2000). Sun et al. (2014) explained that lurkers keep quiet for various reasons and can be incited to participate more by the use of appropriate 'de-lurking' strategies. Indeed, 'lurking' should not necessarily be seen as a negative phenomenon. X. Yang et al. (2017) argued that lurkers, rather than being regarded as passive members, 'consume' the content created by active users in an online community and thus form an indispensable part of that community.

The final issue related to TELL is the difference between netiquette and face-to-face etiquette in the classroom, which should be taken into account when looking at online interactions. Hauck and Hampel (2008) suggested that netiquette is different from etiquette in normal life or in real classrooms. For example, instead of using body language, students might use a smiley face to express their politeness in a synchronous class. Additionally, any praise or inappropriate speech in an online environment, such as an online forum, may remain visible for a long time. In relation to communication behaviour in an online environment, previous studies have indicated that online interactions can lead to a rapid response behaviour and a neglect of social formalities, which may consequently result in misunderstandings or negative emotion (Knight & Masselink, 2008). Despite this, findings from a recent study by Linek and Ostermaier-Grabow (2018) showed that the behaviour of the majority of interactants was deemed to be appropriate. However, there is still an open question of how netiquette supports effective collaboration among students in language learning. With this in mind, this project investigated netiquette as a particular LLS in online language learning and explored how and why students used it in collaborative learning.

2.2 Chinese as a particularly difficult language for English speakers to learn

'Is Chinese difficult to learn or not?' might be a common question that immediately arises when an individual plans to learn Chinese (Mandarin) as a foreign language for the first time. However, it is very hard to give a simple 'Yes' or 'No' answer to this question. On the one hand, the grammar of Chinese is not particularly complicated for English speakers. On the other hand, the sheer number of Chinese characters can result in Chinese being portrayed as a time-consuming foreign language for English speakers to learn. Additionally, English speakers are faced with the significant difficulties of learning Chinese orthography and pronunciation, and the specific acquisition order of the language increases the level of difficulty of Chinese character learning for English first-language speakers (Kan & McCormick, 2014; Shen, 2005; X. Xu, 2022).

Chinese characters have been developing for over 3,000 years and the overall number of Chinese characters currently stands at 87,019, as recorded by the *Zhonghua Chinese Character Dictionary* (中华字海) (B. Zhang, 2002). However, the number of Chinese characters in frequent use by Chinese people in their daily life is only around 3,500. These 3,500 Chinese characters were recorded in the *List of Frequently Used Characters in Modern Chinese* (现代汉语常用字表) and published by the Chinese National Linguistics Work Commission in 1988, which covers 99.48% of the commonly used Chinese characters (B. Zhang, 2002).

According to Y. Hu (1995), 90% of written content in non-scholarly sources (e.g., magazines and books) can be covered by 950 frequently used characters, whilst 99% of such content can be covered by 2,400 frequently used characters (pp. 167–168).

There are three main areas of difficulties in Chinese language learning. The first and foremost one is Chinese orthography (Kan & McCormick, 2014; Shen, 2005; X. Xu, 2022; J. Zhang et al., 2020). Written Chinese characters contain a three-tier orthographic structure: the characters themselves, radicals, and strokes (Shen, 2005). The second area of difficulty in Chinese language learning is pronunciation, caused by the separation between this and the orthographic structure. This is further complicated by the tones in Chinese, especially for beginning-level Chinese learners (Kan & McCormick, 2014). The third area of difficulty is the particular acquisition order of the Chinese language, which increases the challenge of character learning. Shen (2013) indicated that when learning Chinese as a second language, phonological activation occurs at the lexical level whereas, when learning English as a second language, the activation occurs at the pre-lexical level. Thus, Chinese-language learners must retrieve both the syllable and the meaning simultaneously when they face a Chinese character.

The three areas of difficulty in Chinese language learning discussed in this section make Chinese a particularly demanding language for English speakers to learn. In order to address these challenges, online Chinese learners should utilise appropriate LLSs to make their learning more effective. Therefore, knowing what LLSs are more suitable for Chinese learning, and how to apply them more effectively in language learning, are of great value to Chinese language learners.

2.3 LLSs and LLS research

2.3.1 Definition of LLS

LLSs are an important factor impacting online language learning. For a better understanding of the LLSs used by online students, it is necessary to discuss the definitions of LLSs. In the field of second-language acquisition, researchers have been working on the definition of LLS since Rubin (1975) first suggested that researchers should be aware of the strategies adopted by good language learners, referring to them as 'techniques or devices which a learner may use to acquire knowledge' (p. 43). This definition of LLS is very broad, and subsequently O'Malley and Chamot (1990) refined the definition of LLS to 'operations employed by the learner to aid the acquisition, storage, retrieval, and use of information' (p. 8). At the same time, Oxford (1990) defined conscious LLSs as 'specific actions taken by the learner to make learning easier, faster, more enjoyable, more effective, and more transferable to new situations' (p. 8).

In the past three decades, the definition of LLS has been updated by researchers such as Oxford (1990), Cohen (1998), Griffiths (2008), and Cohen (2012). Despite the development of LLS definitions over time, all these LLS scholars have recognised two core features of LLSs; namely, they are based on decisions made by language learners, and they focus on improving language proficiency.

Oxford's (2017) recent definition of LLS emphasised the importance of strategy use in relation to specific learning contexts, as reflected in the following statement:

> LLSs are complex, dynamic thoughts and actions, selected and used by learners with some degree of consciousness in specific contexts in order to regulate multiple aspects of themselves (such as cognitive, emotional, and social) for the purpose of 1) accomplishing language tasks; 2) improving language performance or use; and/or 3) enhancing long-term proficiency. (p. 48)

She also indicated that language learners often use strategies 'flexibly and creatively [... and] combine them in various ways, such as strategy clusters or strategy chains; and orchestrate them to meet learning needs' (p. 48). However, the appropriate use of strategies depends on 'multiple personal and contextual factors' (p. 48). Whilst, as we have seen in this section, there are multiple LLS definitions, the one provided by Oxford (2017) encompasses the key ingredients of addressing the LLS challenge. Because of the clarity of this definition and its clear focus on the LLS issues and challenges, it was adopted in this book.

2.3.2 LLS research

Based on Oxford's definition of LLS, cited in Section 2.3.1, this section will now provide greater detail on the research into LLS and the associated conclusions reached by various key researchers.

In the mid-1970s, research into LLS was described as 'the good language learner' research (Rubin, 1975). Ellis (2008) argued that early studies of successful language learning had focused on the value of teaching quality and lacked the perspective of language learners. This important issue was further recognised in the late 1980s and early 1990s when research began to shift from a teacher-centred to a learner-centred direction. Researchers started to develop specific classifications of LLSs and study individual learner characteristics that influenced learners' use of them, thus reflecting a learner-centred approach, with two of the best known resultant models being those of O'Malley and Chamot (1990) and Oxford (1990).

Oxford's model distinguishes between direct and indirect strategies. Direct strategies 'directly involve the target language' and 'require mental processing of the language', and include memory, cognitive, and compensation strategies (Oxford, 1990, p. 37). Indirect strategies refers to strategies that 'support and manage language learning without (in many instances) directly involving the target language' and include metacognitive, affective, and social strategies (Oxford, 1990, p. 135).

In the last two decades, LLS research has developed further through the use of a sociocultural approach to investigate second- and foreign-language learners' LLSs in different cultures and contexts (X. Gao, 2006, 2008, 2010; Norton & Toohey, 2001; Wenden, 1998). This sociocultural approach highlights the importance of language learners' learning contexts and metacognitive knowledge (X. Gao, 2007). Consequently, language learners' LLS adoption is viewed as a result of individual cognitive decisions and the influences of learning cultures and contexts. X. Gao

(2007) argued strongly for the importance of using such a sociocultural approach in LLS research, since this helps researchers capture the dynamic strategies used by language learners when they are facing different tasks.

The concept of self-regulation is one that has recently begun to find favour. Oxford updated her earlier LLS classification (1990) by distinguishing between strategies (cognitive, affective, and sociocultural) and meta-strategies that reflect the learner's self-regulation of cognition, social interaction, and affect (Oxford, 2011, 2017). She also introduced the Strategic Self-Regulation (S^2R) framework and discussed LLS use in the self-regulation of both mental processes and communicative learning. However, unlike Oxford's (1990) *Strategy Inventory for Language Learning* (SILL), the S^2R framework did not support any measurable indicators for LLS analysis (Oxford, 1990). SILL, as a self-report questionnaire, has been used to assess the frequency of LLS use with a five-point Likert scale (Oxford, 1990), and can accommodate the functions of the S^2R framework (Papadopoulou et al., 2018).

Although there are debates regarding SILL's construct validity, it remains the dominant research instrument in LLS research for gauging language learners' LLS use, not least as it can be modified so that LLSs are located on the behavioural levels (Papadopoulou et al., 2018). Oxford (1990) provided detailed definitions for and explanations of LLS items, and they are broadly aligned with the frameworks in Oxford (2011) and Oxford (2017). Therefore, Oxford's (1990) classification of LLSs was used as the key reference for explaining LLSs in this book. Her classification facilitates an understanding of online students' LLS use and helps shed light on key issues in their learning processes.

When associating LLSs with learning behaviours/actions, it is sometimes challenging to link one learning behaviour/action with just one LLS. When encountering such instances, previous research has adopted the approach of associating those learning behaviours/actions with the LLSs that highlight the most important feature of that behaviour/action. For example, Hurd (2008) identified four affective strategies that 'involve metacognitive knowledge of self' (p. 222) and suggested that researchers should keep the traditional distinction between affective and metacognitive strategies. The same approach was also adopted in this book.

2.3.3 TELL task types and LLS adoption

The choice of LLSs is affected directly by task types, with Oxford (1990) explaining that the task requirements help determine learners' strategy choice. For example, learners might use different LLSs when writing a composition compared with completing a speaking task. TELL task types influence learners' LLSs in the same way. As an illustration of this, L.-S. Huang (2010) explored 20 intermediate distance students' strategy adoption in English speaking through three types of tasks: individual log writing (Group A), tape recordings of post-speaking activities by individual students (Group B), and group dialogues (Group C). The results indicated that different TELL task types can result in different strategy use. However, little is known about online students' LLS use when coping with various learning tasks in online language learning. Given the significant influence of TELL tasks on LLS use, this book is particularly focused on how students used LLSs in completing various tasks in both synchronous and asynchronous learning environments.

2.3.4 LLS training

Oxford (1990) suggested three types of strategy training for language learning: awareness training, one-time strategy training, and long-term strategy training. The purpose of awareness training is to introduce LLSs to students using a short lesson. One-time strategy training involves learning and practising one or more LLSs with language tasks. Long-term strategy training also involves learning and practising LLSs in language tasks, but it takes longer than one-time strategy training and covers more strategies. In long-term strategy training, teachers have to *train* students to use LLSs. Therefore, long-term strategy training is more effective than one-time strategy training. However, some strategy training only provides strategy choices to language learners and lacks an effective way of enabling students to use these strategies (O'Bryan, 2008). Thus, this book was not only concerned with the repertoire of online strategies used by language learners but also explored effective LLSs in order to provide possible solutions for long-term online LLS training.

Language learners can be trained to acquire LLSs as part of the learning process (Dalton & Grisham, 2011; O'Bryan, 2008; Oxford, 2017) and some studies (e.g., Kan & McCormick, 2014; Murday et al., 2008) have revealed that learners have reported positive attitudes toward LLS training in TELL. For instance, O'Bryan (2008) conducted strategy training within TELL to help 22 English-language learners enhance LLS use in online reading through the use of computerised texts with hyperlinked glosses to help language learners' language input, and especially their vocabulary input. The result demonstrated that language learners understood this pedagogy very well after the training.

Strategy training can also be used for specific purposes, such as vocabulary learning. Dalton and Grisham (2011) suggested various vocabulary strategies in the online language-learning environment. For instance, language teachers can introduce students to the use of Wordle (www.wordle.net) to find connections between words. They can also use online information (images, sounds, and background information), for example, by showing such information, themed around a field trip, to language learners in order to help them learn a group of words around the topic of weather. These basic vocabulary strategies can help students memorise new words by creating a mental linkage to memory (Oxford, 1990).

2.4 LLS research in online language learning

Researchers have found that LLS adoption is different to online language learning when compared with other contexts. This section discusses the LLS research of Oxford's (1990) six strategy categories and reviews the literature that focuses on specific LLSs in online language learning, LLS usage in online learning, and online LLS training.

2.4.1 Affective strategies

Recent studies have increasingly accepted the important role of affective strategies in online language learning for maintaining positive learning motivation and reducing learning anxiety (Bosmans & Hurd, 2016; Bown & White, 2010; Hauck & Hampel, 2008; Hurd, 2000). Specifically, as noted by Hauck and Hampel (2008), online students might not be familiar with the communication form in online language learning and face challenges, including the anonymity of the environment and the need for technology support. These challenges encountered when communicating with peers and teachers may lead to unfamiliar learning difficulties in such online environments. Therefore, students involved in online communications need to be aware of the benefits of using affective strategies to reduce learning anxiety from these challenges.

Most of the recent research on affective strategies has focused on measuring the frequencies of strategy use and the different kinds of responses from participants. For example, Altunay (2014) investigated LLS used by Turkish online learners of English and found that the most frequently used affective strategy was 'I give myself a reward or treat when I do well in English', whilst the least frequently used one was 'I write down my feelings in a language learning diary'. Separately, research by Solak and Cakir (2015) indicated that, according to their survey responses, Turkish online students did not pay much attention to affective strategies. When they did so, these students used the affective strategy 'I try to relax whenever I feel afraid of using English' most frequently, and the strategy 'I encourage myself to speak English even when I am afraid of making a mistake' the least. However, these two studies were around English-language learners who were Turkish online students. It is important to understand how Chinese language learners use affective strategies to cope with different learning difficulties.

The learning environment in online flipped language courses may also bring emotional challenges to language learners. Bown and White (2010) examined three online students' emotional regulation in learning Russian as a foreign language in self-directed learning. Their interview data demonstrated that the students showed negative emotions when studying alone, such as feeling overwhelmed at the beginning of the Russian course, when memorising target language forms, and when failing a language test. The students also reported that they invested effort into practising vocabulary writing and reading (cognitive strategies) and carefully scheduled learning time (metacognitive strategies) to develop positive emotions. Such results suggest that the students used cognitive and metacognitive strategies to help motivate their language learning and maintain positive emotions. However, Brown and White's study did not indicate the exact learning context in which the students used the affective strategies. This book has addressed the lack of studies to date that consider not only the frequencies of affective strategy use, but also how these affective strategies are used in different ways in different learning contexts.

2.4.2 Cognitive strategies

Some researchers have reported that distance students use effective cognitive strategies in their self-directed learning (H.-C. Huang et al., 2009; Klapper, 2008;

C. Lee, 2020). According to C. Lee (2020), when students work on writing tasks in an online environment, they commonly employ online searches to find information. This helps them overcome language difficulties and make their writing more engaging. The study also found that these students relied more on their teachers for guidance and suggestions, whilst in an online environment they prefer to search for online resources. This change in strategy use suggests the technology-driven environments have an impact on how students approach their teaching.

For instance, Klapper (2008) offered a range of effective cognitive strategies for self-directed vocabulary learning, such as using word cards, rote learning and rehearsal, and list learning. These cognitive strategies are consistent with Oxford's (1990) cognitive strategies of *'Using resources for receiving and sending messages'* and *'Repeating'*, and the memory strategy of *'Using mechanical techniques'*. Klapper (2008) further explained that distance students might lack access to classroom reviews and tests, and therefore they need to employ these cognitive strategies in self-directed learning. In parallel, H.-C. Huang et al. (2009) found that cognitive strategies were frequently used relating to translation, dictionary, and highlighting key points. These authors believed that online students were likely to employ cognitive strategies that could help them find, evaluate, and use information quickly in self-directed learning.

Both online educational researchers and language learning researchers agree that retrieval practice plays an essential role in online learning. As an example of retrieval practice in language learning, a student's imitation of a native speaker reflects Oxford's (1990) cognitive strategy of *'Repeating'*. In a similar way, Karpicke and Blunt (2011) has published her findings on the importance of retrieval practice for online students in *Science*. These findings showed that such a practice produced a dramatic positive impact on online students' learning achievements. A recent study by Altunay (2014) also found that the most frequently used cognitive strategy by distance English-language learning students was *'Repeating'* by saying or writing new English words several times. However, these researchers did not provide further explanations of when and how online students used these cognitive strategies and the relevant supporting technologies. With this gap in mind, this book investigates online students' use of cognitive strategies and their decisions in relation to the different ways that technological tools could be employed across both asynchronous and synchronous environments.

2.4.3 Social strategies

Researchers have identified two key features in social strategy adoption by learners in online language learning: (1) it is influenced by the development of technologies (Stickler & Lewis, 2008); and (2) it requires language learners to adapt to online language learning and its new forms of social strategies (e.g., netiquette) (Hauck & Hampel, 2008). Studies have also demonstrated the positive aspects of using social strategies by students, such as promoting online collaboration (Akiyama & Saito, 2016; Hadwin et al., 2018; Hauck & Hampel, 2008; Saito, 2005). L. Lee's (2001) study reflected language learners' belief that social strategies are useful in language learning. However, language learners were found to be using social strategies without enthusiasm in online language-learning environments (C. Lai & Gu, 2011). This low enthusiasm might be due to the fact that the students lacked knowledge of social strategy use in an online environment, such as online netiquette.

One issue associated with the low enthusiasm was that students seemed to still use the same social strategies in online collaboration as in face-to-face collaboration. In this respect, findings from L. Lee (2001) have demonstrated that language learners employed communication strategies similar to those used during face-to-face interactions, such as clarification requests and self-corrections. The author then suggested that online students (non-native speakers) need to particularly focus on the importance of improving accuracy in the written form in online collaboration.

Another issue, highlighted by Hauck and Hampel (2008), might be the differences in etiquette between traditional classrooms and online classes. They suggested that online language learners should avoid transferring the same etiquette from traditional classrooms to online classes. In other words, online students should be aware of the advantages of building positive relationships and interacting socially with others, despite the online context, and keeping positive emotions visible in collaborative learning. Online environments lack verbal and non-verbal cues, such as eye contact and body movements, which are regular parts of face-to-face communication. The absence of these cues may lead to misunderstandings in online communication. Hence, online students need to express their attitudes through specific actions, such as responding to others in a timely manner in this online environment. Given the importance of using netiquette to improve effective interactions in online environments and collaboration, '*Netiquette*' was incorporated into the survey questionnaire to explore this social strategy further.

In the study conducted by J. S. Lee and Chen Hsieh (2019), a review of 88 research studies on 'context-aware technology' in foreign-language learning revealed that such technology was found to facilitate interaction and collaborative and cultural learning. The concept of 'context-aware technology', as explained by Lee, encompasses learners' locations, learning environments, and interactions with others. Learning contexts play a crucial role in the use of social strategies by learners, as they enable situated learning and interactions with others, such as teachers and peers, through different technological tools. However, there is a significant dearth of research that is specifically focused on context-specific social strategies in online language learning.

More social strategies have been employed by language learners in synchronous and asynchronous environments since the development of technology in the last two to three decades. According to White (1995), it was found that distance learners had limited engagement with social strategies due to limited chances for interactions with both teachers and other learners. However, White's study was conducted when there was no synchronous technology used in language learning. In contrast, a recent study by Hauck and Hampel (2008) identified affective and social strategy adoption by 25 foreign-language learners through participation in audio-graphic conferencing and blogging online.

However, other studies have indicated that some language learners do not pay great attention to social strategy use in online learning environments (C. Lai & Gu, 2011). C. Lai and Gu (2011) employed an online survey and semi-structured interviews among 279 tertiary-level second/foreign-language learners at the University of Hong Kong. This study identified concerns related to security, difficulties in finding suitable topics, lack of confidence, and fear of receiving feedback on errors as primary factors that hindered learners from participation in social activities through technologies beyond the online classroom setting. These factors illustrate the students' unfamiliarity with social strategies in an online environment. Additionally, the researchers discovered that a majority of the students perceived finding communication opportunities within a traditional classroom environment to be more effective for developing their language skills compared to an online environment. Such a learning belief also reflects a lack of confidence in social strategy use in an online environment.

Research has shown that engaging in collaborative online learning tasks can promote the utilisation of social strategies among learners, facilitating effective communication. Saito (2005) investigated social strategy adoption by Japanese students in collaborative learning using a TELL activity in the form of an internet chat. Such internet chats can provide second-language learners with opportunities to interact with native speakers or advanced learners. Eleven language learners participated in this study at an Australian university. The results showed that, overall, 12 strategies were used when learners saw a new word or expression in their chat exchanges. Most of them preferred asking their chat buddy (29%), classmates (27%), or language teachers (16%) for the answer rather than finding the answer in a dictionary, which provides evidence that, in collaborative learning, learners preferred a quicker way (asking others) to a slower way (checking a dictionary) for the flow of efficient communication. Hauck and Hampel (2008) have suggested that the transfer of affective and social strategies from a face-to-face classroom setting to online environments should not be done directly. They argue that learners need to adapt their communicative skills when interacting with peers and teachers in online environments, such as by sending welcome messages on a blog or sharing personal photos. Consequently, a lack of understanding about selecting appropriate social strategies can impede language learning communications in both the synchronous and asynchronous environments.

Peterson (2008) and Russell and Murphy-Judy (2020) found one social strategy, negotiation of meaning, which is distinctly different from Oxford's social strategies. Peterson discovered that the routine of negotiating meaning was an aspect of students' negotiation in online collaboration via a text-based communicative tool. Students started with repetition and then requested a meaning, and this was followed by a response or reaction to the request. This social strategy use in online collaboration is different from the social strategies (*'Cooperating with peers'*) in Oxford (1990) because of the difference between collaborative learning and cooperative learning. The present work pays particular attention to social strategies for online collaborative learning because of their important role in facilitating collaboration among students.

2.4.4 Memory strategies

Online students' use of memory strategies was explored in two recent studies, Altunay (2014) suggested that online students seemed to be using Oxford's (1990) memory strategy of '*Associating/Elaborating*' to create associations between already known information and the new vocabulary, to help with memorising. Similarly, the results of Solak and Cakir (2015) evidenced that the most frequently used memory strategy of online students was '*Associating/Elaborating*', and the least frequently used memory strategy was '*Using mechanical techniques*'. One possible reason might be that the student-participants in these two studies were all Turkish online students who studied English as a foreign language, and the use of these memory strategies was particular to Turkish students who were English-language learners. Memory strategy use in online Chinese language learning, especially memorising Chinese characters, indicates a clear difference between online learners of English and those learning Chinese (discussed in Section 2.5).

Moreover, studies have already indicated that nowadays online students use fragmented learning time (K. Liang et al., 2018; Zhu et al., 2019), but there is a paucity of LLS research in this regard. Zhu et al. (2019) explained that learners pay more attention to the rich fragmented content in fragmented learning, especially for individual learning, as this is convenient and highly time-efficient with the development of internet technology. The implications of fragmented learning for language learners are that they can take advantage of fragmented time, enabled by technologies, to study anytime and anywhere. Consequently, this might influence online students' LLS use, such as memory and metacognitive strategies. K. Liang et al. (2018) also pointed out that learners may face a massive range and volume of resources, which greatly increases the difficulties they face in fragmented learning. To further understand this learning process, the present book investigates what memory strategies online students used in fragmented language learning.

2.4.5 Compensation strategies

In the literature, many studies have used the term 'communication strategies' rather than 'social' or 'compensation strategies' when referring to LLS use in spoken communication. However, Oxford (1990) used the term 'compensation strategies' to cover strategies adopted by language learners in both speaking and writing situations. For example, the strategy of paraphrasing not only takes place when speaking, but also in the writing process. Such compensation strategies were highlighted in an online context by Shih (2014), which contained two subcategories, guessing intelligently and overcoming limitations.

Oxford, in her definition of compensation strategies, identified a set of detailed strategies, but did not clearly indicate the sequence of compensation strategy use in a collaborative context, nor the relationships between these strategies. However, recent studies have discovered that language learners have a routine of compensation strategy use in speaking when they interact with others, and the routine of these strategies is influenced by different learning environments, types of language learning tasks, and language learners' language proficiency (Shih, 2014). Within this routine of strategy use, Shih (2014) categorised four types of non-verbal compensation strategies and four types of verbal strategies. Shih's study also suggested that non-verbal compensation strategies can be used to support verbal communication, such as to express emotions, or replace words and phrases with non-verbal forms of communication, two strategies which are investigated in Shih's book.

Additionally, the task type would influence the frequency of non-verbal and verbal compensation strategy use for language learners (Shih, 2014). For instance, role-playing tasks helped language learners' language output, and language learners employed more compensation strategies in the role-playing tasks than in the discussion-type tasks. Language proficiency, in addition to influencing the order of strategy use, has also been found to have a close relationship with the frequency of strategy use. Elaborate strategies, such as a paraphrasing strategy, tend to be adopted more frequently by higher-proficiency-level language learners than lower-level students (Shih, 2014). This book investigates what compensation strategies online students uses and how they use these strategies in both Chinese speaking and writing to support collaborative learning.

2.4.6 Metacognitive strategies

Metacognitive strategies have been pointed out to be particularly valuable to online students because, once students understand how to regulate their own learning through the use of strategies, language acquisition should proceed at a faster rate (e.g., H. Chang & Windeatt, 2016; M.-M. Chang, 2007, 2010). For instance, M.-M. Chang (2005) examined whether the use of metacognitive strategies promoted online language learning and consequently improved overall academic achievement. Chang's study demonstrated that less proficient language learners showed the greatest improvement in online language learning. However, language learners have been found to have a lack of knowledge of metacognitive strategies as well as a lack of metacognitive strategy training (M.-M. Chang, 2007). Recent research has also suggested that there is a mismatch between language learners' preference for using compensation strategies and language teachers' expectation that students will use metacognitive strategies in online language learning (S. C. Huang, 2018).

The self-monitoring strategy which belongs to the category of metacognitive strategies, has also been found to be essential for online language learning. Coleman and Webber (2002) described a self-monitoring strategy as a process of having a language learner self-record data to reflect on their learning behaviour in order to adjust their learning activities. In online learning, research has shown a strong relationship between self-monitoring strategy adoption by language learners and the language learners' performance (M.-M. Chang, 2007; Coleman & Webber, 2002; Zimmerman, 1999).

Additionally, metacognitive strategies have been found to contribute to managing affective strategy use. Affect is related to 'emotion, feelings, moods and attitudes, anxiety, tolerance of ambiguity and motivation' (Hurd, 2008, p. 218). Hurd's (2008) investigation of four female distance language learners' use of affective strategies revealed that four metacognitive strategies were adopted to manage their affective strategy use. In another study, M.-M. Chang (2005) introduced a web-based instruction course of metacognitive LLSs to 28 university language learners for one semester, in order to facilitate their motivation. The comparison between the before- and the after-training results showed that language learners had become more confident, challengeable, and responsible, and believed in their efforts more than before.

As mentioned previously, research has revealed that there is a mismatch between language teachers' expectation that language learners will use metacognitive strategies use and language learners' actual preference for compensation strategy use (H.-C. Huang, 2013; Liou, 2000). H.-C. Huang (2013) constructed an online reading strategy training programme for low-proficiency-level Chinese language learners. The results reflected teachers' belief in focusing on using metacognitive strategies, which consisted of self-planning, self-monitoring, and self-checking strategies in reading. However, the language learners relied on compensation strategies, which contained localised actions, such as highlighting, checking dictionaries, taking notes, and using their mother tongue in translation during the reading process. This calls for general and specific LLS training. This book focuses on online students' metacognitive strategy use not only in self-directed learning, but also in collaborative assessment tasks with language partners.

2.4.7 LLSs specific to online learning

Most LLSs used by learners in an online environment can be explained using Oxford's (1990) six categories of LLSs (e.g., Smidt & Hegelheimer, 2004; Ulitsky, 2000). However, the adoption of LLSs by language learners has been influenced by changing technologies, and recent studies have demonstrated that Oxford's categorisation does not cover the whole range of LLSs used by online learners (e.g., Dubreil, 2020; C. Gao & Shen, 2021; Hauck & Hampel, 2008; C. Lai & Gu, 2011; Park & Kim, 2011; Smidt & Hegelheimer, 2004).

Firstly, new LLSs were found in Smidt and Hegelheimer (2004); namely, 'test-taking strategies'. For example, students' preference to answer easy questions first when completing an online listening activity is not one that can be easily classified in any of Oxford's categories. Secondly, a learning action was identified from the interview data of C. Lai and Gu (2011)'s interview data (2004) where one language learner collected phrases from native speakers online, and then checked the dictionary to see if they were in a formal or informal language style. This learning action reflected the student's metacognitive strategy use in online language learning (C. Lai & Gu, 2011). Thirdly, two new reading strategies, which are closely related to online reading, were found in the data of Park and Kim (2011). One was the use of hypermedia, and the other was the use of computer accessories and other functions. Language learners can benefit from using hypermedia in a text presentation in hypertextual reading (Bouvet & Close, 2006).

In another study, Smith's (2000) LLS investigation has demonstrated that Oxford's (2011) categories and SILL might not be able to cover the whole LLS range in TELL, and other strategies can be more effective in a more modern context. Smith used two questionnaires and semi-structured interviews to investigate the factors which influenced successful language learners' embracing of socio-collaborative

CALL at the University of Melbourne. One questionnaire was about individual-student beliefs in relation to teaching and learning, and the other was Oxford's (1990) SILL. The results revealed that language learners adopted a range of well-recognised LLSs in Oxford's LLS categories, especially the cognitive strategies. However, there were three additional LLSs which were beyond the range of Oxford's (1990) LLSs: using one's mother tongue for effective communication, receiving peer feedback, and finding content through relying on keywords. The result also showed three types of LLSs specifically related to TELL: strategies for effective learning resources selection (cognitive strategy), strategies for seeking opportunities to think in the target language (metacognitive strategy), and strategies for quick interaction with websites (not in SILL).

In Hauck and Hampel (2008), a notable LLS specific to online learning environments was used by online students. This study concerned students' strategy use when using online communication tools, such as email, synchronous chat, and threaded discussion, in cooperation with others. Students employed a social strategy related to the communication tools, namely 'Using the tools and modes available to improve communication and interaction' (p. 296), such as showing photos to invite more spontaneous contributions in a conferencing system.

LLS use in online learning environments was also investigated Stickler and Lewis (2008), who discovered 13 new LLSs. The students in their study employed these 13 LLSs in collaboration with native speakers in an email tandem exchange, which refers to students of two different language communities forming a collaborative partnership with the aim of each learning the other's mother tongue and culture.

2.4.8 Summary of LLS research in online language learning

Overall, most strategies used by learners in online language learning can be found in Oxford's (1990) LLS classifications. However, it appears that online learning, which has its own specific characteristics, requires additional categories alongside Oxford's to fully cover online LLSs. Thus, whilst SILL can still be used, it needs to be modified to suit research into LLS use in online learning. Recent studies (such as Dubreil, 2020; C. Gao & Shen, 2021; Hadwin et al., 2018; Hauck & Hampel, 2008; C. Lee, 2020) have explored LLS use in online learning environments, but there is still a huge gap in terms of LLS use associated with technological tools in different learning contexts such as self-directed learning, assessment task completion, and online class participation. Furthermore, most of these studies focused on the use of specific LLSs to support online learning in an asynchronous environment, but not in a synchronous environment. In view of these gaps, this book particularly focuses on students' LLS use across both the asynchronous and synchronous environments.

2.5 An overview of Chinese LLS research

LLS research in the area of English as a second and foreign language has developed very swiftly and systemically, and as such has built an integrated framework with detailed explanations of LLSs. However, the number of studies researching Chinese

LLSs is relatively low. Nevertheless, when reviewing the Chinese LLSs employed by students who speak a European language, two key aspects were found. The first was that students who speak a European language learn Chinese in a specific way. The other was that students use LLSs that are specific to Chinese language learning. Furthermore, when reviewing the literature on Chinese LLSs specific to Chinese learning that are not covered by LLS research relating to English-language learning, it was clear that most of these studies focus on language learning skills, especially LLSs in Chinese character learning. Importantly, not much Chinese LLS research has been done in listening and essay writing or in TELL.

2.5.1 LLS adoption in Chinese language learning

In Chinese LLS research, aspects of European language speakers' LLS adoption in Chinese language learning have been examined in a few key studies (W. Jiang & Wu, 2016; J. Wang et al., 2009; Y. Wang, 2013; Z. Xu, 2010; Zhi & Lu, 2018).

Z. Xu (2010) compared European speakers and Chinese speakers when they learnt a foreign language and found that their strategy adoption and foci were different. These language learners were separated into two groups: a group of 58 adult English-language learners (Chinese speakers), and a group of 66 adult Chinese-language learners (European-language speakers, which included 26 Australians). Xu found that the European-language-speaking group focused on using listening strategies at the beginning proficiency level, and they liked conversations. These students then used more LLSs for reading and writing at the intermediate level after they had accumulated vocabulary. Chinese speakers, on the other hand, learnt English in the opposite way. Their LLS adoptions were therefore influenced by different foci at different levels of language proficiency.

Chinese-language learners also tend to use more social strategies than memory and affective strategies in Chinese learning. Yaomei Wang (Y. Wang, 2013) used the SILL questionnaire to analyse Chinese LLSs among 81 international students from 39 countries who went to China and were preparing for enrolment in Chinese universities. The results revealed that these students used a low frequency of memory strategies and affective strategies, but a high frequency of social strategies. Yaomei Wang (Y. Wang, 2013) deduced that the reason for this use of social strategies was that these students had to use the target language (Chinese) to communicate with others outside the classroom. Wang also suggested that the reasons for using less affective strategies might have included a lack of knowledge of affective strategies and how to use them effectively.

The study by W. Jiang and Wu (2016) supported the result of Yaomei Wang (Y. 2013) relating to European-language-speaking students' social strategy use by comparing 100 Chinese English-language learners and 101 Australian Chinese-language learners' LLSs. They found that Australian students used LLSs with a mean of 3.16 (on a five-point Likert scale) and frequently employed social strategies. The sequence from the most frequently used to the least frequently used LLS categories was: social, metacognitive, compensation, cognitive, and affective.

It has also been found that European-language speakers who valued metacognitive beliefs and strategies in Chinese language learning achieve satisfactory learning outcomes. J. Wang et al. (2009) investigated the effects of metacognitive beliefs and strategy adoption by 45 tertiary-level students learning Chinese as a foreign language at the University of Nottingham in the UK. The results demonstrated that metacognitive beliefs and strategies had a strong impact on learning outcomes. Furthermore, self-efficacy was found to be an important factor in Chinese-language listening performance. As an interactive ability, self-efficacy was found to contribute to oral performance. Thinking about suitable strategies and setting goals were found to be essential to writing performance, and successful students regularly practised writing. The study by Zhi and Lu (2018) also indicated that Western learners employed more metacognitive and social strategies than Asian learners. These results demonstrated that learner autonomy facilitated a strong metacognitive awareness. The studies above suggested that learners of Chinese emphasised using social and metacognitive strategies in their language learning.

2.5.2 Chinese-character-learning strategy use

Chinese-character learning is a challenge for all learners. It requires learners to put effort into practising character writing by following the correct stroke order, memorising radicals, and identifying similar shapes and structures as well. Since the cognitive processing of Chinese-character learning is unique, Chinese-character LLS use is also unique (B. Hu, 2018; Shen, 2005, 2013; Shen & Xu, 2015). Memory, cognitive, and metacognitive strategies have been found to be important and are often employed by language learners in Chinese-character learning (X. Jiang & Zhao, 2001; Shen, 2005).

Many researchers have indicated that memory strategies are essential in Chinese-character learning as it is specific to non-character-background learners, especially for beginners. X. Jiang and Zhao (2001) examined Chinese character-learning strategies among 136 tertiary students who were beginners learning Chinese as a foreign language in China. The results on Chinese-character learning showed that memory strategies were employed frequently by these beginners, who focused on character shapes as a whole and used a rote-reviewing strategy in both writing and recognition. However, they seldom used semantic and phonetic components to help memorise characters, and this was especially the case for non-character-background learners. A recent study by Kan, Owen, and Bax (2018) also demonstrated that the low accuracy of phonetic components pushed non-native Chinese learners into paying attention to the phonological cues in character learning. These findings on character recognition and memorisation have indicated possible processing differences in the strategy use by non-character background learners in Chinese character learning. A recent book by B. Hu (2018) has already identified 11 LLSs that are useful for Chinese-character memorisation. Three out of the 11 strategies are specific for Chinese-character learning, such as 'tracing character strokes', 'making up stories about characters', and 'breaking down characters into components'.

Apart from memory strategies, cognitive and metacognitive strategies have also been found to be frequently adopted for Chinese-character learning. Shen (2005) investigated Chinese-character-learning strategies among 95 English-speaking learners and relevant factors impacting LLS adoption, such as language levels. The results confirmed that 30 strategies in Chinese-character learning were used, and that cognitive strategies were often adopted by Chinese-language learners. For example, students repeated the sound of a character when they first heard it and paid attention to the tone associated with Pinyin. Metacognitive strategies were also adopted by learners, such as the strategies of structured preview and review. The results also revealed that orthographic-knowledge-based strategies (strategies in which students use radical knowledge, graphics, semantics, and phonetics as clues to encode characters) were particularly frequently adopted.

2.5.3 LLS use in Chinese speaking

There is also a paucity of research on LLS use by Chinese-language learners in the development of speaking skills. The studies by Qian and Zhao (2009) and Hsieh (2014) were the two investigations found in the literature that discussed this topic. Both studies compared the strategy use of two groups of Chinese-language learners: learners from a Chinese-character-influenced background or Asian background, such as Japanese, and learners from a non-Chinese-character-influenced background or non-Asian background, such as American. Qian and Zhao (2009) reported on Chinese LLS use among 147 tertiary-level international students at Nanjing Normal University, China. Both non-Chinese and Chinese-character-influenced groups of students were found to have emphasised the importance of gaining speaking proficiency, and most of them adopted a self-monitoring strategy. The non-Chinese-character-influenced group often adopted Chinese language output strategies, such as the adjustment strategy and the cooperation strategy, which are social strategies. Students in the other group (Chinese-character-influenced) emphasised the use of cognitive strategies. This different LLS use suggests that prior learning experience and learner language background influenced the students' LLS use.

Affective strategies and compensation strategies were found to be adopted by the non-Asian background group in Hsieh (2014). Hsieh investigated Chinese oral-communication strategies among 176 Chinese-language learners at a university in Taiwan. The results identified that non-Asian-background language learners tended to use social, affective, and compensation strategies (also known as the conversation maintenance strategies) more than the Asian-background language learners. The results also showed that lower-proficiency learners paid attention to a small part of a conversation (as one LLS) and used this strategy more than higher-proficiency level learners. Higher-proficiency-level language learners were more able to catch the main meaning of a sentence than language learners at lower proficiency levels, and this reduced the frequency of focus-on-a-small-part strategy use.

2.5.4 LLS use in Chinese essay writing

There is also a lack of literature about LLS use in Chinese essay writing. Qian and Zhao (2009) reported that learners who spoke a European language used cognitive strategies and metacognitive strategies in Chinese essay writing. The authors examined Chinese LLS adoption among 119 tertiary-level international students in four universities in China. Overall, the results showed that all the international students adopted the checking and transforming cognitive strategies. However, they seldom used the first-language or cooperation strategies to help them with Chinese essay writing. A possible reason given for this was that the students lacked the opportunities to use the cooperation strategy in teacher-centred classes in China. The researchers also found that the students employed a metacognitive strategy of self-evaluation rather than cooperating with others because their Chinese-language proficiency was low, and therefore they could not critique the work of others very well by using the cooperation strategy.

2.5.5 Chinese LLS use in TELL

It was very difficult to find literature about Chinese LLS use in TELL, and there was no research found regarding Chinese LLS use in online Chinese courses during the course of this research project. J. Wang (2012) investigated how Chinese-language learners used e-dictionaries to learn Chinese vocabulary and demonstrated that a relationship existed between language proficiency and the effectiveness of using e-dictionaries. The author examined the use of e-dictionaries among 20 intermediate and advanced Chinese-language learners in China, finding that intermediate Chinese-language learners can gain more benefits than advanced Chinese-language learners through first-language explanations of Chinese phrases and words in e-dictionaries. The reason for this, Wang suggested, was that intermediate Chinese-language learners needed to expand their knowledge of high-frequency words, whilst the advanced-level Chinese-language learners already had this foundation. The results also reflected the difference between intermediate- and advanced-level Chinese-language learners in reading ability.

However, as TELL advances, new strategies are emerging in Chinese-language learning. For example, Wong et al. (2011) investigated how Chinese-language learners used a mobile-assisted Chinese-character-forming game to assemble characters with the correct radicals. Their study suggested that a gaming strategy might be useful (social scaffold), as participants were required to collaborate with others. Although Wong et al.'s (2011) study represents the beginning of research in this area, in general there remains a gap in our understanding of Chinese-character-learning strategies within TELL.

2.6 Different variables that influence LLS adoption

Research has indicated that there is an association between the use and choice of LLSs and different variables such as learner characteristics, learning experiences, and language proficiency. Chinese LLSs have been found, from the discussions on the Chinese LLS research highlighted so far, to be a specific series of LLSs used by language learners from a European background. In this regard, LLS researchers have paid considerable attention to the language background of language learners. However, there are some learner-related factors that have not received as much attention and could, therefore, be explored further.

2.6.1 Individual differences

Individual difference (ID) research is not a new area in the field of second-language acquisition and is generally seen as a way to gain a deep understanding of foreign-language learners' learning. ID refers to 'characteristics or traits in respect of which individuals may be shown to differ from each other' (Dörnyei, 2005, p. 1). This definition raises a question as to why some foreign-language learners succeed more than others (Ellis, 2012). IDs have been classified into two main categories of attribute, which are: (1) innate differences, such as age, language-learning aptitude, personality, and learning styles, and (2) acquired differences, such as attitudes, motivation, beliefs, and strategy use (Benson & Gao, 2008). In these categories, language learners' strategy adoption is seen as a psychological phenomenon, as it reflects a foreign-language learner's beliefs and preferences (Benson & Gao, 2008).

In online language learning, IDs can certainly result in different LLS use, learning outcomes, and learning preferences. Arispe and Blake (2012) investigated individual-student factors and successful language learning in a hybrid online Spanish course among 51 language learners at the University of California. These individual learner factors contained five personality traits (extraversion, agreeableness, conscientiousness, neuroticism, and openness), and two cognitive factors (verbal and abstract skills). Conscientious learners and low-verbal learners were shown to have benefited from the online language courses because they had clear goals and plans for their learning process. Results also provided evidence that low-verbal language learners might benefit more than high-verbal language learners in an online language course, because these low-verbal students felt less pressure if they made errors in a synchronous environment.

Recent research has also shown that online language-learning design should consider IDs to assist students' online learning. Martinez (2001) believed that learners' IDs led to four types of learning orientation: transforming, performing, conforming, and resistant, which would cause different degrees of learning success. In Martinez's categorisation, transforming learners were aware of their personal strengths and learning ability; performing learners were skilled learners but were reluctant to invest effort into their learning; conforming learners were willing to accept the instructor's management of their learning and relied on others' guidance but lacked critical thinking; and resistant learners doubted others' learning arrangements and had negative learning emotions, leading them to be defensive learners. Martinez's (2001) study showed that IDs influenced learners' LLS use.

2.6.2 Motivation

Motivation is seen as an essential individual learner characteristic that influences outcomes in foreign-language learning, and it is also treated as an important component of ID variable research (Ellis, 2012). Gardner (1985) defined motivation as 'the combination of effort plus desire to achieve the goal of learning the language plus favourable attitudes toward learning the language' (p. 10). Dörnyei (2005) believed that motivational factors can play a more powerful role than language aptitude in foreign-language learning. The possible factors which can influence motivation are the teacher's demands, a high desire to achieve, social pressure, or rewards from parents, and some or all of these can potentially stimulate language learners to put effort into a tedious language-learning process (Gardner, 1985).

Researchers have conducted large-scale studies to investigate the relationship between motivation and LLSs. One study showed that LLS adoption by language learners can be predicted according to their motivation (Oxford & Nyikos, 1989). The findings from another study involving 2,089 foreign-language learners in an American university indicated that motivational strength can lead to a greater level of LLS use (Schmidt & Watanabe, 2001). N.-D. Yang (1999) reported that there was a positive cyclical correlation between learners' belief, motivation, and LLS use.

Relationships have also been found between motivation and metacognitive strategy use. Good distance language learners have been found to have higher motivations and to adopt more metacognitive strategies. Hurd (2000) investigated the characteristics of 'good distance language learners' through questionnaires and face-to-face discussions. Motivation and metacognitive strategy use were identified as two significant factors influencing effective distance language learning. In Hurd's study, good distance language learners were found to be well-organised, have the ability to prioritise, have high learning motivation, and to adopt metacognitive strategies such as emphasising time management and organisation, reflection, and a gradual development of a better awareness of language-learning progress due to the use of LLSs.

The high motivation of good distance language learners has also been described as attributable to a positive feeling towards learning goals that are achieved. In a study of 8,000 beginning-level distance language learners enrolled in a Spanish course with the Open University in the UK, Hurd (2000) discovered that effective language learning is correlated with distance learners' enjoyment and their sense of achieving goals during the learning process. As a result of their enjoyment and sense of goal achievement, the distance learners were motivated in their learning and devoted more effort to completing their assessments.

Although most research in ID literature has investigated the relationship between motivation and LLS use, the word '*motive*' was used in my project for two significant reasons. Firstly, it is difficult to accurately measure motivation as its characteristics (e.g., goal-directed, exhibits positive affect, self-efficacy) are complex, with some being affective and others behavioural (Gardner, 2007). Secondly, this research only asked students to provide their reasons for studying Chinese, therefore 'motive' better describes the questions asked in the survey questionnaire.

2.6.3 Language proficiency

The concept of proficiency combines fluency and accuracy in language learning. Studies have already revealed that language learning tasks in different proficiency levels influenced students' LLS use. For example, high-level language learners can employ relevant strategies to read authentic materials, which are difficult for beginning-to-intermediate language learners because of their complicated grammar, vocabulary, genre-specific style, and cultural references (Garrett, 2009). L. L. Chang (2007) reported a study concerning the use of an authentic Chinese talk show 'Tell it like it is!' (实话实说) in a 14-week Chinese-language course at an Australian university. Chinese idioms and vocabulary were involved in this programme and therefore only high-language-proficiency-level students were able to attend and benefit from the programme. Consequently, the participants in the study used LLSs to learn Chinese idioms in Chinese speaking which beginning-level students would not.

Strategy training in TELL, therefore, needs to consider the various language-proficiency levels and language-learning materials that are appropriate for a particular level of proficiency. Garrett (2009) suggested that language teachers should arrange strategy training for students in tutorials and train them how to learn using authentic materials with strategies in TELL, such as skimming and scanning skills, listening skills, cadence, clause structure, and word choice. Garrett (2009) further suggested that web-based modules of LLSs should be prepared in online learning in order to support language learners according to their proficiency.

Studies have also reported that higher-language-proficiency-level learners adopt more LLSs than lower-language-proficiency-level learners and tend to adopt more metacognitive strategies (Garrett, 2009; Gharbavi & Mousavi, 2012; Griffiths, 2008; Hong-Nam & Leavell, 2006; Oxford & Nyikos, 1989). Oxford and Nyikos's (1989) study of 1,200 language learners in a Midwestern American university demonstrated motivation and language proficiency as two powerful factors that influenced LLS adoption. In their study, higher-language-proficiency learners were shown to have adopted more strategies than lower-language-proficiency learners. Another study by Gharbavi and Mousavi (2012) confirmed Oxford and Nyikos's results, and also demonstrated that advanced-level learners used more compensatory strategies and metacognitive strategies than low-level language learners. The study by Griffiths (2008) echoed the finding that high-proficiency-level language learners employed LLSs more frequently than low-level language learners, based on an analysis of LLS adoption by 131 foreign-language learners.

In *online* language learning, researchers have also explored the relationship between LLS use and language proficiency. In the online reading process, high-proficiency language learners have been found to adopt keyword, prediction, preview, and outline strategies more than low-proficiency language learners (H.-C. Huang et al., 2009). When faced with different difficulty levels of texts, high-proficiency-level students used more social and affective strategies when they read lower-level-difficulty texts. However, low-level students appeared to have no changes in LLS adoption when they were faced with different texts. Overall, studies have tended to reveal a strong relationship between language proficiency and LLS use. This book, therefore, is also based on the assumption that there is a close relationship between language proficiency and LLS use.

2.6.4 Learner autonomy

Learner autonomy (LA) has been defined as 'the ability to take charge of one's own learning' (Holec, 1981, p. 3). This capability requires language learners to consider the learning place, time, process, and content, and thus LA can reflect a psychological control of language learning (Cotterall, 2008). In this respect, LA for foreign-language learning should also consider the features of current technological tools that support LLS use.

Traditionally, LA was seen as the end goal in education. It plays an important role in successful language learning, especially in the learner-centred language-teaching classroom (Holec, 1981; Little, 2000; W. Shi & Han, 2019). Oxford (2008) pointed out that the role of a language learner should be seen as comprising that of a reviewer, a selector, an adaptor, and an inventor in the language-learning process. Thus, a learner-centred curriculum design highlights strategy training to encourage learners to manage and take responsibility for their own learning. As a result, language learners may gain a feeling of achievement from their management of their own learning (Nunan, 1997).

Since the 1990s, technologies have played an important role in the development of learner autonomy in multiple ways (Reinders & Hubbard, 2013). These help language learners promote learner autonomy. Thus, the literature would indicate that LLSs, learner autonomy, and technologies are closely related. For example, language learners can rely on new technologies as a means of developing a planning strategy and a monitoring strategy, and also autonomy. Indeed, the idea of a flipped classroom and technology use may motivate LA research because they are both rooted in learner-centred theories and aim to facilitate language learners' LA as much as possible.

The decisions made by language learners in their selection of technology are related to their LLS adoption, learner autonomy, motivation, and learning effectiveness. Ulitsky (2000) described the complicated relationships between motivation, autonomy, LLSs, and learning effectiveness after they examined 27 foreign-language learners' LLS adoption in a multimedia environment. Specifically, they argued that if learners actively participate in language learning as autonomous learners, it leads them to positive and then to high motivation, which facilitates their LLS use and achievement of improvement in language proficiency. On the other hand, suitable LLSs could lead to high motivation, language proficiency improvement, and enhanced self-esteem. Thus, it is important for language learners to select LLSs in order to mirror the strength of their learner autonomy (Ulitsky, 2000). In addition, in Ulitsky's study, learner autonomy relied on 'software' selection. In other words, the chosen technology must work together with learner autonomy in language learning.

2.6.5 Age

Age is an essential individual learner characteristic that is investigated in LLS research as there are specific characteristics related to adult language learning. Adult language learners who acquire a foreign language through formal language learning in a classroom need to know how to learn a foreign language before they start to learn. However, compared with young language learners, adult learners have prior learning experiences and a broader knowledge of the world (Krashen, 1982). Thus they use conscious consideration when selecting LLSs (Cohen, 1998).

For example, adult language learners tend to adopt cognitive and metacognitive strategies more frequently than younger learners (Nambiar, 2009).

However, there have only been a small number of studies into the LLS use of different-aged adult language learners. Khezrlou (2012) compared cognitive and metacognitive strategy use between 60 young (aged 14–17) and 90 adult (aged 20–30) language learners. This study provided evidence that adult language learners adopted more LLSs than young language learners, especially in foreign-language reading. The results also demonstrated a positive relationship between cognitive strategy use and adult language learners' learning performance.

Age and LLS use were also a topic in the work of Sepasdar and Soori (2014), where the researchers compared 94 primary, guidance, high-school, and university students' LLS use when learning English as their second language. The study revealed that whilst compensation strategies were the most frequently employed by the university students, memory strategies were the least frequently used. University students employed social and affective strategies more frequently than other groups of students.

At an older age, language learners may have an advantage when adopting LLSs as they can use their past learning experience in language learning. A recent study by A. D. Cohen and Li (2013), provided a case study focusing on A. D. Cohen himself as a Chinese language learner. Although he started as a beginning-level Chinese learner at the age of 67, this was the 13th language that Cohen had learnt. Cohen proved to be a successful Chinese language learner because of his positive learning motivation, efforts in learning, and past language-learning experience. For instance, he could link the word-order pattern of Chinese to a similar word-order pattern in a third foreign language. Although he had the challenges of both a reduced long-term memory as an older language learner and the four tones in Chinese-language learning, he still achieved a very good performance in oral tests through careful LLSs selection as an LLS expert which included noticing the word-order pattern, translation, guessing meaning from context, and using the Google Translate app via his iPhone. Therefore, Cohen's past experience in adopting LLSs helped him to consciously select effective LLSs in his language learning.

The study by Montero et al. (2013) found that the study-abroad experience influenced children's but not adults' LLSs. The researchers investigated the relative impact of a three-month study-abroad experience on Spanish-speaking English-language learners' communication strategies, which can be explained as Oxford's (1990) compensation and social strategies. Their results indicated that children developed significantly more effective communication strategies after the study-abroad experience, whilst the influences of experience on adults' communication strategies was limited.

2.7 Summary

This review of the literature on online learning, TELL, and the difficulties in Chinese language learning has sought to provide some background information for the research focus of this book. This literature review indicates that it is generally accepted that students' LLS use is important in understanding their success (or otherwise) in language learning. However, there is still a huge gap in terms of understanding the LLSs that online students use or could use in coping with various challenges in online learning. Specifically, there is a lack of studies on what and how such online students employ the following strategies:

- affective strategies in different ways in self-directed learning;
- cognitive strategies and technological tools in completing various online learning activities and assessment tasks;
- social strategies in collaborative learning;
- memory strategies in fragmented-time learning and Chinese-language learning;
- compensation strategies in both Chinese speaking and writing;
- metacognitive strategies in collaborative learning; and
- LLSs specific to online language learning.

The literature review also found that there are variables affecting the use or preference of LLSs. The variables of language learners' ID, motivation, proficiency level, learner autonomy, and age were discussed in this chapter. Based on the review of these variables, it is clear that there is a shortage of studies focusing on online students' LLS use associated with relevant influencing factors (contextual factors and individual learner factors), such as online environments, motives, different adult age groups, and prior language-learning experience. Hence, this book focuses on the type of LLSs that online Chinese learners use in asynchronous and synchronous environments. It also focuses on both the interactants and characteristics of the specific learning context (e.g. self-directed learning, assessment task completion, and online class participation) as well as individual learner characteristics.

References

Akçayır, G., & Akçayır, M. (2018). The flipped classroom: A review of its advantages and challenges. *Computers & Education, 126*, 334–345. https://doi.org/10.1016/j.compedu.2018.07.021

Akiyama, Y., & Saito, K. (2016). Development of comprehensibility and its linguistic correlates: A longitudinal study of video-mediated telecollaboration. *The Modern Language Journal, 100*(3), 585–609. https://doi.org/10.1111/modl.12338

Altunay, D. (2014). Language learning strategies used by distance learners of English: a study with a group of Turkish distance learners of EFL. *Turkish Online Journal of Distance Education, 15*(3), 291–305. https://doi.org/10.17718/tojde.30083

Anderson, T. (2008). *The theory and practice of online learning* (2nd ed.). Edmonton, Canada: AU Press.

Antoniou, S. (2022). Emergency remote teaching in tertiary education: issues raised, solutions given, and lessons learned. In C. N. Giannikas (Ed.), *Transferring language learning and teaching from face-to-face to online settings* (1st ed., pp. 47–66). Hershey, PA: IGI Global.

Arispe, K., & Blake, R. J. (2012). Individual factors and successful learning in a hybrid course. *System, 40*(4), 449–465.

Baker, J. W. (2000). The classroom flip: Becoming the guide by the side. *Communication Faculty Presentations*. Retrieved from https://digitalcommons.cedarville.edu/media_and_applied_communications_presentations/11

Barnes, S. (2000). What does electronic conferencing afford distance education? *Distance Education, 21*(2), 236–247. https://doi.org/10.1080/0158791000210203

Beatty, K. (2003). *Teaching and researching: Computer-assisted language learning*. London, UK: Pearson Education.

Benson, P., & Gao, X. (2008). Individual variation and language learning strategies. In S. Hurd & T. Lewis (Eds.), *Language learning strategies in independent settings* (pp. 25–40). Bristol, UK: Multilingual Matters.

Bosmans, D., & Hurd, S. (2016). Phonological attainment and foreign language anxiety in distance language learning: A quantitative approach. *Distance Education, 37*(3), 287–301. https://doi.org/10.1080/01587919.2016.1233049

Bouvet, E., & Close, E. (2006). Online reading strategy guidance in a foreign language: Five case studies in French. *Australian Review of Applied Linguistics, 29*(1), 07.01–07.19. https://doi.org/10.2104/aral0607

Bown, J., & White, C. J. (2010). Affect in a self-regulatory framework for language learning. *System, 38*(3), 432–443. https://doi.org/10.1016/j.system.2010.03.016

Brame, C. J. (2013). Flipping the classroom. Retrieved from http://cft.vanderbilt.edu/guides-sub-pages/flipping-the-classroom/

Bruning, R. H. (2004). *Cognitive psychology and instruction* (4th ed.). Upper Saddle River, NJ: Pearson/Merrill/Prentice Hall.

Bush, M. D., & Terry, R. M. (1997). *Technology-enhanced language learning*. Lincolnwood, IL: National Textbook Company.

Chang, H., & Windeatt, S. (2016). Developing collaborative learning practices in an online language course. *Computer Assisted Language Learning, 29*(8), 1271–1286. https://doi.org/10.1080/09588221.2016.1274331

Chang, L. L. (2007). The effects of using CALL on advanced Chinese foreign language learners. *CALICO, 24*(2), 331–353.

Chang, M.-M. (2005). Applying self-regulated learning strategies in a web-based instruction: An investigation of motivation perception. *Computer Assisted Language Learning, 18*(3), 217–230. https://doi.org/10.1080/09588220500178939

Chang, M.-M. (2007). Enhancing web-based language learning through self-monitoring. *Journal of Computer Assisted Learning, 23*(3), 187–196. https://doi.org/10.1111/j.1365-2729.2006.00203.x

Chang, M.-M. (2010). Effects of self-monitoring on web-based language learner's performance and motivation. *CALICO Journal, 27*(2), 298–310.

Clark, R. C., & Mayer, R. E. (2016). *E-learning and the science of instruction: Proven guidelines for consumers and designers of multimedia learning* (4th ed.). Hoboken, NJ: Wiley.

Cohen, A. D. (1998). *Strategies in learning and using a second language*. London, UK: Longman.

Cohen, A. D. (2012). Strategies: The interface of styles, strategies, and motivation on tasks. In S. Mercer, S. Ryan, & M. Williams (Eds.), *Psychology for Language learning: Insights from research, theory and practice* (pp. 136–150). Basingstoke, UK: Palgrave Macmillan.

Cohen, A. D., & Li, P. (2013). Learning Mandarin in later life: Can old dogs learn new tricks? *Contemporary Foreign Language Studies, 396*(12), 5–14.

Coleman, M. C., & Webber, J. (2002). *Emotional and behavioral disorders*. Boston, MA: Pearson Education Company.

Cotterall, S. (2008). Autonomy and good language learners. In C. Griffiths (Ed.), *Lessons from good language learners* (pp. 110–120). Cambridge, UK: Cambridge University Press.

Dalton, B., & Grisham, D. L. (2011). eVoc strategies: 10 ways to use technology to build vocabulary. *The Reading Teacher*, *64*(5), 306–317. https://doi.org/10.1598/RT.64.5.1

Devlin, N. R. F., & Trad, H. (2014). Collaboration as a key for effective teaching: using an online learning environment to help pre-service teachers solve problems across thousands of kilometres. *Special Education Perspectives*, *23*(1), 7–15.

Dörnyei, Z. (2005). *The psychology of the language learner: Individual differences in Second language acquisition*. Mahwah, NJ: Lawrence Erlbaum Associates.

Dubreil, S. (2020). Using games for language learning in the age of social distancing. *Foreign Language Annals*, *53*(2), 250–259.

Ellis, R. (2008). *The study of second language acquisition* (2nd ed.). Oxford, UK: Oxford University Press.

Ellis, R. (2012). *Language teaching research and language pedagogy* (1st ed.). Malden, MA: John Wiley & Sons Inc.

Gao, C., & Shen, H.-Z. (2021). Mobile-technology-induced learning strategies: Chinese university EFL students learning English in an emerging context. *ReCALL*, *33*(1), 88–105.

Gao, X. (2006). Understanding changes in Chinese students' uses of learning strategies in China and Britain: A socio-cultural re-interpretation. *System*, *34*(1), 55–67. https://doi.org/10.1016/j.system.2005.04.003

Gao, X. (2007). Has language learning strategy research come to an end? A response to Tseng et al. (2006). *Applied Linguistics*, *28*(4), 615–620. https://doi.org/10.1093/applin/amm034

Gao, X. (2008). You had to work hard 'cause you didn't know whether you were going to wear shoes or straw sandals! *Journal of Language, Identity & Education*, *7*(3–4), 169–187. https://doi.org/10.1080/15348450802237798

Gao, X. (2010). Autonomous language learning against all odds. *System*, *38*(4), 580–590. https://doi.org/10.1016/j.system.2010.09.011

Gardner, R. (1985). *Social psychology and second language learning: The role of attitude and motivation*. London, UK: Edward Arnold.

Gardner, R. (2007). Motivation and second language acquisition. *Porta Linguarum*, *8*, 9–20.

Garrett, N. (2009). Computer-assisted language learning trends and issues revisited: Integrating innovation. *The Modern Language Journal*, *93*(1), 719–740. https://doi.org/10.1111/j.1540-4781.2009.00969.x

Gharbavi, A., & Mousavi, S. A. (2012). Do language proficiency levels correspond to language learning strategy adoption? *English Language Teaching*, *5*(7), 110–122. https://doi.org/10.5539/elt.v5n7p110

Golonka, E. M., Bowles, A. R., Frank, V. M., Richardson, D. L., & Freynik, S. (2014). Technologies for foreign language learning: A review of technology types and their effectiveness. *Computer Assisted Language Learning*, *27*(1), 70–105. https://doi.org/10.1080/09588221.2012.700315

Griffiths, C. (2008). *Lessons from good language learners*. Cambridge, UK: Cambridge University Press.

Hadwin, A. F., Bakhtiar, A., & Miller, M. (2018). Challenges in online collaboration: effects of scripting shared task perceptions. *International Journal of Computer-Supported Collaborative Learning*, *13*(3), 301–329. https://doi.org/10.1007/s11412-018-9279-9

Hauck, M., & Hampel, R. (2008). Strategies for online learning environments. In S. Hurd & T. Lewis (Eds.), *Language learning strategies in independent settings* (pp. 283–302). Bristol, UK: Multilingual Matters.

Holec, H. (1981). *Autonomy and foreign language learning.* Oxford, UK: Published for and on behalf of the Council of Europe by Pergamon.

Hong-Nam, K., & Leavell, A. G. (2006). Language learning strategy use of ESL students in an intensive English learning context. *System, 34*(3), 399–415.

Hsieh, A. F.-Y. (2014). The effect of cultural background and language proficiency on the use of oral communication strategies by second language learners of Chinese. *System, 45*(1), 1–16. https://doi.org/10.1016/j.system.2014.04.002

Hu, B. (2018). *Manual for teaching and learning Chinese as a foreign language* London, UK: Routledge.

Hu, Y. (1995). *Modern Chinese (*现代汉语*)* (5th ed.). Shanghai, China: Shanghai Education Publishing House.

Huang, H.-C. (2013). Online reading strategies at work: what teachers think and what students do. *ReCALL, 25*(3), 340–358. https://doi.org/10.1017/S0958344013000153

Huang, H.-C., Chern, C.-L., & Lin, C.-C. (2009). EFL learners' use of online reading strategies and comprehension of texts: an exploratory study. *Computers & Education, 52*(1), 13–26. https://doi.org/10.1016/j.compedu.2008.06.003

Huang, L.-S. (2010). Do different modalities of reflection matter? An exploration of adult second-language learners' reported strategy use and oral language production. *System, 38*(2), 245–261. https://doi.org/10.1016/j.system.2010.03.005

Huang, S. C. (2018). Language learning strategies in context. *The Language Learning Journal, 46*(5), 647–659. https://doi.org/10.1080/09571736.2016.1186723

Hurd, S. (2000). Distance language learners and learner support: Beliefs, difficulties and use of strategies. *Links & Letters*(7), 61–80.

Hurd, S. (2008). Affective and strategy use in independant language learning. In S. Hurd & T. Lewis (Eds.), *Language learning strategies in independent settings* (pp. 218–236). Bristol, UK: Multilingual Mattters.

Jacobs, P. (2013). The challenges of online courses for the instructor. *Research in Higher Education Journal, 21,* 1–18.

Jiang, W., & Wu, Q. (2016). A comparative study on learning strategies used by Australian CFL and Chinese EFL learners. *Chinese as a Second Language Research, 5*(2). https://doi.org/10.1515/caslar-2016-0009

Jiang, X., & Zhao, G. (2001). A survey on the strategies for learning Chinese characters among CSL beginners. 初级阶段外国留学生汉字学习. *China Academic Journal, 2001*(4), 10–17.

Kan, Q., & McCormick, R. (2014). Building course cohesion: The use of online forums in distance Chinese language learning. *Computer Assisted Language Learning, 27*(1), 44–69. https://doi.org/10.1080/09588221.2012.695739

Kan, Q., Owen, N., & Bax, S. (2018). Researching mobile-assisted Chinese-character learning strategies among adult distance learners. *Innovation in Language Learning and Teaching, 12*(1), 56–71. https://doi.org/10.1080/17501229.2018.1418633

Karpicke, J. D., & Blunt, J. R. (2011). Retrieval practice produces more learning than elaborative studying with concept mapping. *Science, 331*(6018), 772–775. https://doi.org/10.1126/science.1199327

Khezrlou, S. (2012). The relationship between cognitive and metacognitive strategies, age, and level of education. *Reading Matrix: An International Online Journal, 12*(1), 50.

Klapper, J. (2008). Deliberate and incidental: vocabulary learning strategies in independent second language learning. In S. Hurd & T. Lewis (Eds.), *Language learning strategies in independent settings* (pp. 159–178). Bristol, UK: Multilingual Matters.

Knight, D. D., & Masselink, N. (2008). 'i dont mean too bother u but': Student email and a call for netiquette. *E-Learn Magazine*. Retrieved from http://elearnmag.acm.org/archive.cfm?aid=1379051

Krashen, S. D. (1982). *Principles and practice in second language acquisition*. Oxford, UK: Pergamon.

Lai, C., & Gu, M. (2011). Self-regulated out-of-class language learning with technology. *Computer Assisted Language Learning, 24*(4), 317–335. https://doi.org/10.1080/09588221.2011.568417

Lambropoulos, N., Christopoulou, M., & Vlachos, K. (2006). Culture-based language learning objects: A CALL approach for a ubiquitous world. In P. Zaphiris & G. Zacharia (Eds.), *User centered computer aided language learning* (pp. 22–43). London, UK: Idea Publishing.

Larry, S., & Gary, T. (1997). Netiquette. *Internet Research, 7*, 269–273.

Lee, C. (2020). A study of adolescent English learners' cognitive engagement in writing while using an automated content feedback system. *Computer Assisted Language Learning, 33*(1–2), 26–57. https://doi.org/10.1080/09588221.2018.1544152

Lee, J. S., & Chen Hsieh, J. (2019). Affective variables and willingness to communicate of EFL learners in in-class, out-of-class, and digital contexts. *System, 82*, 63–73. https://doi.org/10.1016/j.system.2019.03.002

Lee, L. (2001). Online interaction: Negotiation of meaning and strategies used among learners of Spanish. *ReCALL, 13*(2), 232–244. https://doi.org/10.1017/S0958344001000829a

Levy, M. (1997). *Computer-assisted language learning: Context and conceptualization*. New York, NY: Clarendon Press.

Levy, M., & Stockwell, G. (2006). *CALL dimensions: Options and issues in computer-assisted language learning*. Mahwah, NJ: L. Erbaum Associates.

Liang, K., Wang, C., Zhang, Y., & Zou, W. (2018). Knowledge aggregation and intelligent guidance for fragmented learning. *Procedia Computer Science, 131*, 656–664. https://doi.org/10.1016/j.procs.2018.04.309

Liang, R., & Chen, D.-T. V. (2012). Online learning: Trends, potential and challenges. *Creative Education, 3*(8), 1332–1335.

Linek, S. B., & Ostermaier-Grabow, A. (2018). Netiquette between students and their lecturers on Facebook: Injunctive and descriptive social norms. *Social Media + Society, 4*(3), 205630511878962. https://doi.org/10.1177/2056305118789629

Liou, H.-C. (2000). Assessing learner strategies using computers: New insights and limitations. *Computer Assisted Language Learning, 13*(1), 65–78. https://doi.org/10.1076/0958-8221(200002)13:1;1-K;FT065

Little, D. (2000). Learner autonomy: Why foreign languages should occupy a central role in the curriculum. In S. Green (Ed.), *New perspectives on teaching and learning modern languages* (pp. 15–23). Clevedon Hall, UK: Multilingual Matters.

Liyanagunawardena, T. R., Adams, A. A., & Williams, S. A. (2013). MOOCs: A systematic study of the published literature 2008–2012. *International Review of Research in Open and Distance Learning, 14*(3), 202–227.

Martinez, M. (2001). Mass customization: Designing for successful learning. *International Journal of Educational Technology, 2*(2).

McDonald, K., & Smith, C. M. (2013). The flipped classroom for professional development: Part I. benefits and strategies. *The Journal of Continuing Education in Nursing, 44*(10), 437–438. https://doi.org/10.3928/00220124-20130925-19

McNally, B., Chipperfield, J., Dorsett, P., Fabbro, L. D., Frommolt, V., Goetz, S., . . . Rung, A. (2017). Flipped classroom experiences: Student preferences and flip strategy in a higher education context. *Higher Education, 73*(2), 281–298.

Montero, L., Serrano, R., & Llanes, À. (2013). The influence of learning context and age on the use of L2 communication strategies. *The Language Learning Journal, 45*(1), 117–132. https://doi.org 10.1080/09571736.2013.853824

Moore, J. L., Dickson-Deane, C., & Galyen, K. (2011). e-Learning, online learning, and distance learning environments: Are they the same? *Internet and Higher Education, 14*(2), 129–135.

Murday, K., Ushida, E., & Chenoweth, N. A. (2008). Learners' and teachers' perspectives on language online. *Computer Assisted Language Learning, 21*(2), 125–142. https://doi.org/10.1080/09588220801943718

Nambiar, R. (2009). Learning strategy research: Where are we now? *Reading Matrix: An International Online Journal, 9*(2), 132.

Norton, B., & Toohey, K. (2001). Changing perspectives on good language learners. *TESOL Quarterly, 35*(2), 307–322. https://doi.org 10.2307/3587650

Nunan, D. (1997). Designing and adapting materials to encourage learner autonomy. In P. Benson & P. Voller (Eds.), *Autonomy & independence in language learning* (pp. 270). London, UK: Longman.

O'Bryan, A. (2008). Providing pedagogical learner training in CALL: Impact on student use of language-learning strategies and glosses. *CALICO Journal, 26*(1), 142–159.

O'Flaherty, J., & Phillips, C. (2015). The use of flipped classrooms in higher education: A scoping review. *The Internet and Higher Education, 25*, 85–95. https://doi.org/10.1016/j.iheduc.2015.02.002

O'Malley, M., & Chamot, A. U. (1990). *Learning strategies in second language acquisition*. Cambridge, UK: Cambridge University Press.

Oxford, R. (1990). *Language learning strategies: What every teacher should know*. Boston, UK: Newbury House.

Oxford, R. (2008). Hero with a thousand faces: Learner autonomy. In S. Hurd & T. Lewis (Eds.), *Learning strategies and learning tactics in independent language learning* (pp. 41–63). Bristol, UK: Second Language Acquisition.

Oxford, R. (2011). *Teaching and researching: Language learning strategies*. London, UK: Routledge.

Oxford, R. (2017). *Teaching and researching language learning strategies: Self-regulation in context* (2nd ed.). New York, NY: Routledge.

Oxford, R., & Nyikos, M. (1989). Variables affecting choice of language learning strategies by university students. *The Modern Language Journal, 73*(3), 291–300. https://doi.org 10.1111/j.1540-4781.1989.tb06367.x

Papadopoulou, I., Kantaridou, Z., Platsidou, M., & Gavriilidou, Z. (2018). The SILL revisited in light of the S2R model of language learning. *The Language Learning Journal, 46*(5), 544–556. https://doi.org/10.1080/09571736.2018.1502739

Park, H.-R., & Kim, D. (2011). Reading-strategy use by English as a second language learners in online reading tasks. *Computers & Education, 57*(3), 2156–2166. https://doi.org/10.1016/j.compedu.2011.05.014

Peterson, M. (2008). Non-native speaker interaction management strategies in a network-based virtual environment. *Journal of Interactive Learning Research, 19*(1), 91–117.

Qian, Y., & Zhao, Q. (2009). Oral output Chinese language learning strategy research among overseas students. In *Chinese language output and learning strategy research among overseas students* (1st ed., pp. 61–80). Beijing, China: World Book Inc.

Reinders, H., & Hubbard, P. (2013). CALL and learner autonomy: Affordances and constraints. In M. Thomas, H. Reinders, & M. Warschauer (Eds.), *Contemporary computer-assisted language learning* (pp. 359–375). London, UK: Bloomsbury Academic.

Rubin, J. (1975). What the 'good language learner' can teach us. *TESOL Quarterly, 9*(1), 41–51. https://doi.org/10.2307/3586011

Russell, V., & Murphy-Judy, K. (2020). *Teaching language online: A guide for designing, developing, and delivering online, blended, and flipped language courses*. London, UK: Taylor and Francis.

Saito, R. (2005). Internet chat as collaborative CALL: language learning strategies in an internet chat class. In B. Bourke, M. Parry, & Y. Watanabe (Eds.), *Innovative practice in Japanese language education* (pp. 55–64). Brisbane, Australia: Queensland University of Technology.

Sales, N. (2013). Flipping the classroom: Revolutionising legal research training. *Legal Information Management, 13*(2013), 231–235.

Schmidt, R., & Watanabe, Y. (2001). Motivation, strategy use and pedagogical preferences in foreign language learning. In Z. Dörnyei & R. Schmidt (Eds.), *Motivation and second language acquisition* (pp. 313–359), Honolulu, HI: University of Hawaii.

Sepasdar, M., & Soori, A. (2014). The impact of age on using language learning strategies. *International Journal of Education and Literacy Studies, 2*(3), 26–31. https://doi.org/10.7575/aiac.ijels.v.2n.3p.26

Shen, H. H. (2005). An investigation of Chinese-character learning strategies among non-native speakers of Chinese. *System, 33*(1), 49–68. https://doi.org/10.1016/j.system.2004.11.001

Shen, H. H. (2013). Chinese L2 literacy development: cognitive characteristics, learning strategies, and pedagogical interventions. *Language and Linguistics Compass, 7*(7), 371–387.

Shen, H. H., & Xu, W. (2015). Active learning: qualitative inquiries into vocabulary instruction in Chinese L2 classrooms. *Foreign Language Annals, 48*(1), 82–99. https://doi.org/10.1111/flan.12137

Shi, W., & Han, L. (2019). Promoting learner autonomy through cooperative learning. *English Language Teaching, 12*(8), 30. https://doi.org/10.5539/elt.v12n8p30

Shih, Y.-C. (2014). Communication strategies in a multimodal virtual communication context. *System, 42*(1), 34–47. https://doi.org/10.1016/j.system.2013.10.016

Siemens, G. (2005). Connectivism: A learning theory for the digital age. *International Journal of Instructional Technology and Distance Learning* (January 2005), 1–9.

Siemens, G. (2008). *Learning and knowing in networks: Changing roles for educators and designers*. Paper presented at the ITFORUM for Discussion (27 January 2008), 1–26.

Smidt, E., & Hegelheimer, V. (2004). Effects of online academic lectures on ESL listening comprehension, incidental vocabulary acquisition, and strategy use. *Computer Assisted Language Learning, 17*(5), 517–556. https://doi.org/10.1080/0958822042000319692

Smith, M. (2000). Factors influencing successful student uptake of socio-collaborative CALL. *Computer Assisted Language Learning, 13*(4–5), 397–415. https://doi.org/10.1076/0958-8221(200012)13:4-5;1-E;FT397

Solak, E., & Cakir, R. (2015). Language learning strategies of language e-learners in Turkey. *E-Learning and Digital Media, 12*(1), 107–120. https://doi.org/10.1177/2042753014558384

Stickler, U., & Lewis, T. (2008). Collaborative language learning strategies in an email tandem exchange. In S. Hurd & T. Lewis (Eds.), *Language learning strategies in independent settings* (pp. 237–261). Bristol, UK: Multilingual Matters.

Stickler, U., & Shi, L. (2013). Supporting Chinese speaking skills online. *System, 41*(1), 50–69. https://doi.org/10.1016/j.system.2012.12.001

Sun, N., Rau, P. P.-L., & Ma, L. (2014). Understanding lurkers in online communities: A literature review. *Computers in Human Behavior, 38*, 110–117. https://doi.org/10.1016/j.chb.2014.05.022

Ulitsky, H. (2000). Language learner strategies with technology. *Journal of Educational Computing Research, 22*(3), 285–322. https://doi.org/10.2190/VLTU-CCXF-NFYL-277H

Wang, J. (2012). The use of e-dictionary to read e-text by intermediate and advanced learners of Chinese. *Computer Assisted Language Learning*, 25(5), 475–487. https://doi.org/10.1080/09588221.2011.631144

Wang, J., Spencer, K., & Xing, M. (2009). Metacognitive beliefs and strategies in learning Chinese as a foreign language. *System*, 37(1), 46–56. https://doi.org/10.1016/j.system.2008.05.001

Wang, Y. (2013). *Chinese language learning strategy adoption by preparatory international students in China*. Beijing, China: World Book Inc.

Wang, Y., & Qi, G. Y. (2018). Mastery-based language learning outside class: Learning support in flipped classrooms. *Language Learning and Technology*, 22(2), 50–74. https://doi.org/10.125/44641

Wenden, A. L. (1998). Metacognitive knowledge and language learning. *Applied Linguistics*, 19(4), 515–537. https://doi.org/10.1093/applin/19.4.515

White, C. (1995). Autonomy and strategy use in distance foreign language learning. *System*, 23(2), 207–221.

Wong, L.-H., Boticki, I., Sun, J., & Looi, C.-K. (2011). Improving the scaffolds of a mobile-assisted Chinese character forming game via a design-based research cycle. *Computers in Human Behavior*, 27(5), 1783–1793. https://doi.org/10.1016/j.chb.2011.03.005

Xu, X. (2022). *Applying mobile technologies to Chinese language learning* [online resource: illustrations (chiefly colour).]. https://doi.org/10.4018/978-1-7998-4876-9

Xu, Z. (2010). *Chinese as foreign language research: Cognitive model and strategy (汉语作为外语的学习研究：认知模式与策略)* Beijing, China: Peking University Press.

Yang, N.-D. (1999). The relationship between EFL learners' beliefs and learning strategy use. *System*, 27, 515–535.

Yang, X., Li, G., & Huang, S. S. (2017). Perceived online community support, member relations, and commitment: Differences between posters and lurkers. *Information & Management*, 54(2), 154–165. https://doi.org/10.1016/j.im.2016.05.003

Zhang, B. (2002). *The new modern Chinese (现代汉语)*. Shanghai, China: Fudan University Press.

Zhang, J., Li, H., Liu, Y., & Chen, Y. (2020). Orthographic facilitation in oral vocabulary learning: Effects of language backgrounds and orthographic type. *Reading and Writing*, 33, 187–206.

Zhi, G., & Lu, X. (2018). A study on Chinese vocabulary learning strategies of second language learners. In J.-F. Hong, Y. Zhang, & P. Liu (Eds.), *Chinese lexical semantics: 20th workshop, clsw 2019* (pp. 428–433). Beijing, China: Springer.

Zhu, J., Chen, P., & Jia, W. (2019). Advantages and disadvantages of fragmented learning and recommendations. *Asian Agricultural Research*, 11(4), 87–92. https://doi.org/10.19601/j.cnki.issn1943-9903.2019.4.020

Zimmerman, B. J. (1999). Commentary: Toward a cyclically interactive view of self-regulated learning. *International Journal of Educational Research*, 31(6), 545–551. https://doi.org/10.1016/S0883-0355(99)00021-X

3 The repertoire of LLSs in online Chinese learning

3.1 Introduction

This chapter presents the LLSs employed by the participants in online Chinese learning. These were obtained from both the student self-reported data and the observed data. The self-reported data, involving the 23 responses from the survey questionnaire and the 10 student interviews, were analysed in three learning contexts: (1) self-directed learning outside the online classes; (2) assessment-task completion (ongoing assessments, a wiki-writing assignment, a speaking assignment, or an oral test) outside the online classes; and (3) online class participation. These three learning contexts related to both asynchronous and synchronous learning environments. The asynchronous environment in learning contexts 1 and 2 consisted of a web-based Discussion Board, wikis, online quizzes, email, and WeChat. The synchronous environment in learning context 3 referred to the Blackboard Collaborate sessions. The participants' use of LLSs from the observed data was presented in the asynchronous and synchronous environments separately. The observed data included data collected from sources such as personal emails, WeChat messages, written-assignment drafts provided by the students, and the tracking data from the Discussion Board.

The LLSs for which data were collected are summarised in Table 3.1, which provides the names of the LLSs, statements describing them, the relevant technological tool(s) related to the corresponding LLS use, the learning context for each LLS use, the data sources and, when applicable, the frequency range of the strategy use (abbreviated as 'Data sources (usage)' in the table), and the participant(s) who used the LLS.

In total, 37 distinct LLSs were identified from the collected data: 33 from the self-reported data, and four found only in the observed data. Of these 37 LLSs, 28 can be found in Oxford's (1990) LLS inventory. The other nine are LLSs that I have proposed as additional to those in the existing LLS taxonomies (including Oxford's), and these are specific to either one of or a combination of the following: online learning, collaborative learning, flipped-classroom learning, and Chinese-language learning.

Table 3.1 Summary of student LLS use

Affective strategies	Statement (paraphrased for brevity)	Technological tool(s)	Learning context	Data source (LLS usage) (H, M, L = high, medium, and low-frequency range of strategy use)	Participant(s)
Taking risks wisely (Oxford, 1990)	Encourage myself to take risks in Chinese learning, such as guessing meanings or trying to speak, even though I might make some mistakes		Self-directed learning outside the online classes	SII (H)	23 survey respondents
	Take risks during conversations with Chinese friends, family, and colleagues			I	S15
Making positive statements (Oxford, 1990)	Encourage myself so that I will continue to try hard and do my best in Chinese learning			SII (H)	23 survey respondents
	Encourage myself to look back on my achievements			I	S12
Discussing your feelings with someone else (Oxford, 1990)	Talk to someone I trust about my attitudes and feelings concerning the language-learning process			SII (M)	23 survey respondents
	Express concerns about language learning to classmates	Forum: Discussion Board (The CAFE)		OII	S36
Rewarding yourself (Oxford, 1990)	Give myself a tangible reward when I have done something well in my Chinese learning			SII (L)	23 survey respondents
Taking steps to minimise anxiety when practising (non-SILL LLS)	Prefer to speak in Chinese with native Chinese speakers who are strangers, such as taxi drivers, or Chinese students in 'English corners', rather than people I know			I	S18

(Continued)

Table 3.1 (Continued)

Cognitive strategies	Statement (paraphrased for brevity)	Technological tool(s)	Learning context	Data source (LLS usage)	Participant(s)
Using resources for receiving and sending messages (Oxford, 1990)	Search online for the meaning of Chinese words I don't know (e.g., using an online dictionary site or Google Translate)	E-dictionary app: Pleco; Google Translate; TrainChinese	Self-directed learning outside the online classes	SII (H)	23 survey respondents S12 S13 S15
		E-dictionary app: Google Translate; Screwit	Assessment-task completion outside online classes (a speaking assignment)	I	S5 S8
	Search for the information online if I do not understand	E-dictionary; Google Translate	Online class participation	SII (H)	23 survey respondents
	Borrow/copy a sentence found by looking up a YouTube video	Videos: YouTube	Assessment-task completion outside online classes (a speaking assignment)	I	S8
	Search for background information on Chinese words online	Website: Google	Self-directed learning outside the online classes	SII (M)	23 survey respondents
Formally practising with the sounds and writing system (Oxford, 1990)	Read aloud to practise for the speaking assignment		Assessment-task completion outside online classes (a speaking assignment or an oral test)	SII (H)	23 survey respondents
Repeating (Oxford, 1990)	Imitate the tones that native Chinese speakers use		Self-directed learning outside the online classes	SII (H)	23 survey respondents
	Imitate the teacher's Chinese speaking	Online teaching platform: Blackboard Collaborate	Online class participation	OI	S9

The repertoire of LLSs in online Chinese learning 57

Strategy category	Strategy	Tool/Resource	Context	Code	Respondents
	Imitate teacher's and Chinese friends' pronunciation	Social media app: WeChat (text and voice messages)	Assessment-task completion outside online classes (a speaking assignment)	I	S5 S9
	Listen to recorded conversations many times	Pimsleur Digital Mandarin language course	Self-directed learning outside the online classes	I	S5 S8
Getting the idea quickly (Oxford, 1990)	Try to understand what I hear or read without translating it word for word into my own language		Self-directed learning outside the online classes	SII (H)	23 survey respondents
Taking notes (Oxford, 1990)	Take notes		Online class participation	SII (M)	23 survey respondents
	Take notes and update lecture notes before and after online classes	Word document; textbook	Online class participation and self-directed learning outside the online classes	I / AD / SIII	S10 / S9 / S10
	Take notes of new words and phrases	Paper notebook	Self-directed learning outside the online classes	I	S14
Learning from other students' written work (Non-SILL LLSs)	Read other students' wiki-writing assessments to learn from them Put comments on other students' wiki-writing assignments because that helps me learn	Wiki	Assessment-task completion outside online classes (a wiki-writing assignment)	SII (L) / SII (L)	23 survey respondents / 23 survey respondents
Practising naturalistically (Oxford, 1990)	Watch Chinese TV programmes and movies; speak Chinese with family members; read novels in Chinese	TV programmes	Self-directed learning outside the online classes	I / SIII	S10 S17 / S8 S10
Analysing contrastively (Oxford, 1990)	Compare sounds in English and Chinese	Online teaching platform: Blackboard Collaborate	Online class participation	OI	S4
Summarising (Oxford, 1990)	Summarise Chinese grammar points in my head as a way to reinforce my understanding		Self-directed learning outside the online classes	SII (M)	23 survey respondents

(*Continued*)

Table 3.1 (Continued)

Social strategies	Statement (paraphrased for brevity)	Technological tool(s)	Learning context	Data source (LLS usage)	Participant(s)
Netiquette (Non-SILL LLS)	Respect my language partner's time when we work together		Self-directed learning outside the online classes	SII (H)	23 survey respondents
			Assessment-task completion outside online classes (ongoing assessments, a speaking assignment)	I	S8
	Respond as soon as possible to my language partner's queries		Assessment-task completion outside online classes (a speaking assignment or an oral test)	SII (H)	23 survey respondents
	Respond to language partner's and the teacher's emails within 24 hours	Email	Assessment-task completion outside online classes (ongoing assessments, a speaking assignment)	I	S9
	Respond to teacher's and classmates' questions quickly	Audio facility via the audio/video panel in Blackboard Collaborate	Online class participation	I	S14
	Respond to language partner's WeChat messages in a timely manner	Social media app: WeChat (text and voice messages)	Self-directed learning outside the online classes	AD	S31 S33 S5 S18 S8
	Prefer keeping the webcam on to let the teacher and other students see me	Audio facility via the audio/video panel in Blackboard Collaborate	Online class participation	SII (M)	23 survey respondents
	Reply to other students' comments on my wiki page		Assessment-task completion outside online classes (a wiki-writing assignment)	I SII (L)	S14 23 survey respondents

The repertoire of LLSs in online Chinese learning 59

	Put comments on other students' wiki-writing assignments to make helpful suggestions		Assessment-task completion outside online classes (a wiki-writing assignment)	SII (L)	23 survey respondents
	Praise a classmate's pronunciation	Online teaching platform: Blackboard Collaborate	Online class participation	OI	S5
	Send greetings and introduce oneself	Forum: Discussion Board (The CAFE)	Self-directed learning outside the online classes	OII	22 students from CHN11, SP1, 2016
Cooperating with peers (Oxford, 1990)	Write the conversation scripts for the speaking assignment together with my language partner		Assessment-task completion (a speaking assignment or an oral test)	SII (H)	23 survey respondents
	Collaborate with a language partner to draft and practise a speaking assignment	Online teaching platform: Blackboard Collaborate	Assessment-task completion (ongoing assessments, speaking assignment)	I	S8 S9 S10 S17
	Discuss the wiki-writing assignment with my language partner		Assessment-task completion outside online classes (a wiki-writing assignment)	SII (H)	23 survey respondents
	Offer or give corrections on my language partner's written draft	Word document	Assessment-task completion outside online classes (ongoing assessments, a speaking assignment)	I	S10
	Organise a WeChat group: switch to using WeChat messaging app	Forum: Discussion Board (The CAFE)	Self-directed learning outside the online classes	OII	22 students from CHN11, SP1, 2016

(*Continued*)

Table 3.1 (Continued)

Social strategies	Statement (paraphrased for brevity)	Technological tool(s)	Learning context	Data source (LLS usage)	Participant(s)
Sharing with other students (Non-SILL LLS)	Share understanding of assessment task or course requirements and Chinese knowledge	Cloud storage app: Google Drive	Assessment-task completion outside online classes (a speaking assignment)	AD	S31, S35
Asking for correction (Oxford, 1990)	Ask my language partner to check my script		Assessment-task completion outside online classes (a speaking assignment or an oral test)	SII (H)	23 survey respondents
	Ask my teacher to provide feedback on my early drafts		Assessment-task completion outside online classes (a wiki-writing assignment)	SII (L)	23 survey respondents
		Social media app: WeChat (text and voice messages)	Assessment-task completion outside online classes (a wiki-writing assignment)	AD	S8
	Encourage other students to leave comments on my Wiki page		Assessment-task completion outside online classes (a wiki-writing assignment)	SII (L)	23 survey respondents
	Seek feedback on initial written drafts from Chinese teacher or friends		Assessment-task completion outside online classes (ongoing assessments, a speaking assignment)	I	S8
	Ask other students to correct me	Online teaching platform: Blackboard Collaborate	Online class participation	SII (L)	23 survey respondents
	Ask my language partner to correct me whenever I make a mistake	Online teaching platform: Blackboard Collaborate	Online class participation	SII (M)	23 survey respondents
	Ask the teacher to correct me	Online teaching platform: Blackboard Collaborate	Online class participation	SII (H)	23 survey respondents
				OI	S8

The repertoire of LLSs in online Chinese learning 61

Strategy category	Strategy	Tool	Activity	Code	Source
Asking for clarification or verification (Oxford, 1990)	If I do not understand, I ask the other students to slow down, repeat, or clarify what was said	Online teaching platform: Blackboard Collaborate	Online class participation	SII (M)	23 survey respondents
	Ask the teacher to verify that I have understood or said something correctly	Online teaching platform: Blackboard Collaborate	Online class participation	SII (M)	23 survey respondents
	Ask the teacher to explain grammar points in ongoing assessments	Social media app: WeChat: images, emojis, text and voice messages	Self-directed learning outside the online classes	AD	S8
	Ask the teacher and the classmates a grammar question in online class	Online teaching platform: Blackboard Collaborate	Online class participation	OI	S19
	Ask questions about assessment tasks and technological problems	Forum: Discussion Board (The CAFE)	Self-directed learning outside the online classes	OII	22 students from CHN11, SP1, 2016
Using the tools available to improve communication and interaction (Non-SILL LLS)	Share photos and comment on photos in a private Chinese friend circle	Social media app: WeChat moments	Self-directed learning outside the online classes	I	S12
	Use different contact tools to interact with different groups of people	Email, WhatsApp, WeChat app	Assessment-task completion outside online classes (ongoing assessments, a speaking assignment)	I	S17
	Use different colours, character fonts, and numbers to remind language partners to focus on important information in a draft	Cloud storage app: Google Drive	Assessment-task completion outside online classes (a speaking assignment or an oral test)	AD	S31 S33 S35

(Continued)

Table 3.1 (Continued)

Social strategies	Statement (paraphrased for brevity)	Technological tool(s)	Learning context	Data source (LLS usage)	Participant(s)
	Type text messages for effective communication		Online class participation	SII (M)	23 survey respondents
	Use emoticons and text chat to interact with others for language learning, such as praising the other students' speaking and answering other students' questions	The emoticons (such as smiley face, LOL, and raised hand) and text messages in the Chat panel in Blackboard Collaborate	Online class participation	OI	S5
	Use emojis to express feelings in the text chat panel	Online teaching platform: Blackboard Collaborate	Online class participation	OI	S5
	Use the user interface elements (e.g., 'away' icon) to show that you are leaving	Online teaching platform: Blackboard Collaborate	Online class participation	OI	S14
Negotiating with other students (Non-SILL LLS)	Negotiate the time and digital location at which practise speaking Chinese	Social media app: WeChat (text and voice messages)	Assessment-task completion (Completing a speaking assignment or an oral test outside online classes)	AD	S31 S33
	Distribute work to complete an assessment task	Cloud storage app: Google Drive	Assessment-task completion (Completing a written draft for a role play in pairs)	AD	S31 S33 S35 S31 S35

Memory strategies	Statement (paraphrased for brevity)	Technological tool(s)	Learning context	Data source (LLS usage)	Participant(s)
Using mechanical techniques (Oxford, 1990)	Use character cards to help memorise new Chinese words		Self-directed learning outside the online classes	SII (M)	23 survey respondents
	Memorise words or characters by listening to flashcard apps over and over	Flashcard functions in learning apps: Intelligent Flashcards STS Chinese; Pinyin Training; Pleco; Google Translate; Youdao; StickyStudy	Self-directed learning outside the online classes	I SIII	S5 S18 S12 S14 S15 S9 S12 S14

The repertoire of LLSs in online Chinese learning 63

Strategy	Statement (paraphrased for brevity)	Technological tool(s)	Learning context	Data source (LLS usage)	Participant(s)
	Make flashcards and use them to memorise words	Self-made flashcard made using PowerPoint software; Flashcard function in a learning app: KTPict CE	Self-directed learning outside the online classes	I SIII	S18
Placing new words into a context (Oxford, 1990)	When learning a new Chinese word, put it in a sentence so I can remember it		Self-directed learning outside the online classes	SII (M)	23 survey respondents
Semantic mapping (Oxford, 1990)	When learning a new Chinese word, list words I know that are related to it and draw lines to show relationships		Self-directed learning outside the online classes	SII (L)	23 survey respondents
Representing sounds in memory (Oxford, 1990)	Memorise phrases by listening to digital resources over and over	Pimsleur Digital Mandarin language course	Self-directed learning outside the online classes	I	S5 S8
	Memorise conversations by listening to voice messages over and over	Social media app: WeChat (text and voice messages)	Assessment-task completion outside online classes (ongoing assessments, a speaking assignment)	I	S5
Creating stories for memorising Chinese character writing (non-SILL LLS)	Memorise Chinese characters by creating stories according to the meaning of strokes in a Chinese character		Self-directed learning outside the online classes	I SIII	S8
Compensation strategies	Statement (paraphrased for brevity)	Technological tool(s)	Learning context	Data source (LLS usage)	Participant(s)
Selecting the topic (Oxford, 1990)	When speaking with other students, I tend to steer the conversation onto a topic for which I know the words		Self-directed learning outside the online classes	SII (M)	23 survey respondents
Using linguistic clues (Oxford, 1990)	Guess the meaning of what is heard			I	S5 S17
Using mime or gesture (Oxford, 1990)	Guess the meaning of the speaker's hand gestures				

(Continued)

Table 3.1 (Continued)

Compensation strategies	Statement (paraphrased for brevity)	Technological tool(s)	Learning context	Data source (LLS usage)	Participant(s)
Getting help (Oxford, 1990)	Ask other students to tell me the right word if I cannot think of it	Online teaching platform: Blackboard Collaborate	Online class participation	SII (L)	23 survey respondents
	Orally use English to ask for the missing words in Chinese when reading a paragraph in the textbook			OI	S15
Providing extra clarification to others in writing for better understanding (Non-SILL LLS)	Provide more information in written drafts to assist a better understanding of each other's writing		Assessment-task completion outside online classes (a speaking assignment or an oral test)	AD	S31 S35

Metacognitive strategies	Statement (paraphrased for brevity)	Technological tool(s)	Learning context	Data source (LLS usage)	Participant(s)
Seeking practice opportunities (Oxford, 1990)	Try to speak Chinese whenever I can		Self-directed learning outside the online classes	SII (M)	23 survey respondents
	Seek opportunities to chat with Chinese native speakers			I	S5 S14 S8
Organising (Oxford, 1990)	Arrange a comfortable environment for studying, to promote learning			SII (H)	23 survey respondents
	Develop a routine so that I study Chinese regularly, not just when there is the pressure of tests			SII (H)	23 survey respondents
	Develop a learning routine			I	S18 S8 S13 S14 S15 S17
	Complete assessment tasks before due dates			SIII	S9
	Schedule fragmented time to learn Chinese vocabulary			SIII	S9
	Schedule a weekly meeting with a Chinese friend			I	S14

Category	Strategy	Tool/Context	Code	Respondents
	Introduce personal information and look for a language partner	Forum: Discussion Board (The CAFE)	OII	15 out of 22 students from CHN11, SP1, 2016
	Build an internal learner network	Social media app: WeChat (text and voice messages)	OII	10 out of 22 students from CHN11, SP1, 2016
	Store drafts of written assignments in Cloud, and share them with language partners and teachers for editing	Cloud storage app: Google Drive	AD	S31 S33 S35
	Send emails for course-related questions	Email	AD	S8 S9 S12 S13 S20
Self-evaluating (Oxford, 1990)	Evaluate the progress I have made in learning Chinese		SII (M)	23 survey respondents
	Record myself speaking by using an audio or video recorder so that I can listen to myself and correct my pronunciation		SII (L)	23 survey respondents
Overviewing and linking with known material (Oxford, 1990)	Review the resources that are recommended in the online Chinese courses		SII (H)	23 survey respondents
Preparing questions for attending online classes (Non-SILL LLS)	Prepare questions in advance to ask in the online classes		SII (M)	23 survey respondents
Self-monitoring (Oxford, 1990)	Read the comments other students leave on my wiki page		SII (L)	23 survey respondents
	Revise my wiki-writing assignment, taking on board the other students' comments and suggestions	Assessment-task completion outside online classes (a wiki-writing assignment)	SII (L)	23 survey respondents
	Try to notice my errors when speaking Chinese and to work out the reason for them	Self-directed learning outside the online classes	SII (H)	23 survey respondents

3.2 LLSs obtained from the self-reported data

This section includes seven subsections. Subsection 3.2.1 summarises by categories the mean values of the frequency of LLS use from the second part (SII) of the survey questionnaire. Subsections 3.2.2 to 3.2.7 present the detailed analyses by LLS within the categories of affective, cognitive, social, memory, compensation, and metacognitive strategies, respectively. When there are conspicuous correlations between the LLS items within a category, the results of Pearson's r correlation analyses (Evans, 1996) are included to explore the strength and the direction of such correlations. Additionally, each subsection also integrates the qualitative analyses of the data collected from the open-ended survey questions (SIII), the interview data (I), and the additional data (AD) provided by the 10 interviewees. These results complement and help explain the LLSs found in the survey results.

3.2.1 LLS use by category

The mean scores for the six LLS categories, based on the 23 survey responses to the 45 LLS items in the survey questionnaire, are listed in Table 3.2. Overall, the participants did not seem to be heavily reliant on employing any particular LLS category. The 23 survey respondents reported LLS category mean scores from 2.45 to 3.24, with an average score of 2.97. Most of the mean scores for the six categories fall in the range of medium strategy use as per Oxford's (1990) system, indicating that the participants diversified their use of LLS categories.

However, some correlations do exist among the six LLS categories. Table 3.3 presents the correlations for pairs of LLS categories through the Pearson's r correlation test. It can be observed that the strongest category correlation existed between cognitive and affective strategy categories ($r = .78$, strong). This relationship suggested that those survey respondents whose use of cognitive strategies was high also had a high level of use of affective strategies. This result is expected and is consistent with the observation of Hurd et al. (2001), who pointed out that distance students have to maintain their motivation to develop LLSs to facilitate language learning. The same could be observed for two other pairs of LLS categories were also strongly correlated, namely: affective and metacognitive strategies ($r = .69$, strong), and cognitive and memory strategies ($r = .60$, strong).

Table 3.2 Mean scores of LLS use by category for the 23 survey respondents

Strategy category	Mean
Affective	3.09
Cognitive	3.24
Social	3.08
Memory	2.95
Compensation	2.45
Metacognitive	2.98
Overall average	2.97

Table 3.3 Pearson's r correlation analysis results across the six LLS categories reported in the survey questionnaire

LLS category	Affective	Cognitive	Social	Memory	Comp.	Meta.
Affective	1					
Cognitive	.78 (strong)	1				
Social	.43 (moderate)	.24 (weak)	1			
Memory	.51 (moderate)	.60 (strong)	.10 (very weak)	1		
Compensation (Comp.)	.37 (weak)	.52 (moderate)	.38 (weak)	.19 (weak)	1	
Metacognitive (Meta.)	.69 (strong)	.50 (moderate)	.40 (moderate)	.53 (moderate)	.32 (weak)	1

Table 3.3 also shows that the weakest category correlation existed between social and memory-strategy categories ($r = .10$, very weak). This result indicated that the respondents who used more social strategies would be likely to use fewer memory strategies, and vice versa. This result seems probable. The social-strategy items in the survey questionnaire concerned interaction with others, whilst for memory strategies, concentration was needed. In this sense, some participants who chose to use social strategies frequently may also be participants who did not like to spend time alone working on memorisation. For example, Interviewee S5, who focused on improving Chinese pronunciation, chose to mainly interact with others orally (social); she did not like to memorise Chinese-character writing (memory).

3.2.2 Affective strategies

Affective strategies refer to the actions taken by learners to cope with the emotional or motivational difficulties they encounter when learning a foreign language (Oxford, 1990). Such actions may include self-encouraging, taking one's emotional temperature, and discussing one's feelings with someone else.

The respondents rated their use of four of Oxford's (1990) affective strategies: (1) '*Taking risks wisely*'; (2) '*Making positive statements*'; (3) '*Discussing your feelings with someone else*'; and (4) '*Rewarding yourself*'. As illustrated in Table 3.4, the survey respondents employed two strategies with a high-frequency-range use: '*Taking risks wisely*' (median (Mdn) = 4; for self-encouraging during speaking); and '*Making positive statements*' (Mdn = 4; for self-encouraging during the learning process generally). Most respondents (73.9%) rated both these affective strategies as 4 (Generally true of me) or 5 (Always or almost always true of me), and used the strategies for self-directed learning outside the online classes. Table 3.4 also suggests that the respondents preferred to motivate themselves by using the strategy of '*Making positive statements*', rather than by giving themselves a tangible reward.

Table 3.4 Affective strategies reported by the survey respondents

Affective strategy	Questionnaire items relating to LLSs	Learning context	% of scale 1, 2, 3, 4, 5	Median, mean, LLS usage
Taking risks wisely (Oxford, 1990)	I encourage myself to take risks in Chinese learning, such as guessing meanings or trying to speak, even though I might make some mistakes.	Self-directed learning outside the online classes	4.3, 8.7, 13.0, 43.5, 30.4	4, 3.87, H
Making positive statements (Oxford, 1990)	I encourage myself so that I will continue to try hard and do my best in Chinese learning.		4.3, 8.7, 13.0, 65.2, 8.7	4, 3.65, H
Discussing your feelings with someone else (Oxford, 1990)	I talk to someone I trust about my attitudes and feelings concerning the language-learning process.		13.0, 21.7, 39.1, 21.7, 4.3	3, 2.83, M
Rewarding yourself (Oxford, 1990)	I give myself a tangible reward when I have done something well in my Chinese learning.		30.4, 47.8, 0, 17.4, 4.3	2, 2.00, L

In regard to the strategy of '*Discussing your feelings with someone else*', the responses were broadly spread. One possible reason for the different rates of usage of this strategy is that some respondents may have lacked the opportunities to discuss their feelings with other classmates and teachers during their language-learning processes, especially at the exact moment when such a need arose. Another possible reason is that they might not often choose to express their feelings to their friends and families around them because those contacts might lack knowledge of the respondents' learning situations, such as the difficulties of practising Chinese speaking.

The Pearson's *r* correlation analysis results (Table 3.5) show a strong correlation ($r = .62; .60-.80$; 'strong') between '*Taking risks wisely*' and '*Making positive statements*'. This finding shows that the respondents who encouraged themselves to take risks tended to deliberately encourage themselves to study hard and do their best in language learning. It further indicates that the respondents who chose these two LLS items realised the importance of relying upon themselves in self-directed learning outside the online classes. This result was expected, as researchers have discovered that affective strategy use plays an important role in building learner confidence (Hurd, 2008; White, 1995). These researchers claimed that distance students become aware of their own learning abilities and performance by using positive/negative self-evaluations, and subsequently employ the relevant affective strategies to enhance their self-confidence.

By using affective strategies more frequently, the participants might be able to address the learning difficulties they have experienced in collaborating with their

Table 3.5 Pearson's r correlation analysis results across the affective strategies reported in the survey questionnaire

Affective strategy	Questionnaire item relating to LLS	Strategy item no.	1	2	3	4
Making positive statements	I encourage myself so that I will continue to try hard and do my best in Chinese learning.	1	1			
Taking risks wisely	I encourage myself to take risks in Chinese learning, such as guessing meanings or trying to speak, even though I might make some mistakes.	2	.62	1		
Rewarding yourself	I give myself a tangible reward when I have done something well in my Chinese learning.	3	.46	.22	1	
Discussing your feelings with someone else	I talk to someone I trust about my attitudes and feelings concerning the language learning process.	4	.12	-.17	.18	1

language partners, as revealed in the survey responses. In responding to an open-ended survey question, three respondents (S9, S10, S13) reported that the most difficult part of working with a language partner was scheduling meeting times (see Excerpt 3.1). According to the interview data, such learning difficulties cause anxieties for the participants, and these students may employ relevant affective strategies (e.g., '*Making positive statements*' and '*Discussing your feelings with someone else*') when necessary.

> **Excerpt 3.1 Three examples of difficulties in scheduling collaboration with a language partner by S9, S10, and S13**
>
> *S9: Co-ordinating times, having them not disappear, having them actually contribute more than just coming in at the end. I try to do everything, but I can't, so I concentrated on doing things that required to pass the course ... (Survey questionnaire part III, S9, 2015).*
>
> *S10: Scheduling time to align. (Survey questionnaire part III, S10, 2015).*
>
> *S13: The most difficult [part] was managed [managing] the time for both of us to do the exercise at the same time. We set up a proper time for the both [of us] to manage it. (Survey questionnaire III, S13, 2015).*

The results obtained from the interview data, shown in Table 3.6, further confirmed the use of the two affective strategies ('*Making positive statements*' and '*Taking risks wisely*') reported in the survey results. One affective strategy was found which is distinctly different from those already defined by Oxford and other researchers, and was named '*Taking steps to minimise anxiety when practising*'.

It refers to students choosing specific groups of people to practise with, and particular learning activities, in order to reduce their speaking anxiety. This affective strategy was employed by S18, who worked in China as an English teacher. During the interview, he mentioned that he preferred talking with Chinese locals in an English corner (an English-language-learning activity in China that is commonly used by learners to practise oral English on a regular basis) to reduce speaking anxiety. S18 also said that he felt 'more relaxed and productive' when talking in Chinese with strangers (e.g., taxi drivers) than with his Chinese friends or colleagues. This suggested that S18, a beginning-level student, had developed a strategy (a deliberate choice of behaviour) to deal with the psychological challenge he had recognised that he felt in practising Chinese speaking with native speakers with whom he was familiar.

This strategy is different from Oxford's and other researchers' LLSs, and therefore I consider it to be a new strategy. There are two factors which may possibly have contributed to the choice of this strategy. The first is that online students like S18 had limited opportunities to interact with classmates in an online course, and consequently such a learning situation requires autonomous behaviour. The second reason is that his self-esteem prompted S18 to use this strategy as he preferred not to practise Chinese speaking with colleagues but to do so with strangers instead. This strategy involves both cognitive and metacognitive aspects. Students understand their own language-proficiency level (metacognitive aspect), and then choose an easier way to find practice opportunities (cognitive aspect) to reduce learner anxiety (affective strategy) and immerse themselves in learning Chinese.

Interestingly, this behaviour by S18 contrasts with the findings of Wolf and Phung's (2019) research, in which they noted that overseas students viewed daily communication with unfamiliar native speakers as the most difficult task they faced. They found that failure in such communications may result in a range of negative emotions, such as stress, embarrassment, and loss of confidence. This can be observed in the cases of S8, S10, and S17, who experienced such learning difficulties with unfamiliar native speakers when visiting China (e.g., Excerpt 3.2).

Table 3.6 Affective strategies identified in the interview data

Affective strategy	Statement (paraphrased for brevity)	Learning context	Data from	Interviewee
Taking steps to minimise anxiety when practising (LLS for online learning)	Seek to speak in Chinese with native Chinese speakers who are strangers, such as taxi drivers, or Chinese students in 'English corners', rather than people I know.	Self-directed learning outside the online classes	I	S18
Making positive statements (Oxford, 1990)	Encourage myself to look back on my achievements.			S12
Taking risks wisely (Oxford, 1990)	Take risks during conversation with Chinese friends, family, and colleagues.			S15

> **Excerpt 3.2 An example of learning difficulties in Chinese listening when interacting with native speakers by S8 in China.**
>
> S8: When I arrived in China, what I found was, I knew enough to be able to say to a taxi driver 'take me to a hotel', but when they spoke back to me, I couldn't understand a word. Hahaha ... That was very different... Because they have an accent and they speak a different dialect most of the time, and they speak VERY VERY VERY fast. (00:04:07 in the recording, Interview, S8, 2015).

As shown in Excerpt 3.2, the two reasons for S8's difficulty were the native speakers' accents and dialects, and the fact that S8's language proficiency level was low. In S18's case, he worked in China as a teacher and felt nervous about making mistakes when speaking Chinese with colleagues because of concerns over his potential loss of self-esteem. Indeed, the observed data indicated that online students like S18 did make an effort to find ways to minimise their learning anxiety, such as expressing their worries and concerns in virtual spaces (e.g., Discussion Board).

In summary, the participants mainly employed affective strategies to minimise learning anxieties and maintain positive motivation in the learning context of self-directed learning outside the online classes. When facing various learning challenges in such a learning context, the students used affective strategies to solve problems independently ('*Taking risks wisely*' and '*Making positive statements*') rather than seeking help from their friends and families ('*Discussing your feelings with someone else*'). However, these students rarely gave themselves a valuable reward when they had done something well in Chinese learning ('*Rewarding yourself*'). I also found that a distinct affective strategy '*Taking steps to minimise anxiety when practising*' was employed by the participants to create positive affect towards successful language learning.

3.2.3 Cognitive strategies

Cognitive strategies are important in that they help learners with 'putting together, consolidating, elaborating, and transforming knowledge of the language and culture' (Oxford, 2011, p. 46). In total, eight cognitive strategies, seven from the survey responses and one from the interviews, emerged from the self-reported data. In the survey questionnaire, the respondents rated their use of six cognitive strategies selected from Oxford (1990) (i.e., '*Repeating*'; '*Formally practising with sounds and writing systems*'; '*Using resources for receiving and sending messages*'; '*Taking notes*'; '*Summarising*'; and '*Getting the idea quickly*'). Additionally, the seventh strategy of '*Learning from other students' written work*' was added to the survey questionnaire as a strategy specific to collaborative learning. The eighth cognitive strategy, obtained from the interview results, was Oxford's (1990) strategy of '*Practising naturalistically*'. Four of these were cognitive strategies with high-frequency-range use.

The first cognitive strategy with high-frequency-range use was '*Using resources for receiving and sending messages*' (*Mdn* = 5). The respondents applied this strategy to search for answers online during the online classes and in their self-directed learning outside the online classes. All the respondents rated 'I search online for the meaning of Chinese words I don't know' as 4 (Generally true of me) or 5 (Always

Table 3.7 Cognitive strategies reported by the survey respondents

Cognitive strategy	Questionnaire items relating to LLSs	Learning context	% of scale 1, 2, 3, 4, 5	Median, mean, LLS usage
Using resources for receiving and sending messages (Oxford, 1990)	I search online for the meaning of Chinese words I don't know (e.g. using an online dictionary site or Google Translate)	Self-directed learning outside the online classes	0, 0, 0, 78.3, 21.7	5, 4.78, H
	If I do not understand, I search for the information online (e.g. e-dictionary; Google Translate)	Online class participation	14.3, 4.8, 14.3, 33.3, 33.3	4, 3.67, H
	I search for background information on Chinese words online	Self-directed learning outside the online classes	4.3, 30.4, 17.4, 21.7, 26.1	3, 3.35, M
Formally practising with sounds and writing system (Oxford, 1990)	I read aloud to practise for the speaking assignment	Assessment-task completion (a speaking assignment or an oral test)	4.3, 0, 0, 17.4, 78.3	5, 4.65, H
Repeating (Oxford, 1990)	I imitate the tones that native Chinese speakers use	Self-directed learning outside the online classes	4.3, 0, 13.0, 65.2, 17.4	4, 3.91, H
Getting the idea quickly (Oxford, 1990)	I try to understand what I hear or read without translating it word for word into my own language	Self-directed learning outside the online classes	8.7, 4.3, 30.4, 39.1, 17.4	4, 3.53, H
Taking notes (Oxford, 1990)	I take notes	Online class participation	23.8, 14.3, 14.3, 19.0, 28.6	3, 3.14, M
Summarising (Oxford, 1990)	I summarise Chinese grammar points in my head as a way to reinforce my understanding	Self-directed learning outside the online classes	4.3, 30.4, 47.8, 8.7, 8.7	3, 2.87, M
Learning from other students' written work (LLS for collaborative learning)	I read other students' wiki-writing assessments to learn from them	Assessment-task completion outside online classes (a wiki-writing assignment)	47.8, 13.0, 21.7, 13.0, 4.3	2, 2.30, L
	I put comments on other students' wiki-writing assignments because that helps me learn		56.5, 26.1, 8.7, 8.7, 0	1, 1.74, L

or almost always true of me). This result is very much as expected. Researchers have discovered that distance students employ this strategy to find, evaluate, and use information quickly in online learning, as they lack interactions with teachers and other students (H.-C. Huang et al., 2009; Klapper, 2008).

The second cognitive strategy with high-frequency-range use was *'Formally practising with sounds and writing system'* (*Mdn* = 5). The respondents frequently read aloud to practise scripts in Chinese to prepare for completing the speaking assignment or for the oral test. This result explains the importance of this strategy in helping students with their preparation for assessments. Chinese as a tonal language requires students to practise the tones and pronunciations of Chinese characters to become proficient. Reading aloud, as suggested by Kelly (1992), is more effective than reading silently when practising speaking a foreign language.

The strategy of *'Repeating'* (*Mdn* = 4) was the third cognitive strategy with a high-frequency-range use. In the survey questionnaire, it refers to the respondents' imitating native speakers' pronunciation in the context of self-directed learning outside the online classes. The students used this strategy to improve their pronunciation and tones. This finding is not surprising. Shen (2005) also recommended that Chinese-language learners repeat the sound when a Chinese character is first introduced. Similarly, the study carried out by Hurd (2000) among distance-learning students evidenced that the most frequently used strategy was that of 'Repeat words and phrases out loud'. Additionally, the survey results supported the observations made by O'Malley and Chamot (1990) that beginning- and intermediate-level language learners, which represented the demography of the survey respondents in my project, employed this strategy most frequently.

The fourth cognitive strategy with high-frequency-range use employed by the respondents was *'Getting the idea quickly'* (*Mdn* = 4). This strategy was aimed at extracting the main idea in listening and reading without word-for-word translation in self-directed learning. As the online students were confronted with a large volume and diversity of learning resources, they needed to use this strategy to quickly understand the learning resources available and identify which were most appropriate for the particular task they faced. Therefore, this strategy was employed by students to enhance the effectiveness of their learning.

At the medium-frequency-range use level, there were two cognitive strategies: *'Taking notes'* (*Mdn* = 3) and *'Summarising'* (*Mdn* = 3) (see Table 3.7). Whilst both strategies shared the same median, they demonstrated completely different distribution patterns. The *'Summarising'* strategy followed a distribution pattern clustered around the mean. The *'Taking notes'* strategy, on the other hand, exhibited a polarised distribution. In other words, some respondents preferred to concentrate on listening, whilst others chose to take notes even though all the online classes were recorded by Blackboard. It is likely that learners with a higher language-proficiency level would engage more with this strategy use, whilst lower-level learners would focus on listening to the lectures rather than taking notes. For example, Interviewee S10, whose proficiency level of listening comprehension was high, adopted this strategy.

74 *The repertoire of LLSs in online Chinese learning*

On the low-frequency-range use spectrum, the survey results reported the cognitive strategy of '*Learning from other students' written work*' (*Mdn* = 2). This strategy was listed in the survey questionnaire as a cognitive strategy specific to collaborative learning. The online Chinese courses were designed in such a way that they required the students to comment on each other's writing whilst working in pairs or groups of three on their written assignment in a wiki-supported online writing space. This was to encourage the students to learn from their peers and improve their Chinese writing through collaboration. This low rating differs from the findings of a recent study by Krishnan et al. (2018), which revealed students' positive attitudes towards learning from others in collaborative writing. The low-frequency-range use of this strategy reported in this research, as suggested by the interviewee S12, reflected the students' lack of confidence in providing corrections and comments due to their low proficiency levels, or their inclination to protect their language partner's self-esteem.

The analyses of other data sources (interview data, additional data, and responses to the open-ended questions in the survey questionnaire) revealed four cognitive strategies, as shown in Table 3.8. Three of the four appeared in the survey questionnaire: '*Using resources for receiving and sending messages*'; '*Repeating*'; and '*Taking notes*'. The reappearance of these three strategies affirmed the relatively high-frequency use of these strategies. These data sources also showed that three interviewees employed the cognitive strategy of '*Practising naturalistically*', which refers to the interviewees actively making use of authentic Chinese resources for self-directed learning, such as watching Chinese TV programmes and movies, reading novels, and chatting with family members in Chinese. The interviewees who reported using the strategy felt that these learning activities were beneficial to building their vocabulary and improving their Chinese speaking, which aligns with Oxford's (1990) belief that this cognitive strategy is valuable to all levels of language learning.

It should be stressed that specific digital resources (other than reference resources such as dictionaries) were highlighted by six (out of ten) interviewees (S5, S8, S9, S12, S13, S15) as being helpful in improving the effectiveness of their cognitive strategy use, especially '*Using resources for receiving and sending messages*' and '*Repeating*' strategies (Table 3.8). These digital resources relate to content-based learning materials both in the form of an app and web-based resources, for example Pimsleur Digital Mandarin (a digital Mandarin course), Intelligent Flashcard STS Chinese, and StickyStudy.

Furthermore, the interviewees reported using different resources for different purposes. For instance, S5 selected flashcard apps from a large range of choices to suit her needs for learning vocabulary and practising pronunciation. She decided to use two flashcard apps: Short-Term Spoken Chinese (an app accompanying the textbook used in the course) and Pinyin Training (an app for mastering tones). The Short-Term Spoken Chinese app allowed her to review the vocabulary list in the textbook and imitate the pronunciation, whilst the Pinyin Training app helped her improve her accuracy in Pinyin pronunciation.

Excerpt 3.3 provides an example of using '*Repeating*' and '*Structured reviewing*' offered by S8, who repeatedly listened to the MP3 resources from Pimsleur

Table 3.8 Cognitive strategies identified in the interview data

Cognitive strategy	Statement (paraphrased for brevity)	Technological tool	Learning context	Data from	Interviewee
Using resources for receiving and sending messages (Oxford, 1990)	Search online for the meaning of Chinese words	E-dictionary app: Pleco; Google Translate; TrainChinese	Self-directed learning outside the online classes	I	S12 S13 S15
		E-dictionary app: Google Translate; Screwit	Assessment-task completion outside online classes (a speaking assignment)	I	S5 S8
	Borrow/copy a sentence found by looking up a YouTube video	Videos: YouTube	Assessment-task completion outside online classes (a speaking assignment)	I	S8
Repeating (Oxford, 1990)	Listen to recorded conversations many times	Pimsleur Digital Mandarin language course	Self-directed learning outside the online classes	I	S5 S8
	Imitate teacher's and Chinese friends' pronunciation	Social media app: Social media app: WeChat (text and voice messages)	Assessment-task completion outside online classes (a speaking assignment)	I	S5 S9
Taking notes (Oxford, 1990)	Take notes before and after online class	Word document; textbook	Online class participation	I AD SIII	S10 S9 S10
	Take notes of new words and phrases	Notebook	Self-directed learning outside the online classes	I	S14
Practising naturalistically (Oxford, 1990)	Watch Chinese TV programmes and movies; speak Chinese with family members; read novels in Chinese	TV	Self-directed learning outside the online classes	I SIII	S10 S17 S8 S10

and imitated the native speakers in the conversations. In the interview, he also mentioned that he had used this learning resource for a year. Such repeated actions suggest that S8 was trying to practise (a cognitive strategy of '*Repeating*') and memorise (a memory strategy of '*Structured Reviewing*') grammar items and vocabulary in learning conversations. The learning behaviours of overlearning and imitating served two learning motives, one of practising and the other of memorising. This result supported Oxford's (2017) description of how LLS can be combined in various ways, such as 'strategy clusters or strategy chains' (p. 48).

76 *The repertoire of LLSs in online Chinese learning*

> **Excerpt 3.3 An example of using 'Repeating' and 'Structured reviewing' by S8**
>
> *S8: ... I think it was very very useful ... was a ... and that was a show like a podcast, whereby it runs one in Beijing, one in Shanghai, and they run a daily podcast. Some are normal Chinese speed, but then they break it down slowly ... so it's a conversation, usually kind of funny with some humour. And then they break it down and do the vocabulary, and the grammar, that was a great way to progress from just these standard MP3 audio classes. (00:04:57 in the recording, Interview, S8, 2015).*

In summary, the participants reported that they had employed a diverse repertoire of cognitive strategies to practise Chinese listening, speaking, reading, and writing in all the three learning contexts. They used cognitive strategies in a variety of language-learning activities and assessment tasks in independent learning, and particularly relied on using relevant cognitive strategies to search for answers on websites and language-learning apps to solve problems in both asynchronous and synchronous environments. The collaborative learning activities were expected to influence how the students used cognitive strategies, and to particularly increase the use of the cognitive strategy '*Learning from other students' written work*' to improve their writing skills. However, my research indicated that the students were reluctant to use this strategy in their collaboration, and the reasons behind this are perceived to be worthy of further investigation.

3.2.4 Social strategies

Social strategies are used in learning a foreign language through communication with others (Oxford, 1990). For online language learning, researchers have discovered that learners need to adapt to online learning environments by using new forms of social strategies, such as 'Using the tools and modes available to improve communication and interaction' (Hauck & Hampel, 2008). According to the self-reported data, the category of social strategies appeared to be important to online language learning. Table 3.9 summarises the use of the five social strategies included in the survey questionnaire.

As shown in Table 3.9, three of the five social strategies were from Oxford (1990): (1) '*Cooperating with peers*'; (2) '*Asking for correction*'; and (3) '*Asking for clarification and verification*'. The other two, '*Netiquette*' and '*Using tools available to improve communication and interaction*', were added to the questionnaire for this research as strategies specific to online learning. Overall, the survey results suggested that the participants employed the social strategies to different degrees to interact with their language partners, peers, and teachers in the three learning contexts.

I identified '*Netiquette*' in the survey questionnaire as a social strategy that was distinctly different from those of other researchers; the respondents used this

Table 3.9 Social strategies reported by the survey respondents

Social strategy	Questionnaire items relating to LLSs	Learning context	% of scale 1, 2, 3, 4, 5	Median, mean, LLS usage
Netiquette (LLS specific to online learning)	I respect my language partner's time when we work together	Self-directed learning outside the online classes	0, 0, 8.7, 30.4, 60.9	5, 4.52, H
	I respond as soon as possible to my language partner's queries	Assessment-task completion outside online classes (a speaking assignment or an oral test)	8.7, 4.3, 13.0, 26.1, 47.8	4, 4.00, H
	I prefer keeping the webcam on to let the teacher and other students see me	Online class participation	26.1, 17.4, 17.4, 21.7, 8.7	3, 2.67, M
	I reply to other students' comments on my wiki page	Assessment-task completion outside online classes (a wiki-writing assignment)	52.2, 26.1, 8.7, 8.7, 4.3	1, 1.87, L
	I put comments on other students' wiki-writing assignments to help them with my suggestions		56.5, 21.7, 13.0, 8.7, 0	1, 1.70, L
Cooperating with peers (Oxford, 1990)	I write the conversation scripts of the speaking assignment together with my language partner	Assessment-task completion outside online classes (a speaking assignment or an oral test)	8.7, 21.7, 4.3, 26.1, 39.1	4, 3.65, H
	I discuss the wiki-writing assignment with my language partner	Assessment-task completion outside online classes (a wiki-writing assignment)	17.4, 13.0, 13.0, 30.4, 26.1	4, 3.35, M
Asking for correction (Oxford, 1990)	I ask my language partner to check my script	Assessment-task completion outside online classes (a speaking assignment or an oral test)	8.7, 21.7, 21.7, 17.4, 30.4	4, 3.57, H
	I ask my teacher to provide feedback on my early drafts	Assessment-task completion outside online classes (a wiki-writing assignment)	39.1, 26.1, 13.0, 13.0, 8.7	2, 2.26, L
	I encourage other students to leave comments on my wiki page		56.5, 17.4, 17.4, 8.7, 0.0	1, 1.78, L

(*Continued*)

Table 3.9 Continued

Social strategy	Questionnaire items relating to LLSs	Learning context	% of scale 1, 2, 3, 4, 5	Median, mean, LLS usage
	I ask my language partner to correct me whenever I make a mistake	Assessment-task completion outside online classes (a speaking assignment or an oral test)	8.7, 21.7, 21.7, 17.4, 30.4	3, 3.39, M
	I ask the teacher to correct me	Online class participation	21.7, 8.7, 4.3, 47.8, 8.7	4, 3.14, M
	I ask other students to correct me		39.1, 17.4, 8.7, 21.7, 4.3	2, 2.29, L
Asking for clarification or verification (Oxford, 1990)	If I do not understand, I ask the teacher to explain/repeat	Online class participation	17.4, 0, 17.4, 34.8, 21.7	4, 3.48, M
	If I do not understand, I ask the other students to slow down, repeat, or clarify what was said		17.4, 8.7, 21.7, 30.4, 13.0	3, 3.14, M
	I ask the teacher to verify that I have understood or said something correctly		21.7, 4.3, 26.1, 30.4, 8.7	3, 3.00, M
Using tools available to improve communication and interaction (LLS specific to online learning)	I type text messages for the purpose of effective communication	Online class participation	13.0, 8.7, 26.1, 30.4, 13.0	3, 3.24, M

strategy at a high-frequency range (*Mdn* = 5). The concept of netiquette relates to etiquette in an online environment (Hauck & Hampel, 2008). In the survey questionnaire, the strategy '*Netiquette*' involves respecting a language partner's time, responding in a timely way, keeping the webcam turned on in online classes, and replying to other students' comments on a wiki page.

One interesting observation from the survey results is that the participants used the '*Netiquette*' strategy items in different ways and to different degrees. As presented in Table 3.9, the strategy item of respecting others' time during collaboration appeared to be the most frequently used item (high-frequency-range use, $M = 4.52$). Most respondents (91.3%) rated this item at 4 (Generally true of me) or 5 (Always or almost always true of me). Respecting others' time could entail responding to others in a timely fashion in email and WeChat exchanges, as well as showing up at the agreed time when recording dialogues together or preparing for oral tests in the Collaborate Homework Rooms. Similarly, the respondents rated the strategy item about responding promptly to a language partner's queries at a high frequency of use ($M = 4.00$).

One less frequently used strategy item, keeping the webcam on to show one's face in the online classes, received a medium-frequency-range use ($M = 2.67$). The webcam is an important feature in online language learning. However, less than one third of the respondents (30.4%) rated this item at 4 or 5, whilst 43.5% rated it at 1 or 2. One interviewee (S10) claimed that she thought it was unnecessary and inconvenient as she studied in a bedroom. Kozar's (2016) study provided similar reasons in that online students reduced their use of webcams because of self-consciousness and privacy concerns. However, Kozar (2016) suggested that it is important to use the webcam, as it may reduce the learners' aloneness in online language learning. Doing so also increases the number of opportunities to use nonverbal cues during interactions, such as nodding one's head.

The other social strategy specific to online learning, '*Using tools available to improve communication and interaction*', received a rating of medium-frequency-range use ($Mdn = 3$) (Table 3.9). This strategy is similar to 'Using the tools and modes available to improve communication and interaction' in Hauck and Hampel (2008). Nearly half (43.3%) of the respondents rated the strategy item as 4 (Generally true of me) or 5 (Always or almost always true of me). However, the observed data showed that this strategy use may be influenced by the size of the online class. For instance, students would not use this strategy much if there were only a few students in the class; rather, they preferred to interact with the teachers and other students orally instead of using text chat.

There were three noticeable correlations among the questionnaire items in social strategies based on Pearson's r-correlation-analysis results. The first noticeable correlation existed between two strategy items: asking teachers for correction ('*Asking for correction*'), and asking teachers to verify the student's understanding or speaking ('*Asking for clarification or verification*') in online classes ($r =.84;.80–1.0$; 'very strong'). Such a strong correlation suggested that the respondents tended to apply the same frequency of use to asking teachers for corrections and asking for verification in online classes.

The second noticeable correlation appeared in the strategy item pair of asking questions via text chat (non-vocal) ('*Using tools available to improve communication and interaction*'), and the strategy item of asking teachers (vocal) for further explanation or repetition ('*Asking for clarification or verification*') in online classes ($r =.77;.60-.79$; 'strong'). This result revealed that the respondents who frequently asked questions via non-vocal communications also preferred to ask the teacher to explain or repeat what they did not understand via vocal communication.

The third noticeable correlation occurred between the strategy item of asking other students to slow down, repeat, or clarify what had been said ('*Asking for clarification or verification*') and that of asking teachers to verify whether the student had understood or said something correctly in online classes ('*Asking for clarification or verification*') ($r =.74;.60-.79$; 'strong'). This result demonstrated that the respondents who tended to ask other students for verification would also ask the teacher for verification as well.

Further evidence about the use of social strategies from the students' interviews, additional data, and classroom observations is summarised in Table 3.10. The strategy of '*Using the tools available to improve communication*' was found to be used not only by the respondents in the learning context of online class participation, but also in the other two learning contexts, as reported from the interview data. For instance, two interviewees (S12 and S17) reported that they used WeChat to send voice messages, text messages, images, and emojis, in English, Chinese Pinyin, and Chinese characters. Such uses typified the respondents' use of available tools by applying various functions in software and apps to enhance interactions with others.

Table 3.10 Social strategies identified in the interview, observed and additional data

Social strategy	Statement (paraphrased for brevity)	Technological tool	Learning context	Data from	Participant
Netiquette (LLS specific to online learning)	Respect my language partner's time when we work together		Assessment-task completion outside online classes (ongoing assessments, a speaking assignment)	I	S8
	Respond quickly: responding to the language partners' and the teacher's emails within 24 hours	Email		I	S9
	Respond to teacher's and classmates' questions quickly;	Audio facility via the audio/video panel in Blackboard Collaborate	Online class participation	I	S14
	Keeping the webcam on	Audio facility via the audio/video panel in Blackboard Collaborate		I	S14
Cooperating with peers (Oxford, 1990)	Collaborate with a language partner to draft and practise a speaking assignment	Online teaching platform: Blackboard Collaborate room	Assessment-task completion outside online classes (ongoing assessments, a speaking assignment)	I	S8 S9 S10 S17
	Offer or give corrections on the language partner's written draft	Word document		I	S10
Asking for correction (Oxford, 1990)	Seek feedback on initial written draft from Chinese teacher or friends		Assessment-task completion outside online classes (ongoing assessments, a speaking assignment)	I	S8
Asking for clarification or verification (Oxford, 1990)	Ask the teacher to explain grammar points in ongoing assessments	Social media app: WeChat: images, emojis, text and voice messages		AD	S8

Using the tools available to improve communication and interaction (LLS specific to online learning)	Use emoticons and text chat to interact with others for language learning, such as praising the other students' speaking, and answering other students' questions	The emoticons (such as smiley face, LOL, and raised hand) and text messages in the Chat panel in Blackboard Collaborate	Online class participation	OI	S5
	Share photos and comments on the photos in a private Chinese friend circle	Social media app: WeChat moments	Self-directed learning outside online classes	I	S12 S14
	Use different contact tools to interact with different groups of people	Email, WhatsApp, WeChat	Assessment-task completion outside online classes (ongoing assessments, a speaking assignment)	I	S17

The self-reported data revealed that the participants employed a significant number of social strategies and diversified their use in the three learning contexts. These social strategies were adopted by the students to discuss and negotiate ideas, share information and resources, and coordinate their collaboration. As part of this process, the participants tried various interactive tools, apps, and social media to enhance the effectiveness of their social-strategy use. Most of the social strategies found in the data were used for online collaboration, which indicated that the students employed social strategies for efficient interactions in collaborative learning. In other words, online learning environments and collaborative learning produced marked impacts on the students' social-strategy selection and use.

3.2.5 Memory strategies

Language learners use memory strategies, such as creating mental linkages, applying images and sounds, and carefully reviewing, in order to remember important information (Oxford, 1990). According to the collected data in this project, memory strategies were mainly used in the contexts of self-directed learning and assessment-task completion. There was no evidence that these participants employed memory strategies in online classes. In the survey questionnaire, the participants responded to three strategy items which reflected three of Oxford's (1990) LLSs: '*Using mechanical techniques*'; '*Placing new words into a context*'; and '*Semantic mapping*' (Table 3.11). Additionally, Oxford's memory strategy of '*Representing sounds in memory*', and a specific Chinese-character-learning strategy, '*Creating stories for memorising Chinese character writing*' were found from the qualitative data (see Table 3.12).

Table 3.11 Memory strategies reported by the survey respondents

Memory strategy	Questionnaire items relating to LLSs	Learning context	% of scale 1, 2, 3, 4, 5	Median, mean, LLS usage
Using mechanical techniques (Oxford, 1990)	I use character cards to help memorise new Chinese words	Self-directed learning outside the online classes	17.4, 13.0, 26.1, 21.7, 21.7	3, 3.17, M
Placing new words into a context (Oxford, 1990)	When I am learning a new Chinese word, I put it in a sentence, so I can remember it		4.3, 26.1, 39.1, 8.7, 21.7	3, 3.17, M
Semantic mapping (Oxford, 1990)	When I am learning a new Chinese word, I list words I know that are related to it and draw lines to show relationships		21.7, 39.1, 13.0, 17.4, 8.7	2, 2.52, M

The survey respondents used all three memory strategies at medium-frequency range in self-directed learning outside the online classes. Of these three strategies, two share the same mean and median scores, albeit with different distribution patterns. One strategy is '*Using mechanical techniques*' ($M = 3.17$) which refers to using character cards to help memorise new Chinese words. The other strategy is '*Placing new words into a context*' ($M = 3.17$), which refers to memorising a Chinese word in a sentence. The third strategy '*Semantic mapping*' is only just at the medium-frequency range ($M = 2.52$), and indeed over 60% of the respondents rated it as 1 (Never or almost never true of me) or 2 (Generally not true of me). Through these statistics, we can see that whilst all three memory strategies were at medium-frequency-range use, these were not greatly used by most of the participants in self-directed learning.

The Pearson's *r*-correlation results showed that the correlations were either very weak or weak between the three memory strategies. A very weak correlation ($r = .04$;.00-.19; 'very weak') existed between the two strategy items which corresponded to the two memory strategies of '*Placing new words into a context*' and '*Semantic mapping*'. A similar situation pertained between '*Semantic mapping*' and '*Using mechanical techniques*' ($r = .13$;.00-.19; 'very weak'). A weak correlation ($r = .27$;.20-.39; 'weak') was found between '*Placing new words into a context*' and '*Using mechanical techniques*'. All these correlation results indicated that the respondents might have used memory strategies differently in self-directed learning to suit their needs.

The qualitative results reinforced the conclusion drawn from the survey results. These qualitative data involved the interview (I) and the open-ended questions in the survey (SIII), as shown in Table 3.12. One of the three memory strategies in the survey questionnaire, '*Using mechanical techniques*', reappeared in the results from the qualitative data. The qualitative data also suggested that the interviewees used the strategy '*Representing sounds in memory*'. In addition, '*Creating stories*

Table 3.12 Memory strategies identified in the interview data and the open-ended questions from the survey questionnaire

Memory strategy	Statement (paraphrased for brevity)	Technological tool	Learning context	Data from	Participant
Using mechanical techniques (Oxford, 1990)	Memorise words or characters by listening to flashcard apps over and over	Flashcard functions in learning apps: Intelligent Flashcards STS Chinese; Pinyin Training; Pleco; Google Translate; Youdao; StickyStudy	Self-directed learning outside the online classes	I SIII	S5 S18 S12 S14 S15 S9 S12 S14
	Make flashcards and use them to memorise words	Home-made flashcards, created using PowerPoint software; Flashcard function in a learning app: KTPict CE		I SIII	S18
Representing sounds in memory (Oxford, 1990)	Memorise phrases by listening to digital resources over and over again	Pimsleur Digital Mandarin language course		I	S5 S8
	Memorise conversations by listening to voice messages over and over again	Social media app: WeChat (text and voice messages)	Assessment-task completion outside online classes (ongoing assessments, a speaking assignment)	I	S5
Creating stories to memorise Chinese character writing (LLS for Chinese-language learning)	Memorise Chinese characters by creating stories reflecting the meaning of strokes in a Chinese character		Self-directed learning outside the online classes	I SIII	S8

to memorise Chinese character writing' emerged from the interview data as a new memory strategy specific to Chinese-language learning.

As shown in Table 3.12, more than half of the interviewed students (S5, S9, S12, S14, S15, S18) used various learning tools (e.g., flashcard apps) to memorise Chinese words, thereby employing the strategy of '*Using mechanical techniques*'.

However, this strategy embraced a much richer content in this project when compared with that originally proposed by Oxford (1990), as the interviewees used a variety of tools and resources to support their learning. Most of them were online learning tools and resources, such as flashcard functions in apps (e.g., Intelligent Flashcards STS Chinese, KTPict CE, Pleco, and StickyStudy), and digital resources (such as Pimsleur for conversation in Chinese).

Self-evidently, these types of learning tools save learners from having to make paper flashcards and facilitate the use of visual and auditory input for learners to learn and review vocabulary with. Such benefits clearly help learners improve the effectiveness of '*Using mechanical techniques*'. In this sense, the interviewees' use of the flashcard functions was also related to the cognitive strategy of '*Repeating*' to imitate the pronunciation. Therefore, the use of the flashcard function appears to cut across cognitive- and memory-strategy categories.

The qualitative data also revealed a new memory strategy of '*Creating stories to memorise Chinese character writing*', which was specific to Chinese-language learning. According to Interviewee S8, a student on the higher-beginning-level course, the most difficult aspect of learning Chinese characters was memorising how to write them, as he often 'quickly forgot'. He commented that this LLS was very effective. Excerpt 3.4 exemplifies how he created a story to memorise the character 质 in the word 质量 <quality>.

Excerpt 3.4 An example of 'Creating stories for memorising Chinese character writing' by S8

S8: ... and also a lot of the learning aids, they tell you to learn some silly little stories about the word to remember it, so – for example, 质量 <quality>, ... it has the radical for cliff, it has the radical for shell, and maybe I think it is the character ten, ..., so the story I learnt was, 质量 ... climbing down the cliff to collect ten quality shells, and I think that was the story I made up to remember it. (00:52:30 in the recording, Interview, S8, 2015).

S8's example of memorising 质 showed that he used his knowledge of the radicals (十 and 贝) in the character of 质 as cues to create his own idiosyncratic stories about the character. Hence, I named this strategy '*Creating stories for memorising Chinese character writing*' and added it to the memory-strategy category. However, as the use of this strategy often relies on one's prior knowledge of radicals or characters, the frequency of employment is likely to be influenced by learners' language-proficiency level. These findings are consistent with Shen's (2005) study on Chinese-character learning. In her study, she created a strategy inventory for Chinese-character learning which included the strategy item 'Finds the connection between the new character and previously learned radicals in terms of sound, meaning, and shape for character learning' (p. 57).

In summary, the participants' memory-strategy use was limited in quantity and was only found to be employed in the self-directed learning context. Similar to social-strategy use, the qualitative data indicated that technology enriched the ways that memory strategies were used, thus enhancing the effectiveness of these strategies. As a result, the participants used memory strategies in Chinese learning in different and more varied ways than those in which memory strategies were defined in Oxford (1990). For example, the memory strategy '*Creating stories to memorise Chinese character writing*' was focused specifically on memorising Chinese characters. The participants in this research were also found to be studying and memorising words in a variety of ways and applying different types of language-learning apps to suit their learning motives and needs; consequently, they developed personalised use of memory strategies.

3.2.6 Compensation strategies

Compensation strategies are used by learners to make up for missing knowledge whilst listening, reading, speaking, or writing (Oxford, 1990). As presented in Table 3.13 and Table 3.14, four compensation strategies were reported by the participants, two from the survey questionnaire and two from the interview data. These four strategies are: (1) '*Selecting the topic*'; (2) '*Using linguistic clues*'; (3) '*Using mime or gesture*'; and (4) '*Getting help*'. These compensation strategies were employed by the participants in the learning contexts of self-directed learning and online class participation, as well as assessment-task completion (Table 3.14).

From the survey data, the strategy of '*Selecting the topic*' can be seen to be at medium-frequency-range use ($Mdn = 3$), but is only just inside that range ($M = 2.61$). This result suggested that '*Selecting the topic*' was not a commonly employed strategy when talking with others in Chinese. This is unsurprising, given that this strategy cannot realistically be expected to be in high-frequency-range use among beginning-level learners (who represented the majority of the survey respondents) as they are unlikely to be able to converse freely on any topic in Chinese.

Table 3.13 Compensation strategies reported by the survey respondents

Compensation strategy	Questionnaire items relating to LLSs questionnaire	Learning context	% of scale 1, 2, 3, 4, 5	Median, mean, LLS usage
Selecting the topic (Oxford, 1990)	When speaking with other students, I tend to steer the conversation onto a topic for which I know the words	Self-directed learning outside the online classes	13.0, 34.8, 34.8, 13.0, 4.3	3, 2.61, M
Getting help (Oxford, 1990)	I ask other students to tell me the right word if I cannot think of it	Online class participation	34.8, 26.1, 4.3, 9.5, 19.0	2, 2.28, L

86 *The repertoire of LLSs in online Chinese learning*

Table 3.14 Compensation strategies identified in the interview data

Compensation strategy	Statement (paraphrased for brevity)	Learning context	Data from	Inter- viewee
Using linguistic clues (Oxford, 1990)	Guess the meaning of what is heard in Chinese, in the absence of complete knowledge of vocabulary	Self-directed learning outside the online classes	I	S5 S17
Using mime or gesture (Oxford, 1990)	Guess the meaning of the speaker's hand gestures			

The interview data also showed students' adoption of two other compensation strategies described by Oxford (1990), which had not been included in the questionnaire: '*Using linguistic clues*' and '*Using mime or gesture*', as shown in Table 3.14. They used these two strategies to communicate with native speakers, such as Chinese friends and family members, in daily communication. By doing so, they benefited from using these compensation strategies during interactions. For instance, Interviewee S5 talked about an example which showed that she used the strategy of '*Using linguistic clues*', as shown in Excerpt 3.5. S5's description demonstrated that she needed to have a certain amount of vocabulary knowledge to support her subsequent guessing. This interview result is in accord with a study by Karbalaei and Negin Taji (2014), who indicated that language proficiency level is an essential factor which influences learners' compensation strategy use.

Excerpt 3.5 An example of 'Using linguistic clues' by S5 in daily conversations with a Chinese girl

S5: So, for example, I asked the girl in Chinese what she would like to drink, and she answered, and I guessed it was apple juice ... Because I know 'apple' in Chinese, and there wasn't any other thing in the fridge, so ... (00:43:00 in the recorded interview, S5, 2015).

In summary, the students employed a small number of compensation strategies when collaborating with others. The observed data demonstrated that online collaboration was a factor influencing the students' compensation strategy use, which is further discussed in Section 3.3.1.

3.2.7 Metacognitive strategies

Metacognitive strategies enable students to coordinate their own learning process (Oxford, 1990). Researchers have indicated that metacognitive strategies are especially valuable for achieving success in online language learning (Chang, 2007, 2010; Solak & Cakir, 2015). In the survey questionnaire, the respondents rated five

The repertoire of LLSs in online Chinese learning 87

out of the 11 metacognitive strategies in Oxford's (1990) taxonomy: (1) *'Seeking practice opportunities'*; (2) *'Organising'*; (3) *'Self-evaluating'*; (4) *'Overviewing and linking with already known material'*; and (5) *'Self-monitoring'* (see Table 3.15). Additionally, Table 3.15 contains the strategy of *'Preparing questions for attending online classes'*, which was added to the survey questionnaire as a strategy specific to flipped-classroom learning. The survey results at strategy item level evidenced that some metacognitive strategies were heavily used by the participants for self-directed learning outside the online classes.

Table 3.15 Metacognitive strategies reported by the survey respondents

Metacognitive strategy	Questionnaire items relating to LLSs	Learning context	% of scale 1, 2, 3, 4, 5	Median, mean, LLS usage
Organising (Oxford, 1990)	I arrange a comfortable environment for studying, to promote learning	Self-directed learning outside the online classes	0, 8.7, 17.4, 56.5, 17.4	4, 3.83, H
	I have developed a routine so that I study Chinese regularly, not just when there is the pressure of tests		4.3, 13.0, 17.4, 39.1, 26.1	4, 3.70, H
Overviewing and linking with known material (Oxford, 1990)	I review the resources that are recommended in the online Chinese courses		4.3, 13.0, 26.1, 34.8, 21.7	4, 3.57, H
Self-evaluating (Oxford, 1990)	I often evaluate the progress I have made in learning Chinese		8.7, 13.0, 39.1, 34.8, 4.3	3, 3.13, M
	I record myself speaking by using an audio or video recorder so that I can listen to myself and correct my pronunciation		34.8, 30.4, 26.1, 0, 8.7	2, 2.17, L
Seeking practice opportunities (Oxford, 1990)	I try to speak Chinese whenever I can		0, 21.7, 43.5, 26.1, 8.7	3, 3.22, M
Preparing questions for attending online classes (LLS for flipped-classroom learning)	I prepare questions in advance to ask in the online classes		17.4, 30.4, 39.1, 8.7, 4.3	3, 2.52, M
Self-monitoring (Oxford, 1990)	I try to notice my errors when speaking Chinese and to work out the reason for them		0, 13.0, 17.4, 52.2, 17.4	4, 3.74, H
	I read the comments other students leave on my wiki page	Assessment-task completion outside online classes (a wiki-writing assignment)	47.8, 13.0, 21.7, 13.0, 4.3	2, 2.13, L
	I revise my wiki-writing assignment taking on board the other students' comments and suggestions on it		56.5, 21.7, 8.7, 8.7, 4.3	1, 1.83, L

The first high-frequency-range use metacognitive strategy was '*Organising*' (*Mdn* = 4), which was employed by the respondents in self-directed learning outside the online classes in respect of two related strategy items. One was to arrange a learning environment for self-directed learning (*M* = 3.83), and the other was to develop a learning routine to study Chinese regularly (*M* = 3.70). These survey results suggested that the majority of the respondents understood the importance of managing a comfortable learning environment and of developing a learning routine for their studies. Language learning requires constant and regular practice to gain proficiency. Therefore, maintaining a learning routine is undoubtedly important to successful distance language learning as it helps students maintain constant and regular practice and thereby to become proficient.

The second high-frequency-range use metacognitive strategy was '*Overviewing and linking with known material*' (*Mdn* = 4) which was utilised by the respondents to review and learn the recommended resources in the online Chinese courses. These learning resources included texts and exercises in their textbooks, the prerecorded mini-lecture videos, the PowerPoint slides of the online classes, and online quizzes. More than half of the respondents (56.5%) gave a rating of 4 (Generally true of me) or 5 (Always or almost always true of me) to the strategy item 'I review the resources that are recommended in the online Chinese courses'. These survey results indicated that the respondents' metacognitive strategy use was influenced by the design of the online courses as these courses provided them with a range of learning resources and tools for self-directed learning. The flipped-classroom approach adopted in these courses also required the students to master the basic content each week before coming to their online classes.

The third high-frequency-range strategy was '*Self-monitoring*' (*Mdn* = 4). This strategy was used to a different extent in two language-learning contexts. In the context of self-directed learning, one strategy item, noticing the errors when speaking Chinese and working out the reason for them, appeared with a high-frequency-range strategy use (*M* = 3.74). Nearly 70% of respondents (69.6%) gave a rating of 4 (Generally true of me) or 5 (Always or almost always true of me) to this strategy item.

In contrast, in the context of assessment-task completion (a wiki-writing assignment), two strategy items appeared to have low-frequency-range usage. These two strategy items were reading the comments other students leave on the wiki page (*M* = 2.13); and revising the wiki-writing assignment taking on board the other students' comments and suggestions on it (*M* = 1.83).

The survey results on these two strategy items indicated that the respondents lacked interactions on the wiki page, which was confirmed by my observation of this assessment task. Rarely did the students provide comments and suggestions on other students' work. However, there was evidence that they interacted with their language partners by using other software, for example, Google Drive, Word documents, and email. The use of these technological tools will be further discussed in Section 3.3.1.

The strategy of '*Preparing questions for attending online classes*', which had a medium-frequency-range usage (*Mdn* = 3), referred to whether online learners prepared questions in advance to ask others in the online classes. This strategy was listed as a metacognitive strategy specific to flipped-classroom learning in the survey questionnaire. Almost half of the respondents (47.8%) gave a rating of 1 (Never or almost never true of me) or 2 (Generally not true of me) in respect to this strategy. One contributing factor might be that it was not compulsory for the students to attend these online classes, thus some students lacked the motivation to prepare any questions.

Among all the metacognitive strategy items in the survey questionnaire, Pearson's r correlations suggested that three strategy items had particularly strong correlations with each other in the context of self-directed learning outside the online classes. The correlation results showed that the strategy of '*Overviewing and linking with known material*' was strongly correlated with the strategy of '*Self-monitoring*' ($r = .68$); the strategy of '*Self-monitoring*' was strongly correlated with the strategy of '*Self-evaluating*' ($r = .63$); and the strategy of '*Self-evaluating*' was strongly correlated with the strategy of '*Overviewing and linking with known material*' ($r = .65$). Such strong correlations were to be expected, as the more the students reviewed the learning resources, the more likely they would evaluate and monitor their language learning, and vice versa. According to Chang (2007), online students who used the strategy of '*Self-monitoring*' paid more attention to their own learning behaviours in reading the learning materials.

The qualitative data from the interview and the open-ended questions, as listed in Table 3.16, provided further evidence to support the survey results that the interviewees emphasised the importance of using the metacognitive strategies of '*Organising*' and '*Seeking practice opportunities*'. Six interviewees (S8, S13, S14, S15, S17, S18) reported organising learning routines which involved a variety of learning activities. They also considered the time involved and the suitability of various learning and communication tools for these learning activities. For example, S8's daily routine involved finding opportunities to talk with native Chinese speakers, listening to MP3 recordings and podcasts in Chinese, watching TV programmes for children, and undertaking online Chinese courses on YouTube. S14's routine activities included talking with a Chinese friend once a week and frequently chatting with Chinese colleagues at lunchtime.

In addition, these interview results revealed that the online students created and developed schedules which outlined study times and learning goals. Such findings suggested that most interviewees exhibited a strong sense of responsibility for their own Chinese-language learning and had developed personal processes and techniques to promote their Chinese-language skills.

These findings are consistent with the concept which Bown (2006) named the 'locus of learning'. That is, independent learners believe that they have responsibilities and capabilities to control the language-learning process. These online students were confident in their ability to seek opportunities to practise listening, reading, and speaking. They were autonomous learners and did not hesitate to obtain help from native Chinese speakers. In these interviewees' learning schedules, they considered the possible practice opportunities and organised these opportunities into their learning routines for personalised online learning.

90 The repertoire of LLSs in online Chinese learning

Table 3.16 Metacognitive strategies identified in the interview data and the open-ended questions from the survey questionnaire

Metacognitive strategy	Statement (paraphrased for brevity)	Learning context	Data from	Participant
Organising (Oxford, 1990)	Develop a learning routine	Self-directed learning outside the online classes	I	S8 S13 S14 S15 S17 S18
	Complete assessment tasks before due dates		SIII	S9
	Schedule fragmented time to learn Chinese vocabulary		SIII	S9
	Schedule a weekly meeting with a Chinese friend		I	S14
Seeking practice opportunities (Oxford, 1990)	Seek opportunities to practise their reading, listening and speaking, such as chatting with Chinese native speakers		I	S5 S14 S8

Overall, the participants employed many metacognitive strategies to manage their online learning. These played an important role in the students' online language learning in terms of managing their cognitive- and memory-strategy use. The students' metacognitive strategy use indicated that their particular learning goals and motives were important factors influencing the development of their own specific learning routines for online language learning. The self-reported data also revealed that some participants employed a distinct metacognitive strategy, '*Preparing questions for attending online classes*', for flipped-classroom learning. This finding suggests that the students tried to take on additional responsibilities in order to help them move towards the achievement of successful online language learning.

3.3 LLSs obtained from the observed data

This section reports the participants' LLS use through observations. It contains thematic analyses of the texts of their communication in two learning environments: the asynchronous (Section 3.3.1) and the synchronous environment (Section 3.3.2). The asynchronous environment in this research project refers to four technological tools: Discussion Board, WeChat, Google Drive, and email. Data sources in the asynchronous mode consisted of 155 messages on the Board, 177 screenshots of WeChat conversations, five written drafts on Google Drive for two assessment tasks, and 146 emails between five students (S8, S9, S12, S13, S20) and their teacher for one whole study period. The synchronous environment in this project refers to the online classes, accessed via Blackboard Collaborate. Data sources in the synchronous mode were 24 recordings of online classes in three courses (CHN11, CHN12, CHN222).

3.3.1 LLS adoption observed in the asynchronous learning environment

Nine strategies emerged from the observed data obtained from the asynchronous learning mode: one affective, one metacognitive, one compensation, and six social strategies. Unlike in the findings from the self-reported data, no memory and cognitive strategies were in evidence in the observed data. Whilst most of the nine strategies are in line with the findings in Section 3.2, a number of additional strategies and methods of strategy use were found in the observed data.

Affective strategies

One affective strategy of '*Discussing your feelings with someone else*' was observed on the Discussion Board (The CAFE). This Discussion Board is different from those used in most other learning situations, where students discuss academic content relating to a topic. Rather, the Discussion Board used in the online courses under investigation functioned as a forum which offered the students a venue for socialising with one another without the teacher's supervision. This is perhaps why students were occasionally observed to discuss their feelings there. For example, participant S36 wrote about her feelings towards Chinese learning as follows:

Excerpt 3.6 An example of 'Discussing your feelings with someone else' by S36 on the Discussion Board

S36: I am a farmer and a mum of five. I home educate 4 of them as well as doing online study through OUA to complete a Bachelor of Education. I'm nervous and excited and hopefully by the end of the unit I will be able to write some of the 'intro' in Chinese. (S36, 2016, Discussion Board).

Excerpt 3.6 indicates that S36 was nervous. As she had just started the online Chinese course, she expressed her concerns about learning Chinese as part of her self-introduction to the class. Whilst the reason for her anxiety was not clear, this example suggested that the Discussion Board might help reduce her learning anxiety by providing a less intimidating space for her to express her feelings in than would be the case in a face-to-face interaction. Online students can use online spaces, such as the Discussion Board, to express their emotional or motivational difficulties in the online learning process. For example, students might feel frustrated when encountering technical problems, such as challenges in submitting an online assignment. In this case, the Discussion Board would provide a forum for the students to share the issue and potential solutions, as they might have similar backgrounds and/or first languages, face the same assessment tasks, and have similar issues in using the online learning platform.

Social strategies

The observed data provided evidence that the participants applied six social strategies when using three of the four technological tools: Discussion Board, Google Drive, and WeChat. No social strategy emerged from their email exchanges (Table 3.17). Of these six strategies, two can be classified as Oxford's (1990) social strategies of '*Asking for clarification or verification*' and '*Asking for correction*'. The other four strategies listed in Table 3.17 are LLSs specific to online or collaborative learning.

Table 3.17 Social strategies observed in participants' use of Discussion Board, Google Drive, and WeChat

Social strategy	Example	Reason	Technological tool	Participant
Netiquette (LLS specific to online learning)	Respond to the language partners' WeChat messages in a timely manner	Collaborating with a language partner	Social media app: WeChat (text and voice messages)	S31, S33, S5, S18, S8
	Send greetings and introduce oneself	Socialising and finding a language partner	Forum: Discussion Board (The CAFE)	22 students of CHN11, SP1, 2016
Asking for clarification or verification (Oxford, 1990)	Ask questions about assessment tasks and technical problems	Finding quick answers		
Sharing with other students (LLS for collaborative learning)	Share understanding of assessment task or course requirements and Chinese knowledge	Preparing for a three-minute role play in pairs	Cloud storage app: Google Drive	S31, S35
Asking for correction (Oxford, 1990)	Ask the teacher to provide feedback on the initial written draft			
	Ask the teacher to correct Chinese word usage	Completing ongoing assessments	Social media app: WeChat (text and voice messages)	S8
Using the tools available to improve communication and interaction (LLS specific to online learning)	Use different colours and character fonts to remind language partners to focus on important information in a draft	Collaboratively completing a speaking assignment or an oral test outside online classes	Cloud storage app: Google Drive	S31, S33, S35 S31, S35
Negotiating with other students (LLS for collaborative learning)	Negotiate the time and online venue for practising Chinese speaking with their peers	Collaboratively completing a speaking assignment or an oral test outside online classes	Social media app: WeChat (text and voice messages)	S31, S33
	Distribute work to complete an assessment task	Completing a written draft for a role play in pairs	Cloud storage app: Google Drive	S31, S33, S35 S31, S35

A common way of starting interaction with others in an asynchronous environment such as the Discussion Board is to introduce oneself and exchange some personal background and/or information with peers. Such greetings and self-introductions as those used by the students in CHN11 reflected the use of the social strategy *'Netiquette'* (see Table 3.17). An example of such an introduction is shown in Excerpt 3.6. These findings are similar to those in Stickler and Lewis (2008), who demonstrated that the online students in their study would be willing to give personal information in order to build social connections as part of the development of collaboration. Using the social strategy of *'Netiquette'*, as Hauck and Hampel (2008) have pointed out, helps online learners make and maintain contact with others, find out each other's learning interests, and develop an identity within a group. Findings from the observed data also showed that the *'Netiquette'* strategy assisted students in finding a suitable language partner. Consequently, this strategy can be linked to the metacognitive strategy of *'Organising'*, as students shared their personal information to find a language partner who preferably lived in a similar time zone and had a similar learning schedule, language learning background, and learning goals.

Among the 15 CHN11 (SP1, 2016) students who posted on the Discussion Board, 11 of them provided their personal information when seeking a language partner to match up with. This strategy use was also encouraged by the assessment tasks as students were required to find a language partner to practise Chinese speaking and writing, as well as to complete a speaking or wiki-writing assignment. The sequencing of the social strategy *'Netiquette'* (e.g., sending greetings, introducing personal background) followed by the metacognitive strategy *'Organising'* (e.g., finding a suitable language partner) could be particular to the online learning environments of these courses.

The findings in Table 3.17 also provided evidence that the students used the strategy of *'Asking for clarification or verification'* on the Discussion Board. This strategy was used for assessment-task completion and to solve technological problems. The questions that these students asked were typically about the technique for accessing a PDF document, assessment-task requirements, and the vocabulary range of an oral exam. From these posts, it can be seen that the students used asynchronous communications to make up for the lack of face-to-face interaction. The Discussion Board provided the students opportunities to connect with their peers and receive feedback. An asynchronous environment such as the Discussion Board proved to be an important way of keeping the students engaged in the online Chinese courses.

In a similar vein, the findings from communications in WeChat also showed that the participants used a number of social strategies to compensate for the lack of face-to-face interaction with their peers. For example, Figure 3.1 demonstrates how two participants (S31 and S33) used *'Netiquette'*, *'Sharing with other students'*, *'Negotiating with other students'*, and *'Using the tools available to improve communication and interaction'* in their WeChat exchanges when completing their speaking assignment of a 1.5-minute oral presentation to introduce a friend.

These two students used the strategy *'Netiquette'* to respond to the language partner's WeChat messages in a timely fashion. The strategy *'Negotiating with*

94 The repertoire of LLSs in online Chinese learning

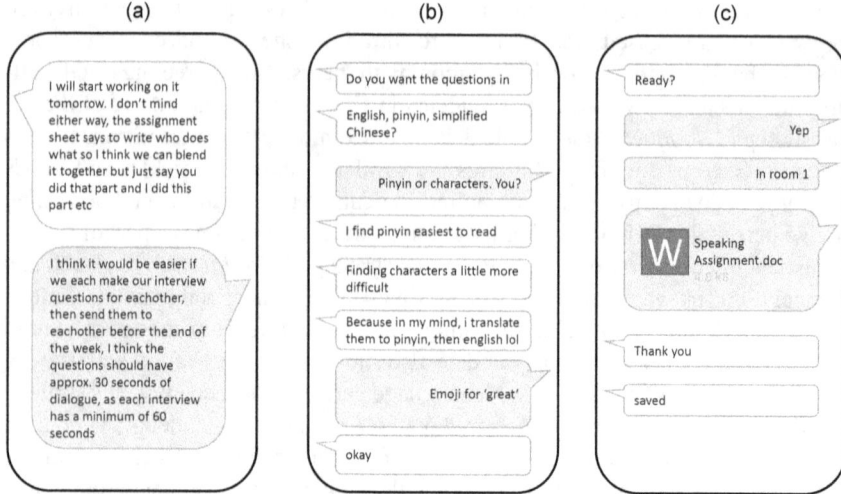

Figure 3.1 Examples of student exchanges via WeChat (reproduced screenshots, provided by S31 and S33, CHN11, 2016)

(a) An example of negotiating work distribution
(b) An example of negotiating the written form
(c) An example of sending reminders and file transfer

other students' was employed to negotiate workload distributions (Figure 3.1a), what languages to use for script writing (Figure 3.1b), and the time and online venue at which to meet and practise Chinese speaking (Figure 3.1c). They also used '*Sharing with other students*' to share their understanding of the course requirements (Figure 3.1a).

In addition, these students employed the strategy of '*Using the tools available to improve communication and interaction*' to transfer their drafts of the writing assignment using the file-transfer function in WeChat (Figure 3.1c). By using the asynchronous environment in WeChat and transferring the written drafts, S31 and S33 interacted with each other before they switched to the synchronous environment in Blackboard to practise Chinese speaking. These observed data indicate that the participants used the asynchronous tools to compensate for the lack of face-to-face interaction with their language partners.

In the Microsoft Word document, S31 and S33 used different colours, fonts, and font sizes to remind language partners to focus on important information in the written draft (Figure 3.2). S33 used bold letters to show his part of the written work, S31 used blue colour to highlight important information that he deleted a Pinyin of 'shi' in a sentence. These actions can also be seen as the social strategy of '*Using the tools available to improve communication and interaction*' for collaboration.

Two social strategies stand out as they do not fit well into any existing LLS classifications. Rather, they are heavily influenced by the collaborative learning in these Chinese-language courses. The first strategy is '*Sharing with other students*', which refers to students sharing learning resources and sharing their understanding

Planned conversation in Pinyin.

Conversation 1

S31: Wo shi Aodaliya liu2xue2sheng1. Wo Xuéxí (sounds like shashe) hànyǔ

S33: Wo3 shi4 de2guo2 liu2xue2sheng1. Wo3 ye3(shi was deleted) **xue2xi2 han4yu3**

S31: Ni hao ma

S33: Wo3 hen3 hao3. Ni3 ne

S31: Wo ye3 (also) hen hao

Figure 3.2 An example of '*Using the tools available to improve communication and interaction*' between two students in completing a speaking assignment (a Word document provided by S31 and S33, CHN11, 2016)

of course requirements and Chinese knowledge with language partners in order to facilitate the collaboration.

The second strategy is '*Negotiating with other students*', which refers to distributing work, setting deadlines, and selecting communication tools to complete assessment tasks with language partners. Such negotiations can also be understood as Oxford's (1990) metacognitive strategy of '*Organising*' as it helps organise two students' learning schedules via negotiation. In this case, WeChat allowed the students to negotiate (social) and arrange language learning (metacognitive) with language partners. Similarly, responding to a language partner's messages in a timely fashion and using emojis ('*Netiquette*') reflects an aspect of affective strategies to maintain a positive motivation for online learning. These two actions were classified as social strategies here to emphasise their collaborative nature in a social interaction process.

In total, four social strategies ('*Netiquette*'; '*Sharing with other students*'; '*Negotiating with other students*'; and '*Using tools available to improve communication and interaction*') can be grouped together as a subcategory, 'Collaborating with others'. These four strategies are distinctly different from Oxford's (1990) subcategory 'Cooperating with others', which contains two social strategies '*Cooperating with peers*' and '*Cooperating with proficient users of the new language*', and they expand the social-strategy categories that have been identified in the literature. In short, and as discussed earlier in Section 2.1.1, collaborative learning requires individual students to work together to build knowledge and achieve a common goal, whereas cooperative learning relies on individual contributions which are simply assembled together on completion (Hammond, 2016).

Metacognitive strategies

The observed data indicated that the participants employed the metacognitive strategy of '*Organising*' when working with the four technological tools; namely,

Board, WeChat, Google Drive, and email (Table 3.18). Oxford (1990) defined '*Organising*' as 'understanding and using conditions related to optimal learning of the new language; organising one's schedule, physical environment (e.g., space, temperature, sound, lighting), and language learning notebook' (p. 139). As discussed in Section 3.2.7, this strategy was used by the survey respondents at a high-frequency range, in terms of arranging a comfortable environment for studying and developing a learning routine. This section further investigates how the students used this strategy in the learning contexts of self-directed learning and assessment-task completion outside the online classes.

When the participants selected different technological tools with which to arrange their study, they used the metacognitive strategy of '*Organising*'; but at the same time, they also used social strategies. As shown in Table 3.18, a prime example is that when the participants used '*Organising*' to find a language partner, they also used the social strategy of '*Netiquette*' to introduce themselves on the Discussion Board. Another example is how the participants used '*Organising*' to change from using the Discussion Board to using WeChat for greater convenience. This action was also related to the social strategy of '*Using tools available to improve communication and interaction*', as it strengthened the relationship between students by using WeChat's multiple interactive functions, such as sending both audio and text messages. Similarly, using '*Organising*' to email questions about

Table 3.18 Metacognitive strategy adoption when using Board, WeChat, Google Drive, and email

LLS	Example	Reasons	Learning context	Technological tool	Participants
Organising (Oxford, 1990)	Introduce personal information and look for a language partner	Finding a language partner	Assessment-task completion	Forum: Discussion Board (The CAFE)	15 out of 22 students of CHN11, SP1, 2016
	Build a small learner group	Changing from Discussion Board to using the WeChat messaging app	Self-directed learning outside the online classes	WeChat messaging app	10 out of 22 students of CHN11, SP1, 2016
	Store drafts of written assignments in the Cloud, and share them with language partners and teachers for editing	Completing a written draft with language partners	Assessment-task completion	Cloud storage app: Google Drive	S31, S33, S35
	Send emails about course-related issues	Asking teachers course-related questions	Self-directed learning outside the online classes	Email	S8, S9, S12, S13, S20

course-related issues was related to the social strategy of '*Asking for clarification or verification*'.

Moreover, the students' strategy use of '*Organising*' seemed to be shifting over time from technical problems to course-related problems. For instance, the majority of the emails provided by the five participants (S8, S9, S12, S13, S20) were about the assessment tasks and related to the strategy of '*Organising*'. These students wrote emails to the teacher to request extensions, ask about the range of vocabulary for a test, ask for confirmation of assignment submissions, or ask about the final course grades. These data suggested that the students had a good level of information technology literacy and familiarity with the online learning platform, and this differed from the findings from earlier research, which had indicated that questions about technical problems were frequently asked (Hauck & Hampel, 2008).

The students in CHN11 (SP1, 2016) provided further evidence on how their improved information technology literacy level changed their use of technological tools, as a result of implicitly using the metacognitive strategy of '*Organising*'. The students in CHN11 (SP1, 2016) originally used the Discussion Board to find language partners, but later changed to WeChat, where a class group was built. The students posted a total of 27 topic items on the Discussion Board between 25 February and 27 May 2016, with two of these at the end of February, and then 23 in March. The students only posted one topic item each month in April and May, after one student had started a WeChat group and 10 students expressed their interest in joining the group. After that, none of these 11 students posted on the Discussion Board. These data indicated that, as the students become more aware of the availability and the capability of various technological tools, they might select tools that are outside those provided as part of the courses in order to enjoy more effective and convenient communications.

Compensation strategies

From the observed data, one compensation strategy was found to be distinctly different from those already defined by Oxford and other researchers. This is named '*Providing extra clarification to others in writing for better understanding*', and refers to cases in which the students provided more information in the written drafts to assist a better understanding of each other's writing. For instance, Excerpt 3.7 provides evidence that two students (S31, S35) discussed what should be used in the script in order to make it easy to read. Figure 3.3 shows that the written drafts turned out to be written in English, Chinese characters, and Pinyin with tones. Again, the simultaneous use of multiple strategies was observed in Excerpt 3.7 and Figure 3.3. S31 negotiated ('*Negotiating with other students*') with S35 that colours should be used to highlight important information in the draft ('*Using the tools available to improve communication and interaction*'). S35 echoed this suggestion and mentioned that he had also used Pinyin for ease of reading and pronunciation ('*Providing extra clarification to others in writing for better understanding*').

> **Excerpt 3.7 An example of 'Negotiating with other students' by S31 and S35**
>
> *S31: If its [it's] alright, I would like to colour code different parts of the text to make it easier on the eyes.*
> *S35: Hey S31, sounds great. I have added the pingyu [Pinyin] version so it is easier to read and pronounce.*
> *(Data source: Additional data provided by S31 and S35, a written conversation exchange between S31 and S35 in the comment area on Google Drive, regarding the speaking assignment draft, June 2016)*

S31: What do you do every day?

你每天做什么？

Nǐ měitiān zuò shénme?

S35: Most days, it looks like this: I go to work every day, and at night I study Chinese. I am busy at work and at studying. To relax, I like to read books and watch television

平常, 我常常做这些: 我每天去上班, 在晚上我学习汉语. 我忙于工作和学习. 放松, 我喜欢阅读 和 看电视

Tōngcháng qíngkuàng xià, wǒ jīngcháng zhèxiē zuò: Wǒ měitiān wǎnshàng wǒ hěn máng de gōngzuò hé xuéxí hanyu wǒ xuéhuì fàngsōng, wǒ xǐhuān dúshū hé kàn diànshì.

Figure 3.3 An example of '*Providing extra clarification to others in writing for better understanding*' by S31 and S35 (a written draft of a speaking assignment provided by S31 and S35, Google Drive, June 2016)

S31 later explained in the interview that they used this method to avoid misunderstanding when exchanging the written drafts. The English explanation and the Chinese characters helped S35 understand S31's Chinese sentences more accurately. They provided Pinyin with tones because the Chinese characters do not contain phonetic information to indicate their pronunciation, and a large number of homophones exist among Chinese characters. Pinyin with tones helped them to know how to pronounce the characters. It also improved their pronunciation when they practised speaking Chinese alone. These actions were identified as a compensation strategy of '*Providing extra clarification to others in writing for better understanding*' because it compensated for the lack of linguistic cues (i.e., pronunciation and tones) in writing and speaking.

3.3.2 *LLS adoption observed in the synchronous learning environment*

This section presents the participants' strategy use observed in the online classes supported by Blackboard Collaborate (i.e., in a synchronous environment). As shown in Figure 1.2, teachers can use the content area as a whiteboard to present PowerPoint slides and work with students by typing, writing, and highlighting on it. Additionally, students can use the Chat panel to input text messages and emojis as part of their participation in the class. They can also use the Participants panel to express their status, such as 'away' and 'raise hand'.

The observed data from the online classes emanated from 24 recordings of online classes from three courses, namely, CHN11 and CHN12 (beginning level), and CHN222 (intermediate level). Each recording was 1–2 hours in duration. The students were observed to have employed seven LLSs in these classes: two cognitive strategies, four social strategies, and one compensation strategy, as shown in Table 3.19. The rest of this section will use examples to illustrate how the students employed these strategies.

The strategy of '*Repeating*' was commonly used. Five out of eight students employed this cognitive strategy in the beginning-level class CHN11 during one session. As shown in Figure 3.4, these five students imitated the teacher's pronunciation

Table 3.19 LLS Use in online classes obtained from the observed data

LLS	Example	Collaborate classroom functions	LLS category	Participant(s)
Repeating (Oxford, 1990)	Imitate the teacher's Chinese	Audio facility via the audio/video panel	Cognitive	S1, S4, S6, S7, S8 in CHN11, SP3, 2015; S9 in CHN12, SP3, 2015
Analysing contrastively (Oxford, 1990)	Compare sounds between English and Chinese			S4 in CHN11, SP3, 2015
Getting help (Oxford, 1990)	Orally use English to ask the missing words in Chinese when reading a paragraph in the textbook	Audio facility via the audio/video panel	Compensation	S15 in CHN222, SP3, 2015
Asking for correction (Oxford, 1990)	Translate between English and Chinese to get immediate feedback from the teacher	Audio facility via the audio/video panel	Social	S8 in CHN12, SP3, 2015
Asking for clarification and verification (Oxford, 1990)	Ask a grammar question in online class	Use audio facility and text messages in the Chat panel		S19 in CHN11, SP3, 2015
Netiquette (LLS specific to online learning)	Praise a classmate's pronunciation	Use emojis and text messages in the Chat panel		S5 in CHN11, SP3, 2015
Using tools available to improve communication and interaction (LLS specific to online learning)	Use the user interface elements (e.g., 'away' icon) to show that you are leaving	Use icons in the Participants panel		S14 in CHN11, SP3, 2015
	Use emojis to express feelings (e.g., smiley face) in text chat	Use emojis and text messages in the Chat panel		S5 in CHN11, SP3, 2015

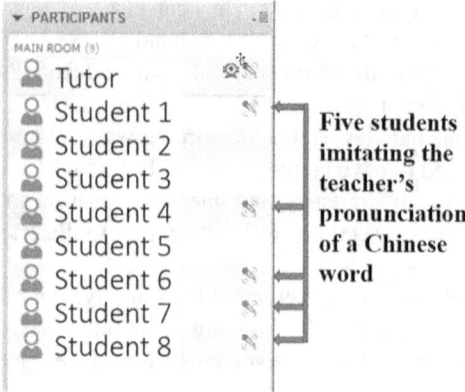

Figure 3.4 An example of using *'Repeating'* by five students. (00:49:00 in the recording; Lesson 2; CHN11, SP3, 2015)

of a Chinese word '不好听' (English meaning: not nice to listen to). The teacher did not require the students to imitate her pronunciation; however the five students repeated the words after the teacher. They imitated the sound correctly in tones, intonation, and pronunciation. S9 in CHN12, another beginning-level student, also reported in the interview that he often imitated the teacher's pronunciation in the online classes in order to improve his own pronunciation.

The cognitive strategy of *'Analysing contrastively'* was used by S4, as shown in Excerpt 3.8, to help pronounce 'shi'. Oxford (1990) defined this strategy as 'comparing elements (sounds, vocabulary, grammar) of the new language with elements of one's own language to determine similarities and differences' (p. 46). S4 started with intensive listening to the sound 'shi', separated the sound into syllables, and then found the English sound 'sh' in 'ship', 'shark', and 'short' to compare with the Chinese sound 'shi'.

Excerpt 3.8 An example of 'Analysing contrastively' by S4

T1: Number 10 is 'shí'.
S4: shí.
S4: Like ship.
T1: Yeah, ship.
S4: Ship, shark, or short...
T1: No, not shark, not that big.
S4: Oh, you are right, not that long, shí. Yes, it's more like ship.
(01:29:00 in the recording, Lesson 1, CHN11, SP3, 2015).

The compensation strategy of *'Getting help'* was used by S15 to ask a teacher to provide the missing information. This student explicitly asked the teacher for help by saying, 'Oh, I can't remember this character', when he was reading a paragraph in a textbook. The importance of the teacher as the source of information, ready to help online students with their language-learning problems and difficulties, was highlighted in the observed data.

The social strategy of '*Asking for correction*' was employed by a student (S8) to translate between English and Chinese and obtain immediate feedback. The following example (Excerpt 3.9) shows how the student learnt the sentence structure of 'A 是A，不过 … <It is / does …, but …>'.

Excerpt 3.9 An example of 'Asking for correction' by S8

T2: 这件衣服好看是好看，但是太贵了！ *<These clothes are attractive but are too expensive.>*
S8: It's good looking, but it's too expensive?
T2: 对。*<Correct.>*
S8: In my case, 我的衣服不好看，但是很便宜。*<My clothes are not attractive but very cheap.>*
(00:31:30 in the recording, Lesson 14, CHN12, SP3, 2015)

The conversation in Excerpt 3.9 shows how the student first translated the teacher's Chinese into English to show his understanding of the sentence structure in such a way as to invite the teacher's correction. He then provided another sentence in Chinese to show his understanding of the meaning of the sentence structure. In this example, the teacher and the student had a tacit collaborative understanding, and therefore the teaching and learning process was an efficient way of learning the target sentence structure. This strategy use was highlighted by Hung and Higgins (2016), who observed that students often used this strategy in online classes in order to ensure their output was correct.

There were many examples of employing the social strategy of '*Using the tools available to improve communication and interaction*' in the online classes to support the collaboration process. These tools refer to the participants' use of the built-in icons in the Participants panel or typing texts and sending emojis in the Chat panel via Blackboard Collaborate. In the Participants panel, teachers and students can use four built-in icons to engage with online teaching. These icons are a smiley face, a status icon, a raise-hand icon, and polling, shown as items 2–5 in Figure 3.5. For example, if a student clicks the raise-hand icon, the teacher's Participants panel will show a red coloured hand and a number to indicate that this student wants to speak.

Compared with using the built-in icons in the Participants panel, the students' interactions in the Chat panel appeared more flexible and richer in expression. In the Chat panel, the students employed the strategy '*Using the tools available to improve communication and interaction*' by typing texts and sending emojis as

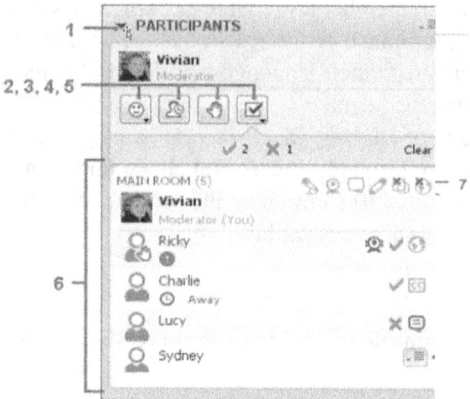

Figure 3.5 The example of the teacher's Participants panel in Blackboard Collaborate (Screen capture of Blackboard Collaborate, 2018) 1. Expand/Collapse icon; 2. Smiley face; 3. Away icon; 4. Raise hand icon; 5. Polling response menu; 6. Participant list; 7. Global permissions

part of their participation in the online classes. For example, in Figure 3.6, S1 and S5 used the 'thumbs-up' and 'smiley face' emojis, which helped create a supportive, encouraging environment to make up for the lack of facial expressions in online learning. These emojis conveyed messages which helped the students express themselves effectively in a visual style instead of a verbal style. By using these emojis, the online students were able to communicate and interact with others in the classroom in a much quicker, more light-hearted and expressive way.

Figure 3.6 also shows that S5 combined text message with emojis to praise S7's Chinese pronunciation by saying 'You're louder and clearer', with a smiley face attached. The praise was effective as it was specific, timely, and descriptive in that it showed S5's awareness of S7's improvement in pronunciation. The use of emojis and the encouragement phrases shows '*Netiquette*' (a social strategy) with an affective aspect. These observed data suggest that the online students took advantage of the tools offered by the online classroom to make their interactions more expressive, and to create an encouraging atmosphere.

Another example of the combined use of strategies is evident in Figure 3.6. S19 employed the strategy of '*Asking for clarification and verification*' to ask the teacher a grammar question, but used a smiley face at the end of his question to soften his tone, thereby offering a prime example of '*Using the tools available to improve communication and interaction*'. These observations indicate that the online students understood the value of using both verbal and non-verbal Collaborate Classroom functions (e.g., text messages and emojis) to achieve effective collaboration.

Switching from speech to text may also have helped the online students enhance the effectiveness of their collaboration. Figure 3.7 shows that the participants

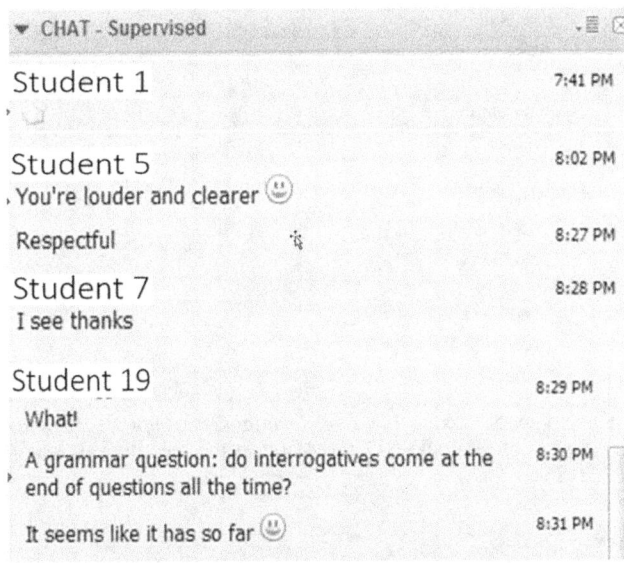

Figure 3.6 An example of 'Using the tools available to improve communication and interaction' and 'Asking for clarification and verification' by S1, S5, S7, S19 (00:41:00 in the recording, Lesson 2, CHN11, SP3, 2015)

solved the problem of occasional internet lag by using the Chat panel in the online class. In this case, the teacher noticed there was a serious internet lag after she asked the question 'How do you travel from France to Italy?' The teacher quickly texted the message 'lag ...' and S14 also reported the same problem. S17 then answered the question in the Chat panel using Chinese characters, '我们从法国到意大利开车,' which means 'We travel from France to Italy by car'. These observed data suggest that the online students used the Chat panel, which provides an asynchronous method of interaction in the synchronous environment, to increase the opportunities to participate in the online classes and achieve effective collaborative learning.

Overall, the participants' use of two cognitive, one compensation, and four social strategies were obtained from the observed data. The students used these strategies in activities such as engaging in learning activities, getting feedback from teachers, improving Chinese pronunciation, and socialising. Such strategies reveal that the participants facilitated the creation and maintenance of a collaborative learning environment by using various technological tools. The main tools used by the participants included both vocal (e.g., audio) and non-vocal tools (e.g., texts, emojis, built-in icons) because of their relative ease of use, their ability to meet students' communication needs (e.g., built-in icons), and their ability to support spontaneous interactions (i.e. audio and text messages).

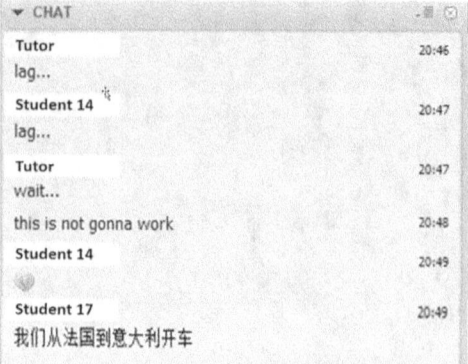

Figure 3.7 An example of '*Using the tools available to improve communication and interaction*' by S14 and S17 (00:44:00 in the recording, Lesson 5, CHN222, SP3, 2015)

3.4 Summary

This chapter has added to the current knowledge of online students' use of LLSs and how they use LLSs in different ways. A contextualised picture provided through the data analyses has shown that the students employed a wide repertoire of LLSs in online Chinese learning. The use of these strategies provides evidence that the participants applied the LLSs with varying frequencies to suit their learning needs and goals in different learning contexts.

In the context of self-directed learning, the students studied alone for most of the time and had flexibility in managing and controlling their learning activities. They employed a wide repertoire of LLSs in relation to the six LLS categories in this learning context. By contrast, in the contexts of assessment-task completion and online class participation, the students mainly used cognitive and social strategies to assist their online Chinese learning. There was no evidence of the use of memory or affective strategies in these two learning contexts. Such results indicate that students' strategy use was highly context-bound.

Among the 37 LLSs identified in this research project, 28 were drawn from Oxford's (1990) taxonomy. The remaining nine strategies were found to differ from Oxford's LLSs in terms of online learning, collaborative learning, flipped-classroom learning, and Chinese-language learning. The nine LLSs, one affective, one cognitive, four social, one memory, one compensation, and one metacognitive, reflect how students created LLSs to memorise Chinese characters, minimised learning anxieties in Chinese speaking, made use of the particular functions of the online learning environments, tools, and apps, and collaborated with language partners in completing assessment tasks. The use of these strategies also reflects the challenges of online learning in general, and Chinese learning in particular. Furthermore, these strategies were mediated by technology as well as by the collaboration engendered in the course designs and were well suited to the flipped-classroom approach adopted in the courses under investigation.

The analyses of self-reported data in Section 3.2, which comprised both survey and interview data, revealed the frequency of LLS use, and classified strategies into high-, medium-, and low-frequency ranges of use in the three learning contexts. The quantitative analyses also explored the possible correlations between LLS items within each LLS category. By applying Pearson's *r*-correlation analyses, a number of strong or very strong correlations between LLS items were found in the affective, cognitive, social, and metacognitive categories. These correlations suggest that language learners might benefit from using the correlated strategies in pairs or in clusters.

The observed data in Section 3.3, primarily interactions between students, language partners, and teachers in both the synchronous and asynchronous learning environments, further explained and complemented the findings obtained from the self-reported data in Section 3.2. Strategy use by the participants around social, cognitive, compensation, and metacognitive categories was identified in both the asynchronous and synchronous environments. Whilst most of the LLSs found in the observed data are consistent with the findings in Section 3.2, there are some strategies which are interesting because students used them differently and with different technological tools. Additionally, the observed data provided evidence that enables us to develop a deeper understanding of questions such as how the students employed these strategies, which technological tools were selected for what purposes, and the use sequence of the strategies in collaborative learning.

The findings in this chapter also revealed some differences in strategy use from those identified by Oxford (1990), which reflect the technologies used and the requirements of collaborative language learning. Both the quantitative and the qualitative data demonstrated that technology particularly enhanced the effectiveness of the students' cognitive-, memory-, and social-strategy use. In particular, these data showed that the participants created a cluster of social strategies to discuss and negotiate ideas, share information and resources, and coordinate their collaboration.

References

Bown, J. (2006). Locus of learning and affective strategy use: Two factors affecting success in self-instructed language learning. *Foreign Language Annals, 39*(4), 640–659. https://doi.org/10.1111/j.1944-9720.2006.tb02281.x

Chang, M.-M. (2007). Enhancing web-based language learning through self-monitoring. *Journal of Computer Assisted Learning, 23*(3), 187–196. https://doi.org/10.1111/j.1365-2729.2006.00203.x

Chang, M.-M. (2010). Effects of self-monitoring on web-based language learner's performance and motivation. *CALICO Journal, 27*(2), 298–310.

Evans, J. D. (1996). *Straightforward statistics for the behavioral sciences.* Pacific Grove, CA: Brooks/Cole Pub.

Hammond, M. (2016). Online collaboration and cooperation: The recurring importance of evidence, rationale and viability. *Education and Information Technologies, 22*(3), 1005–1024. https://doi.org/10.1007/s10639-016-9469-x

Hauck, M., & Hampel, R. (2008). Strategies for online learning environments. In S. Hurd & T. Lewis (Eds.), *Language learning strategies in independent settings* (pp. 283–302). Bristol, UK: Multilingual Matters.

Huang, H.-C., Chern, C.-L., & Lin, C.-C. (2009). EFL learners' use of online reading strategies and comprehension of texts: An exploratory study. *Computers & Education*, *52*(1), 13–26. https://doi.org/10.1016/j.compedu.2008.06.003

Hung, Y.-W., & Higgins, S. (2016). Learners' use of communication strategies in text-based and video-based synchronous computer-mediated communication environments: Opportunities for language learning. *Computer Assisted Language Learning*, *29*(5), 901–924.

Hurd, S. (2000). Distance language learners and learner support: Beliefs, difficulties and use of strategies. *Links & Letters*, (7), 61–80.

Hurd, S. (2008). Affective and strategy use in independent language learning. In S. Hurd & T. Lewis (Eds.), *Language learning strategies in independent settings* (pp. 218–236). Bristol, UK: Multilingual Mattters.

Hurd, S., Beaven, T., & Ortega, A. (2001). Developing autonomy in a distance language learning context: Issues and dilemmas for course writers. *System*, *29*(3), 341–355. https://doi.org/10.1016/S0346-251X(01)00024-0

Karbalaei, A., & Negin Taji, T. (2014). Compensation strategies: Tracking movement in EFL learners' speaking skills. *GIST Education and Learning Research Journal*, (9), 88.

Kelly, P. (1992). Does the ear assist the eye in the long-term retention of lexis? *IRAL – International Review of Applied Linguistics in Language Teaching*, *30*, 137–145.

Klapper, J. (2008). Deliberate and incidental: Vocabulary learning strategies in independent second language learning. In S. Hurd & T. Lewis (Eds.), *Language learning strategies in independent settings* (pp. 159–178). Bristol, UK: Multilingual Matters.

Kozar, O. (2016). Perceptions of webcam use by experienced online teachers and learners: A seeming disconnect between research and practice. *Computer Assisted Language Learning*, *29*(4), 779–789. https://doi.org/10.1080/09588221.2015.1061021

Krishnan, J., Cusimano, A., Wang, D., & Yim, S. (2018). Writing together: Online synchronous collaboration in middle school. *Journal of Adolescent & Adult Literacy*, *62*(2), 163–173. https://doi.org/10.1002/jaal.871

O'Malley, M., & Chamot, A. U. (1990). *Learning strategies in second language acquisition*. Cambridge, UK: Cambridge University Press.

Oxford, R. (1990). *Language learning strategies: What every teacher should know*. Boston, UK: Newbury House.

Oxford, R. (2011). *Teaching and researching: Language learning strategies*. London, UK: Routledge.

Oxford, R. (2017). *Teaching and researching language learning strategies: Self-regulation in context* (2nd ed.). New York, NY: Routledge.

Shen, H. H. (2005). An investigation of Chinese-character learning strategies among non-native speakers of Chinese. *System*, *33*(1), 49–68. https://doi.org/10.1016/j.system.2004.11.001

Solak, E., & Cakir, R. (2015). Language learning strategies of language e-learners in Turkey. *E-Learning and Digital Media*, *12*(1), 107–120. https://doi.org/10.1177/2042753014558384

Stickler, U., & Lewis, T. (2008). Collaborative language learning strategies in an email tandem exchange. In S. Hurd & T. Lewis (Eds.), *Language learning strategies in independent settings* (pp. 237–261). Bristol, UK: Multilingual Matters.

White, C. (1995). Autonomy and strategy use in distance foreign language learning. *System*, *23*(2), 207–221.

Wolf, D. M., & Phung, L. (2019). Studying in the United States: Language learning challenges, strategies and support services. *Journal of International Students*, *9*(1), 211–224. https://doi.org/10.32674/jis.v9i1.273

4 Factors influencing LLS adoption

4.1 Introduction

The previous chapter investigated the repertoire of language-learning strategies (LLSs) adopted by the research participants and how they used those LLSs in online language learning. However, it did not specifically address the factors that impacted the reported LLS use. Therefore, this chapter aims to explore the relationships between the participants' LLS use and some potentially influencing factors in two major sections: the characteristics of the three learning contexts and interactants (Section 4.2), and the individual-learner characteristics of the participants (Section 4.3). The data analyses were based on the data obtained from the responses to the survey questionnaire and from the 10 student interviews. These analyses were also supplemented by data from the online class observations, and notes taken by one participant.

4.2 The impact of the learning contexts and interactants on the participants' LLS use

This section reports the analyses of two sources of potentially influencing factors on the participants' LLS use in the three learning contexts: the asynchronous or synchronous nature of the environment (Section 4.2.1); and the categories of interactants involved in the language-learning process (Section 4.2.2). The asynchronous environment refers to the two learning contexts that did not require the simultaneous participation of the students and teachers, that is, self-directed learning and assessment-task completion outside the online classes. The synchronous environment refers to the online classes via Blackboard Collaborate, which required the students and teachers to engage in learning activities at the same time. The categories of interactants concerned those within the Chinese courses, namely the students themselves, their peers (i.e., other students in the course, especially language partners), and the teachers, as well as people external to the online courses who might be able to speak Chinese, such as family members, colleagues and friends. In these interactions, the interaction with students themselves was described as 'learner-self interaction' in Soo and Bonk (1998, p. 3) which refers to the learner's self-reflection on the learning content, learning process, and LLS use.

4.2.1 The impact of the asynchronous and synchronous environments on the participants' LLS use

In the asynchronous environment, the participants were able to arrange self-paced learning activities in the form of studying the provided learning resources, interacting with their peers and teachers, and completing the assessment tasks. Such activities involved using a web-based Discussion Board, wiki, online quizzes, email, and WeChat as the technological tools supporting the courses. Students also used other tools such as Google Drive, YouTube, and language-learning apps. The synchronous environment relied on Blackboard Collaborate, in which the participants interacted with their peers and teachers simultaneously during the online classes.

Whilst this distinction is made for the overall asynchronous and synchronous environments, it should be noted that asynchronous interactions could also occur in the synchronous environment. For example, during an online class, it was observed that there were occasions when a student asked the teacher a question by typing in the Chat panel and received a delayed text response from the teacher. On the other hand, synchronous interactions could also happen in the asynchronous environment, such as the participants engaged in conversations with their peers in order to practice and complete the speaking assignment.

Based on the results of all the collected data (Table 3.1) in relation to the six LLS categories, Table 4.1 counts the number of different LLSs identified as being used in the asynchronous and synchronous environments. It should be noted that as some strategies were employed by the participants in both the asynchronous and the synchronous environments, the total number of LLSs in each category is not a simple summation of the numbers of LLSs used across the two environments.

In the asynchronous environment, the participants employed 35 out of 37 LLSs, which represented 94.6% of all the LLSs considered in this research project. Two LLSs ('*Analysing contrastively*' and '*Getting help*') were not found to be used in the asynchronous environment. The cognitive strategy '*Analysing contrastively*' was defined in Oxford (1990) as 'comparing elements (sounds, vocabulary, grammar) of the new language with elements of one's own language to determine similarities

Table 4.1 The number of different LLSs used in the asynchronous and synchronous environments, by LLS category

LLS category	Number of different LLSs used in the asynchronous environment	Number of different LLSs used in the synchronous environment	Total number of LLSs considered in this project, by category
Affective	5	0	5
Cognitive	8	4	9
Social	7	4	7
Memory	5	0	5
Compensation	4	1	5
Metacognitive	6	0	6
Total (number and %)	35 (94.6%)	9 (24.3%)	37

and differences' (p. 46). The compensation strategy '*Getting help*' refers to asking help when undertaking a language task (Oxford, 1990). These definitions indicate that these two strategies could also be employed in an asynchronous environment, although such use was not found in this research project.

More broadly, such a wide repertoire of LLS employment suggests that the asynchronous environment did not restrict the repertoire of the participants' LLS use. This was to be expected given that the flipped-classroom approach adopted in the courses required the students to work consistently in the asynchronous environment, to pre-learn online resources such as the prerecorded mini-lecture videos and lecture notes, and to master the basic content before class and complete various assessment tasks.

In the synchronous environment, however, the participants only employed LLSs from cognitive, social, and compensation categories, with none from the affective, memory, and metacognitive categories. The nine (one compensation, four cognitive, and four social,) strategies found in the synchronous environment represented approximately 24.3% of the total repertoire of LLSs considered in this project. Again, the observed strategy repertoire was consistent with the course design and with the flipped-classroom approach, which required teachers to use the online classroom to check students' understanding of the prerecorded mini-lecture videos, guide them to practise what they had learnt from these lectures, and encourage them to interact and collaborate with others synchronously.

As a result, the participants mainly adopted cognitive strategies when participating in learning activities, social strategies when interacting and collaborating with others, and one compensation strategy to overcome the lack of appropriate vocabulary in Chinese. In the online classes, it was to be expected that there would be little time for the use of metacognitive and memory strategies, as students were intensely engaged in completing various interactive activities. Whilst there were no observed data regarding affective-strategy use, this did not necessarily mean that no affective strategies were employed, as the students and teachers may have used the private chat setting in the Blackboard Collaborate classroom, which was not observable. Also, the duration of the weekly online classes was only 1.5–2 hours, which may have limited the opportunity for students to use metacognitive, memory, and affective strategies.

Both the interview and the observed data revealed that the participants not only used a smaller repertoire of strategies in fewer categories in the synchronous environment, but also used these strategies less frequently. In the asynchronous environment, 12 LLSs had a high-frequency-range use, whilst in the synchronous environment there was only one social strategy, '*Asking for correction*', that attained a high-frequency-range use.

The 12 high-frequency-range use LLSs in the asynchronous environment were in affective, cognitive, social, and metacognitive categories. They were: two affective strategies ('*Taking risks wisely*' and '*Making positive statements*'); four cognitive strategies ('*Using resources for receiving and sending messages*'; '*Formally practising with sounds and writing systems*'; '*Repeating*'; and '*Getting the idea quickly*'); three social strategies ('*Netiquette*'; '*Cooperating with peers*'; and

'*Asking for correction*'); and three metacognitive strategies ('*Organising*'; '*Overviewing and linking with already known material*'; and '*Self-monitoring*'). Again, the use of these strategies suggested that the asynchronous environment allowed the students to have more time and opportunities to employ a wider repertoire of LLSs in the four LLS categories than the synchronous environment.

As this section focuses on the impact of the characteristics of learning environments on LLS use, the following paragraphs discuss how the participants used cognitive and social strategy categories differently in the two learning environments. (There was only one strategy in the third strategy category, i.e., the compensation category, used in the synchronous environment.) Of the nine cognitive strategies considered overall, the participants employed eight in the asynchronous environment and five in the synchronous environment. Table 4.2 lists examples of how the participants used the cognitive strategies in the two learning environments, based again on the results presented in Table 3.1.

The four strategies of '*Using resources for receiving and sending messages*', '*Repeating*', '*Taking notes*', and '*Learning from other students' written work*' were employed in both environments but used in different ways. For example, in the synchronous environment, the participants employed '*Using resources for receiving and sending messages*' to check, probably very briefly, the meaning of Chinese words online via e-dictionaries. In the asynchronous environment, the participants reported that they applied the strategy in a wider range of activities, such as searching for background information on Chinese words using e-dictionaries.

YouTube was reported to be another important resource that the participants used when adopting this strategy. One student (S8) reported that he listened to the conversations repeatedly on the YouTube videos he found, imitated the speakers' pronunciation, tones, and intonation, collected some Chinese words and phrases, and wrote down important word orders, before drafting his script for the speaking assignment. In this process, it became apparent that he used a number of strategies together with the strategy of '*Using resources for receiving and sending messages*', such as '*Repeating*', '*Taking notes*', '*Placing new words into a context*', and '*Representing sounds in memory*'.

The differences in using the same cognitive strategy '*Using resources for receiving and sending messages*' in various learning environments further suggested that the participants' cognitive strategy use was influenced by the learning environments. Although other factors should also be taken into consideration, such as the availability of resources and the types of technology used, time restrictions in these environments played a key role in the differences in this strategy use. In a synchronous environment, the students did not have enough time to use multiple resources simultaneously to assist their learning. On the other hand, the asynchronous environment has fewer restrictions and greater flexibility to support the extended use of this strategy when compared with the synchronous environment.

Four other cognitive strategies were found to be used in the asynchronous environment only, and one exclusively in the synchronous environment. The four cognitive strategies used in the asynchronous environment were '*Formally practising with sounds and writing system*', '*Getting the idea quickly*', '*Practising*

Table 4.2 Cognitive strategy use in the asynchronous and synchronous learning environments

Cognitive strategies	Examples in the asynchronous environment	Examples in the synchronous environment
Using resources for receiving and sending messages (Oxford, 1990)	Search online for the meaning of Chinese words I don't know (e.g., e-dictionary; Google Translate) in self-directed learning and in assessment-task completion Collect, select, and modify conversations in a series of YouTube videos online in assessment-task completion Search for background information on Chinese words online via Google in self-directed learning	Search for the information online (e.g., e-dictionary; Google Translate) if I do not understand something during online class participation
Repeating (Oxford, 1990)	Imitate teacher and Chinese friends' pronunciation via WeChat voice messages in assessment-task completion Listen to recorded conversations many times by using Pimsleur (a digital Mandarin course) in self-directed learning	Imitate the teacher's Chinese speaking via Blackboard Collaborate in online class participation.
Taking notes (Oxford, 1990)	Take notes of new words and phrases by using a Word document, or paper notebook in self-directed learning	Take notes in online classes and then compile these notes for future review
Formally practising with sounds and writing system (Oxford, 1990)	Read aloud to practise for the speaking assignment in assessment-task completion	
Getting the idea quickly (Oxford, 1990)	Try to understand what I hear or read without translating it word for word into my own language in self-directed learning	
Learning from other students' written work (LLS for collaborative learning)	Read other students' wiki-writing assessments to learn from them in assessment-task completion Put comments on other students' wiki-writing assignments because that helps me learn in assessment-task completion	Put comments on other students' wiki-writing assignments to help them with my suggestions in assessment-task completion
Practising naturalistically (Oxford, 1990)	Watch Chinese TV programmes and movies; speak Chinese with family members; read novels in Chinese in self-directed learning	
Summarising (Oxford, 1990)	Summarise Chinese grammar points in one's mind as a way to reinforce my understanding in self-directed learning	
Analysing contrastively (Oxford, 1990)		Compare sounds between English and Chinese in online class participation

naturalistically', and '*Summarising*'. The one LLS that was not found in the asynchronous environment, '*Analysing contrastively*', as noted earlier in this section, *could* also be used. Clearly, the students' language practice was facilitated by the flexibility offered in the asynchronous environment, as it provided the students with not only enough learning time, but also various learning places, online learning resources, and technologies to engage with the relevant learning activities. For instance, the participants used the video clips and the online quizzes provided by the courses as required by the flipped-classroom approach, and they collaborated with their language partners through a range of technologies in completing the assessment tasks designed for the online courses. In this respect, the asynchronous environment engendered an appropriate environment for these students to apply various cognitive strategies in their self-paced learning.

The participants also used seven social strategies in the asynchronous and synchronous environments. Four were employed in both learning environments, and the remaining three were used only in the asynchronous environment as listed in Table 4.3, which also contains various technological tools that the participants employed in the strategy-use examples.

The participants employed three social strategies ('*Negotiating with other students*', '*Sharing with other students*', and '*Cooperating with peers*') only in the asynchronous environment. The students used these strategies to better collaborate with their language partners to complete the assessment tasks (e.g., the speaking assignment of a role play), such as negotiating meeting times and digital places, distributing work, and sharing their understanding of task and assessment requirements.

Whilst similar behaviour could be conducted in the synchronous environment, evidence was lacking that the students used these social strategies in this context. Based on the online class observations, a likely explanation is that the teacher organised the learning activities and guided the students' learning in the online classes. As a result, there was no need, and not enough time, for the students to employ these social strategies in the synchronous environment. By contrast, in the asynchronous environment, the students needed to take more responsibility for their own learning as well as in their collaboration with their language partners, and they have more time to do so.

From Table 4.3, we can also see that the participants selected different technological tools in different learning environments in order to improve their interactions with peers and teachers. For example, in the asynchronous environment, the students mainly used email, text and voice messages in WeChat, and posts on the Discussion Board for the two social strategies of '*Asking for correction*' and '*Asking for clarification or verification*'. Most of these tools are asynchronous tools. In the synchronous environment, the students mainly used the audio and video facilities in the Participants panel whilst occasionally sending texts and emojis in the Chat panel. Whilst some asynchronous interactions occurred in the synchronous environment (such as sending text messages to ask teachers for assistance), they were used by the students in addition to their primary synchronous interactions in online classes. These findings suggest that the participants' social strategy use, and

Table 4.3 Social strategy use in the asynchronous and synchronous learning environments

Social strategies	Asynchronous environment		Synchronous environment		
	Examples	Tool(s)	Examples		Classroom functions
Netiquette (LLS specific to online learning)	Respond to the language partners' and the teacher's emails within 24 hours in assessment-task completion	Email	Respond to teacher and students' questions quickly in online class participation		Audio facility via the audio/video panel
	Respond to the language partners' WeChat messages in a timely way in assessment-task completion	Social media app: WeChat (text and voice messages)	Usually keep the webcam on to let the teacher and other students see me in online class participation		Video facility via the audio/video panel
	Send greetings and introduce oneself in self-directed learning	Forum: Discussion Board (The CAFE)			
Asking for correction (Oxford, 1990)	Ask my teacher to provide feedback on my early drafts in self-directed learning	Email	Ask other students to correct me in online class participation		Audio facility via the audio/video panel
	Encourage other students to leave comments on my wiki page in self-directed learning	Forum: Discussion Board (The CAFE)	Ask my language partner to correct me whenever I make a mistake in online class participation		Audio facility via the audio/video panel
Asking for clarification or verification (Oxford, 1990)	Ask the teacher to correct my Chinese words in assessment-task completion	Social media app: WeChat (text and voice messages)	Ask the others to slow down, repeat, or clarify what was said if I do not understand something in online class participation		Audio facility via the audio/video panel
			If I do not understand, I ask the other students to slow down, repeat, or clarify what was said in online class participation		Audio facility via the audio/video panel
			Ask the teacher to verify that I have understood or said something correctly in online class participation		Audio facility via the audio/video panel
	Ask questions about assessment tasks and technological problems in self-directed learning	Forum: Discussion Board (The CAFE)	Ask the teacher and the classmates a grammar question in online class		Text messages via the Chat panel

(*Continued*)

Table 4.3 Continued

Social strategies	Asynchronous environment			Synchronous environment		
	Examples	Tool(s)		Examples		Classroom functions
Using the tools available to improve communication and interaction (LLS specific to online learning)	Share photos and comments on the photos on a private Chinese friend circle in self-directed learning	Social media app: WeChat moments		Type text messages for effective communication in online class participation		Text messages via the Chat panel
	Use different contact tools to interact with different groups of people in assessment-task completion	Email, WhatsApp, WeChat app		Use emoticons and texts chat to interact with others for language learning, such as praising the other students' speaking, and answering other students' questions in online class participation		Emoticons and text messages via the Chat panel
	Use different colours, character fonts, and numbers to remind language partners to focus on important information in a draft in assessment-task completion	Cloud storage app: Google Drive		Use emojis to express feelings in the text Chat panel in online class participation		Emojis via the Chat panel
				Use the user interface elements (e.g., 'away' icon) to show whether or not I am present in online class participation		User interface elements (e.g., 'away' icon) in the Participants panel
Negotiating with other students (LLS for collaborative learning)	Negotiate the time and digital location to practise Chinese speaking in assessment-task completion	Social media app: WeChat (text and voice messages)				
	Distributing work to complete an assessment task in assessment-task completion	Cloud storage app: Google Drive				
Sharing with other students (LLS for collaborative learning) Cooperating with peers (Oxford, 1990)	Share understanding of requirements and Chinese knowledge in assessment-task completion	Cloud storage app: Google Drive				
	Discuss the wiki-writing assignment with my language partner in assessment-task completion					
	Offer or give corrections on my language partner's written draft in assessment-task completion	Word document, email				
	Organise a WeChat group: switching to using the WeChat messaging app in self-directed learning	Forum: Discussion Board (The CAFE)				

the associated selection of tools to support their strategy adoption, were influenced by the synchronous/asynchronous nature of the learning environments.

In conclusion, this section has provided insights into the problems of how LLSs were identified and their different manifestations in the various learning contexts. The asynchronous or synchronous nature of the learning environment was clearly an influencing factor in the participants' LLS use. The asynchronous environment allowed the participants to have more time and flexibility to reflect on and improve their performance of learning activities and assessment tasks. Consequently, they employed a wide repertoire of LLSs in these learning activities. However, in the synchronous environment, students employed a limited repertoire of LLSs (cognitive, social, and compensation strategies) and applied them less frequently, due to the comparatively short and concentrated online time in the synchronous environment.

The results also indicate that flexibility in time and place in the asynchronous environment offered opportunities for the students to select suitable tools for effective learning, interact with others, and apply critical thinking in their learning process. The synchronous environment, on the other hand, required them to respond quickly to different learning activities by following the teachers' instructions. Therefore, students are expected to self-direct and manage their learning in the asynchronous environment to ensure learning success.

4.2.2 *The impact of the interactants on the participants' LLS use*

This section focuses on the participants' LLS use, which was potentially influenced by the categories of people with whom they interacted, and how their LLS use was shaped by these interactants in different learning contexts. The interactants concerned were the student her/himself, their language partner (for completing assessment tasks), their peers (the other students in the course), their teachers, and people external to the courses.

Table 4.4 shows the LLSs the participants used in relation to different interactants based on the results in Table 3.1. These results suggest that the participants' strategy use varied significantly when they interacted with different interactants.

The participants employed the broadest repertoire of LLSs (19) when they studied alone, and this figure represents 51.4% of the total number of the LLSs considered in this project. These 19 LLSs were restricted to the four LLS categories of affective, cognitive, memory, and metacognitive strategies. There were no social and compensation strategies used when the individuals studied alone, as these two types of strategies required interactions with other people. On the other hand, memory strategies were reported to be used by the participants only when they studied alone.

The participants used the lowest number of LLSs (six), with no affective, memory, or compensation strategies, when interacting with their teachers. The absence of affective, memory, and compensation strategies when interacting with teachers was anticipated. This is because it was easier for the students to revert to English when interacting with their teachers, as the teachers could speak English, and consequently the students did not need to employ compensation strategies.

Table 4.4 The number of LLSs used when interacting with different interactants

LLS category	Number of LLSs used					Total number of LLSs in category (considered in this project)
	alone	with a language partner	with a teacher	with peers	with external people	
Affective	3	0	0	1	3	5
Cognitive	8	1	1	0	1	9
Social	0	6	4	4	1	7
Memory	5	0	0	0	0	5
Compensation	0	1	0	1	3	5
Metacognitive	3	2	1	2	3	6
Total (number and %)	19 out of 37 (51.4%)	10 out of 37 (27.0%)	6 out of 37 (16.2%)	8 out of 37 (21.6%)	11 out of 37 (29.7%)	37

Furthermore, the duration of online classes was shorter than that of classes in the face-to-face language courses, hence there were fewer opportunities for the application of affective, memory, or compensation strategies.

Moreover, Table 4.4 provides evidence that the number of LLSs used in each LLS category seemed to be affected by the interactants with whom the participants interacted. Firstly, the participants' affective strategies tended to involve only student-self, peers, and external people. There was no evidence that the use of these strategies involved their teachers or language partners during assessment-task completion. Researchers have already argued that distance students should use a wide repertoire of affective strategies to enhance their self-confidence in distance learning (Hurd, 2008; White, 1995). In this respect, online students could consider expanding their use of affective strategies when interacting with their teachers and language partners.

Secondly, the students used eight out of the nine cognitive strategies, and all memory strategies (five out of five), only when studying alone. These results matched the fact that these two categories of strategies required the lowest level of interactions with other people.

Thirdly, the participants used the highest number of compensation strategies (three out of five strategies) when interacting with external people, followed by interaction with peers and language partners (both one out of five). Such results indicated that the students might need to employ compensation strategies more when interacting with external people, possibly because unfamiliar topics might be more likely to be introduced in these interactions, or it was not possible for them to use their first language to communicate with the external people.

Fourthly, the number of metacognitive strategies used by the participants seemed to be relatively evenly spread across the different categories of interactants. For example, these students scheduled their due dates with their language partners ('*Organising*') in completing a collaborative assessment task. This example suggested that students schedule their own learning time, taking into account the other's time during collaboration.

As it was to be expected, when the participants interacted with different interactants (language partners, teachers, and their peers), they were found to use the seven social strategies differently, as shown in Table 4.5. When interacting with all the interactants, the participants used three social strategies to show respect ('*Netiquette*'), ask for feedback on writing and speaking tasks ('*Asking for correction*'), and facilitate effective communication with their peers and teachers ('*Using the tools available to improve communication and interaction*').

However, three social strategies ('*Cooperating with others*', '*Sharing with other students*', and '*Negotiating with other students*') were found to be only used when the participants were collaborating with their language partners in assessment-task completion. The students used these three strategies to write the conversation scripts for the speaking assignment together ('*Cooperating with others*'), share their understanding of requirements of a collaborative assessment task ('*Sharing with other students*'), and negotiate time, digital location, and work distribution ('*Negotiating with other students*'). Such results are in accord with the study by Saito (2005), which indicated that collaborative online learning tasks can encourage learners to employ specific social strategies. The seventh social strategy, '*Asking for clarification or verification*', was used by the students to collaborate with their teachers and peers in self-directed learning and in online classes. Such differences in using the social strategies indicate that the students chose different social strategies to suit their learning needs and purposes, and employed these social strategies according to the task requirements and the learning contexts they were working in.

It was notable that the social strategy '*Asking for correction*' was used differently when the respondents asked for corrections from different people in different learning contexts, as shown in Table 4.6. The respondents used the strategy at a high-frequency-range strategy use ($M = 3.57$) to ask for their language partners' corrections when completing the assessment tasks. However, they used the strategy at a low-frequency range when seeking assistance from teachers ($M = 2.26$) and peers ($M = 1.78$) for the same tasks. By contrast, when participating in the online classes, the respondents were keen to ask for the teachers' corrections directly ($M = 3.14$; medium-frequency-range strategy use), but they were less likely to ask other students for corrections ($M = 2.29$; low-frequency-range strategy use). These results suggested that the respondents developed learning-context awareness when using this social strategy and applied it to maximise their learning. One driving factor behind this type of awareness was that the online classes were only held once a week and the students needed to use them to seek immediate feedback from their teachers. There was more spontaneity and immediacy in the need to understand in synchronous interactions; therefore the students were more likely to seek help from the teachers if they were struggling to understand or speak Chinese.

Furthermore, the interview data provided evidence that the participants used the strategies of '*Asking for correction*' and '*Negotiating with other students*' by

Table 4.5 The use of social strategies in relation to different categories of interactants

Social strategies	Examples of different LLS use when working		
	with a language partner	with a teacher	with peers (except language partners)
Netiquette (LLS specific to online learning)	Respect my language partner's time when we work together in self-directed learning and assessment-task completion	Respond to the teacher's emails within 24 hours in assessment-task completion	
		Usually keep the webcam on to let the teacher see me in online class participation	Usually keep the webcam on to let the other students see me in online class participation
Cooperating with peers (Oxford, 1990)	Write the conversation scripts of the speaking assignment together with my language partner in assessment-task completion		
Sharing with other students (LLS for collaborative learning)	Share understanding of requirements and Chinese knowledge in assessment-task completion		
Asking for correction (Oxford, 1990)	Ask my language partner to check my script in assessment-task completion	Ask my teacher to provide feedback on my early drafts in assessment-task completion	Encourage other students to leave comments on my wiki page in assessment-task completion
		Ask the teacher to correct me in online class participation	Ask other students to correct me in online class participation

Factors influencing LLS adoption 119

Strategy	Examples
Asking for clarification or verification (Oxford, 1990)	Ask the teacher to verify that I have understood or said something correctly in online class participation
	Ask the teacher a grammar question in online class participation
	Ask questions about assessment tasks and technological problems via email in self-directed learning
	Ask the others to slow down, repeat, or clarify what was said if I do not understand in online class participation
	If I do not understand, I ask the other students to slow down, repeat, or clarify what was said in online class participation
	Ask the other students a grammar question in online class participation
Using the tools available to improve communication and interaction (LLS specific to online learning)	Use different colours, character fonts, and numbers to remind language partners to focus on important information in a draft via Google Drive in assessment-task completion
	Share photos and comment on the photos in a private Chinese friend circle via WeChat moments in self-directed learning
	Use emoticons (such as smiley face, LOL, and raised hand) and text chat to interact with others for language learning, such as praising other students' speaking, and answering other students' questions in online class participation
	Use the user interface elements (e.g., 'away' icon) to show whether I am present
Negotiating with other students (LLS for collaborative learning)	Negotiate the time and digital location to practise Chinese speaking in assessment-task completion
	Distribute work to complete an assessment task

Table 4.6 Use of the social strategy 'Asking for correction' in relation to three categories of interactants in different learning contexts

Asking for correction	Interactants	Learning context	% of scale 1, 2, 3, 4, 5	Median, Mean, LLS usage
I ask my language partner to check my script	Language partners	Assessment-task completion outside online classes (a speaking assignment or an oral test)	8.7, 21.7, 21.7, 17.4, 30.4	4, 3.57, H
I ask my language partner to correct me whenever I make a mistake	Language partners		13.0, 21.7, 0, 26.1, 39.1	3, 3.39, M
I ask my teacher to provide feedback on my early drafts	Teachers	Assessment-task completion outside online classes (a wiki-writing assignment)	39.1, 26.1, 13.0, 13.0, 8.7	2, 2.26, L
I encourage other students to leave comments on my wiki page	Peers		56.5, 17.4, 17.4, 8.7, 0.0	1, 1.78, L
I ask the teacher to correct me	Teachers	Online class participation	21.7, 8.7, 4.3, 47.8, 8.7	4, 3.14, H
I ask other students to correct me	Peers		39.1, 17.4, 8.7, 21.7, 4.3	2, 2.29, L

selecting different learning tools to interact with different categories of interactants. For example, S17 was conscious of selecting suitable communication tools which consequently influenced the effectiveness of her communication. She claimed that email was seen as a formal professional tool used to communicate and show respect to others, whilst WeChat was seen as a personal tool for more convenient communication. She normally negotiated meeting times and discussed the assessment tasks with her language partner via WeChat ('*Negotiating with other students*') but consulted with the teachers on the earlier drafts of her assessment tasks via email ('*Asking for correction*'). Although email can be used, and was actually used by some other students, to send messages as a casual communication tool, S17 drew a distinct line between these communication tools. Such a tool-selection approach suggested that the student had prior knowledge of learning-tool selection and this influenced her interactions with different interactants.

Overall, the categories of interactants with whom the learners interacted could be seen as influencing their LLS use in different learning contexts. Specifically, the students used most of the cognitive strategies and all the memory strategies when studying alone in self-directed learning. By contrast, the students employed compensation and social strategies when interacting with others, especially with native Chinese speakers. At the same time, in self-directed learning, their affective-strategy use tended to involve only themselves, peers, and external individuals, but not their teachers. Lastly, the results indicated that the students might benefit from developing a clear awareness of using different social strategies with teachers and peers, and thereby selecting different communication tools for effective collaborative learning.

4.3 The impact of individual-learner characteristics on the participants' LLS use

Many researchers believe that individual-learner characteristics play a crucial role in LLS adoption. For the purpose of conducting quantitative analyses to identify relationships between individual-learner characteristics and LLS use in this project, the 23 questionnaire respondents were divided into two groups (Yes/No groups) with respect to each learner characteristic under consideration. These characteristics, summarised in Table 4.7, are

- six language-learning motives, from the six responses to the survey question 'Why are you learning Chinese as a foreign language?'
- four learning goals, from the four responses to the survey question 'What level are you aiming at in your Chinese studies?'
- age; and
- the length of prior learning of Chinese.

In Table 4.7, 'Yes' indicates the respondents had chosen the listed motive or goal, or were under 30 years old, or had had less than six months of studying Chinese; whilst 'No' indicates otherwise. Only the characteristics that appeared to be key

Table 4.7 Grouping of the 23 survey respondents by the 12 learner characteristics under consideration

Response options	Yes (%)	No (%)
Motive		
For pleasure and interest	16 (70%)	7 (30%)
I hope to use it in my present or future work	15 (65%)	8 (35%)
As an intellectual challenge	13 (57%)	10 (43%)
To improve my career prospects	13 (57%)	10 (43%)
To be able to communicate when visiting a Chinese-speaking country	12 (52%)	11 (48%)
To be able to communicate with Chinese-speaking friends or family	11 (48%)	12 (52%)
Language-learning goal		
I just want to get a taste of language and culture	5 (22%)	18 (78%)
I would like to be able to use Chinese for simple conversations and obtaining information when travelling in a Chinese-speaking country	7 (30%)	16 (70%)
I would like to live and work in a Chinese-speaking country and be able to speak it in most everyday life situations	9 (39%)	14 (61%)
I would like to attain a very high level of proficiency and be able to work as a translator/interpreter or teach Chinese	12 (52%)	11 (48%)
Age at time of survey (years)		
Under 30 years old (younger adult students)	7 (30%)	16 (70%)
Length of prior learning of Chinese		
Less than six months (less experienced students)	13 (57%)	10 (43%)

factors that influenced the participants' LLS use are discussed. As a result, the following four factors are discussed in this section:

- The motive of desiring to be able to communicate with Chinese-speaking friends or family;
- The learning goal of attaining a very high level of proficiency and being able to work as a translator/interpreter or teach Chinese;
- Age;
- The length of prior learning of Chinese.

4.3.1 Motives for learning Chinese and LLS use

Researchers have widely and persistently claimed that one important influencing factor in language learners' LLS adoption is motivation, as discussed in Section 2.6.2. They also believed that language learners who had strong motivation would put additional effort into the language-learning process. In this study, rather than seeking to measure the students' motivation (a complex construct) and to investigate its relationship to their LLS use, their motives for learning Chinese and their learning goals were used instead.

To examine the influences of motives for learning Chinese on LLS adoption, the participants were asked to respond to the survey question 'Why are you learning Chinese as a foreign language?', with six answer options, of which they could tick as many as were applicable. Those participants who answered 'Yes' to the option 'to be able to communicate with Chinese-speaking friends or family' were assumed to have Chinese friends or family around them and therefore to have a goal of becoming able to communicate with them in Chinese.

The mean scores between the 'Yes' and 'No' groups to the learning motive 'to be able to communicate with Chinese-speaking friends or family' were compared and Mann–Whitney U tests were conducted to see whether there were statistically different between-group differences. The investigation across the six LLS categories revealed that the motive showed notable, and sometimes statistically significant (at $p <= 0.05$), differences in the respondents' use of affective, cognitive, and metacognitive strategies.

The Mann–Whitney U tests on the frequency of use of affective strategies between the 'Yes' and the 'No' groups for this motive, as shown in Table 4.8, did not indicate any statistically significant differences ($p <= 0.05$). However, the mean scores suggest that the respondents for whom learning Chinese was important in order to communicate with friends and family ('Yes' group) used the four affective strategies in the table less frequently than the 'No' group. A possible explanation is that the 'No' group, who lacked the opportunities and urgency implied in communicating with friends and family, might need to employ the affective strategies more frequently in order to keep motivating themselves in self-directed learning.

In particular, the Mann–Whitney U tests as applied to the two affective strategies of *'Discussing your feelings with someone else'* and *'Rewarding yourself'* show asymptotic significance values of 0.08 and 0.06 respectively, which are close

Table 4.8 Comparison of affective LLS frequencies by learning motive 'To be able to communicate with Chinese-speaking friends or family' ($N = 23$)

Affective strategy	LLS item in the survey questionnaire	Learning context	Mean of student group		Asymp. Sig. (p)
			Yes (48%)	No (52%)	
Taking risks wisely (Oxford, 1990)	I encourage myself to take risks in Chinese learning, such as guessing meanings or trying to speak, even though I might make some mistakes	Self-directed learning outside the online classes	3.81	3.91	.38
Making positive statements (Oxford, 1990)	I encourage myself so that I will continue to try hard and do my best in Chinese learning		3.45	3.65	.87
Discussing your feelings with someone else (Oxford, 1990)	I talk to someone I trust about my attitudes and feelings concerning the language-learning process		2.36	3.25	.08
Rewarding yourself (Oxford, 1990)	I give myself a tangible reward when I have done something well in my Chinese learning		1.63	2.33	.06

Note: 'Yes' means 'chose this motive'; 'No' means 'did not choose this motive'.

to the significance threshold of $p <= 0.05$. In this research, '*Discussing your feelings with someone else*' means to talk with others to express feelings about online language-learning with the aim of reducing one's learning anxieties when studying independently. The mean score of the 'Yes' group ($M = 2.36$) is in the low-frequency range of strategy use, whilst the mean score of the 'No' group ($M = 3.25$) is at the high end of the medium-frequency range of strategy use. This difference suggests that the respondents who had more opportunities to use Chinese to communicate with native Chinese speakers had less need to use affective strategies when compared with the respondents who had fewer opportunities. One of the interviewees provided an example to illustrate this. In the interview, S17 (in the 'Yes' group) mentioned that she lived in a Chinese-speaking family and always used Chinese to interact with her parents-in-law. She gave a rating of 1 (Never or almost never true of me) to the questionnaire item related to the strategy of '*Discussing your feelings with someone else*'. The use of the strategy '*Rewarding yourself*' shows a similar trend, where the 'Yes' group ($M = 1.63$) used the strategy less than the 'No' group ($M = 2.33$).

The motive 'to be able to communicate with Chinese-speaking friends or family' also appeared to significantly influence the students' use of two cognitive strategies in self-directed learning, namely, '*Summarising*' and '*Using resources for receiving and sending messages*' (see Table 4.9).

As listed in Table 4.9, the 'Yes' and the 'No' groups used the two cognitive strategies of '*Summarising*' ($p = .02$, $p <= 0.05$) and '*Using resources for receiving and sending messages*' ($p = .05$, $p <= 0.05$) with statistically significant frequency differences. In the survey, the first strategy refers to summarising Chinese grammar

Table 4.9 Significant differences in the use of two cognitive strategies in relation to the motive 'To be able to communicate with Chinese-speaking friends or family' (*N* = 23)

Cognitive strategy	LLS item in the survey questionnaire	Learning context	Mean of student group		Asymp. Sig. (p)
			Yes (48%)	No (52%)	
Summarising (Oxford, 1990)	I summarise Chinese grammar points in my head as a way to reinforce my understanding	Self-directed learning outside the online classes	2.36	3.33	.02
Using resources for receiving and sending messages (Oxford, 1990)	I search for background information on Chinese words online		2.82	3.83	.05

Note: 'Yes' means 'chose this motive'; 'No' means 'did not choose this motive'.

points in one's own mind, and the second strategy refers to looking up background information on Chinese words online. The mean score comparison results suggested that the 'Yes' group used the two cognitive strategies less frequently than did the 'No' group. These results indicate that the 'Yes' group of students could easily receive explanations relating to vocabulary items and grammar points through communication with native Chinese speakers, rather than by looking up the words in e-dictionaries and summarising grammar points by themselves.

S17 is a case in point. This student gave a rating of 2 (Generally not true of me) for both '*Summarising*' and '*Using resources for receiving and sending messages*'. She lived in a Chinese family and always participated in conversations in Chinese at home, as shown in Excerpt 4.1.

Excerpt 4.1 The benefits of being exposed to a Chinese-language environment according to S17

S17: No, I don't struggle to understand what people speak so much anymore, just because my in-laws have been speaking to me in Mandarin for years now. I am quite attuned to understanding what they are saying. I lived overseas for ten years, and you start to understand that a lot of language isn't to do with what people are saying, but the context or what the conversation is. So you start to learn how to anticipate what they probably will be saying, and to predict the direction of the language. So even if you don't understand every word, you can generally understand the meaning of what's being said, and fill in the blanks. (00:07:15 in the recording, Interview, S17, 2015)

Excerpt 4.1 illustrates that S17 had adapted to the Chinese-speaking environment, and therefore benefited from practising Chinese speaking in daily conversations. This practice helped her to read the environment and situation so that appropriate Chinese words could be understood during communication. In environments such as this one, S17 developed situational awareness and therefore relied less on '*Using resources for receiving and sending messages*' or '*Summarising*'.

At the same time, the daily conversations mentioned above provided evidence that S17 employed a cognitive strategy, '*Practising naturalistically*'. This cognitive strategy refers to a learner using the language in natural and realistic settings, such as participating in a conversation (Oxford, 1990).

Excerpt 4.2 shows an example of how she used this strategy to learn a Chinese word, 毛病 (which means 'problem'), by listening to the word and asking her husband the meaning. In S17's case, the readily available help, such as checking with her husband, also contributed to her less frequent use of '*Using resources for receiving and sending messages*' or '*Summarising*', compared with that of other students.

Excerpt 4.2 An example of 'Practising naturalistically' by S17

S17: It's a situation that I won't be able to select to have a conversation about something that I go [to the internet] and find out the words ... or if I hear a word a lot of times, then I'll ask my husband what that word is, like 毛病 <problem>. My father-in-law would often use 毛病 in a sentence if there's a problem, ... and eventually I start[started] to know this means 'problem'. (00:20:21 in the recording, Interview, S17, 2015)

The motive of being able to communicate with Chinese-speaking friends or family also appeared to influence the respondents' use of two metacognitive strategies. Table 4.10 shows that there are marked differences in the use of the two metacognitive strategies between the 'Yes' and 'No' groups of respondents, with one of them ('*Overviewing and linking with known material*') being statistically significant.

The 'Yes' group used both the strategy '*Overviewing and linking with known material*' and the strategy '*Self-evaluating*' less frequently than did the 'No' group. The Mann–Whitney U test results show that the differences between the two groups for the former strategy use are statistically significant ($p = 0.05$, $p <= 0.05$), and are just short of statistical significance ($p = .10$) in regard to the latter. At first these results might appear counter-intuitive. The respondents who selected this motive seemed to be putting less effort into managing and organising their work in the courses. However, the 'Yes' group was assumed to have better access to Chinese-speaking people and therefore might be less reliant on the course materials and

Table 4.10 Differences in the use of two metacognitive strategies in relation to the motive 'To be able to communicate with Chinese-speaking friends or family' (N = 23)

Metacognitive strategy	LLS item in the survey questionnaire	Learning context	Mean of student group		Asymp. Sig. (p)
			Yes (48%)	No (52%)	
Overviewing and linking with known material (Oxford, 1990)	I review the resources that are recommended in the online Chinese courses	Self-directed learning outside the online classes	3.09	4.00	.05
Self-evaluating (Oxford, 1990)	I often evaluate the progress I have made in learning Chinese		2.73	3.50	.10

Note: 'Yes' means 'chose this motive'; 'No' means 'did not choose this motive'.

activities. This might also explain why they tended to use the relevant metacognitive strategies less frequently when studying course materials than the 'No' group of students.

The interview data provided supporting evidence that the students who lived in Chinese-speaking families did not just rely on the online Chinese courses to improve Chinese speaking and writing. S10 and S17, who chose this motive option, reported in the interviews that they studied the course materials only to reinforce their memory of vocabulary. They both had long-term learning experience and Chinese was one of their family languages. In the interview, S17 recalled that she had learnt a large number of Chinese characters previously. Similarly, S10 mentioned that she had been studying traditional Chinese since she was very young, and she hoped that she could learn to recognise simplified Chinese characters through online Chinese courses. As shown in Excerpt 4.3, and unlike other students, S10 focused more on the practical value of learning Chinese rather than focusing on her marks in the assessment tasks.

> **Excerpt 4.3 An example of using the strategy 'Self-evaluation' by S10**
>
> *S10: So I listened and also read the characters to see if I [understood them], and I noticed that the more I learn, the more characters I can understand on the bottom [on-screen scripts]. So that's how I know that I am really learning, because I can start to read the characters and also, when my little one has a Chinese nanny, I can understand a bit more. And I know, because my parents and my in-laws, when we have dinner, they speak Mandarin, my in-laws especially, I can understand even more, so that's how I know that [I'm] making progress. (00:38:48 in the recording, Interview, S10, 2015)*

In sum, the motive of being able to communicate with Chinese-speaking friends or family was found to be an influencing factor to the participants' use of four affective, two cognitive, and two metacognitive strategies. The students with a less powerful motive for using Chinese to communicate with others needed to employ these strategies more frequently in order to keep themselves motivated, summarise grammar points in their minds, find background information on Chinese words online, review the recommended resources, and self-evaluate their learning progress in self-directed learning. Whilst the results seem counter-intuitive, selecting this motive may imply that the participants have better access to Chinese-speaking people, and therefore have more options available to support their learning. All these findings suggest that language-course designers and teachers may better support the students with this motive by providing additional learning activities inside the online Chinese courses and guiding them to resources outside these courses.

4.3.2 Learning goals and LLS use

Learning goals refer to the reasons behind engaging in language-learning behaviour which may predict learners' strategy use (Oxford, 1990). When students pursue these goals they are concerned with improving their competence, understanding the learning materials, gaining knowledge, or developing a new skill (Han & Lu, 2018). However, few studies have been conducted on online Chinese learners to examine the relations between learning goals and strategy use.

Therefore, in order to examine the possible influence of learning goals on LLS adoption, the participants were asked to respond to the survey question 'What level are you aiming at in your Chinese studies?' with four learning-goal options, as shown in Table 4.7. Interview and statistical analysis results suggest that the learning goals, especially that of 'I'd like to attain a very high level of proficiency and be able to work as a translator/interpreter or teach Chinese', might influence how the participants used memory, metacognitive, and social strategies in different learning contexts.

Two examples from the interview data (S18 and S14) demonstrate how learning goals affected these students' use of two memory strategies. These two memory strategies were used by the students to memorise words and phrases by '*Using mechanical techniques*', such as flashcards, and '*Placing new words into a context*', such as a sentence. S18, a beginning-level student, confirmed his learning goal as follows: 'I'd like to live and work in a Chinese-speaking country and be able to speak Chinese in most everyday life situations'. In the interview, S18 explained that he wanted to expand his vocabulary in order to be able to conduct basic communication as quickly as possible. He therefore made the cards in PowerPoint slides to memorise the meaning and pronunciation of new words, and 'used the cards everywhere' ('*Using mechanical techniques*'). This idea of memorising vocabulary was rooted in his belief in 'cross training' (a term used by S18 to describe his using of flashcards to learn vocabulary by comparing English and Chinese meanings). These results reflect that considerable effort was invested by the student in employing a memory strategy for building vocabulary with a specific learning goal.

128 *Factors influencing LLS adoption*

S14, whose learning goal was different from that of S18, stated in his interview that he aimed to achieve the highest level of Chinese-language-learning proficiency possible. He provided an example of his notes in vocabulary learning, as shown in Figure 4.1, which articulated one cognitive and one memory strategy. He first took notes about the characters, their meanings, pronunciation, and sentence examples (*'Using resources for receiving and sending messages'*) from the Pleco app, which contains the features of an e-dictionary and flashcards. After that, he organised the information related to the vocabulary, such as by making sentences with new words (*'Placing new words into a context'*), as shown in Figure 4.1, which shows seven aspects of S14's note-taking in relation to a Chinese word. He:

- wrote the Chinese characters, words, and Pinyin with tone marks;
- wrote the English meaning of the Chinese characters and words;
- made sentences using the Chinese characters and words;
- used different colours (pencil, black ink, and highlighter) to show the words and their meaning;
- highlighted important information related to a word;
- noticed the homonyms of Chinese words; and
- learnt new characters through association.

Compared with the use of the strategy '*Using mechanical techniques*', which was mostly employed for rote learning, S14's note-taking explicitly demonstrated how he adopted the strategy of '*Placing new words into a context*' in associative learning. As shown in Figure 4.1, when he learnt 厉害 <serious, terrible, severe>, he also associated it with other words containing the same character 害 to help memorise the meaning of 害, such as 伤害 <hurt>, 杀害 <kill>. This may have helped him strengthen his memory and deepen his understanding of 害 and expand his vocabulary at the same time. This memory-strategy use evidenced that this student memorised vocabulary in contexts (e.g., in phrases and sentences) and used the strategies of '*Analysing contrastively*', '*Semantic mapping*', and '*Using linguistic clues*'. The approach taken by S14 matches Nation's (1994) suggestion that

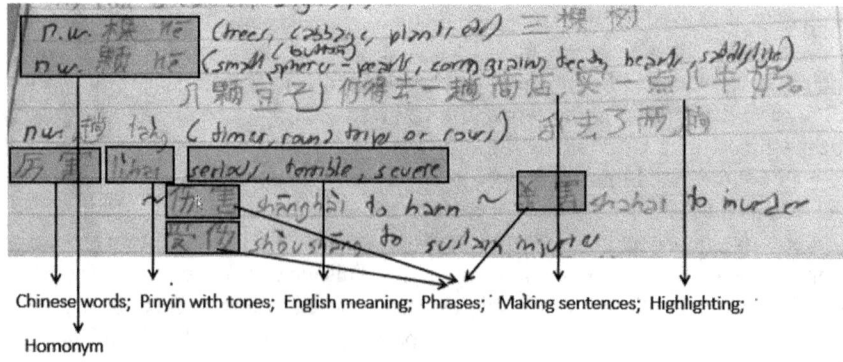

Figure 4.1 Example of notes using LLSs for vocabulary learning by S14

language learners should memorise vocabulary items by noticing their associations rather than rote learning. Figure 4.1 therefore presents an example of using a cluster of LLSs concurrently.

The survey results showed that the learning goal 'I would like to attain a very high level of proficiency and be able to work as a translator/interpreter or teach Chinese' affected how frequently memory strategies were used. The mean scores comparison results indicated that interesting differences exist in the use of two memory strategies: '*Using mechanical techniques*' and '*Placing new words into a context*' (see Table 4.11). Whilst the Mann–Whitney U test results did not show significant differences between the two groups of respondents, the 'No' group used character cards to help memorise new Chinese words ('*Using mechanical techniques*'; $M = 3.45$) more frequently than the 'Yes' group ($M = 2.92$); by contrast, the 'No' group ($M = 2.82$) used the strategy '*Placing new words into a context*' less frequently than the 'Yes' group ($M = 3.50$).

These survey results suggest that the students who had higher expectations of their Chinese-language learning were more willing to spend time on finding associations between words and grouping words, but less reliant on using flashcards to memorise words. Oxford (1990) and Brown (2007), among others, claimed that words and phrases need to be learnt in context in order to enhance the effectiveness of memorisation and they believed that contextualised and meaningful memorisation was the most effective method of second-language learning. The application of the two memory strategies by the 'Yes' group demonstrates this approach.

With respect to metacognitive strategies, the learning goals were found to be influencing how some of the students used the strategy of '*Organising*'. S8's learning goal expressed in the survey was: 'I would like to live and work in a Chinese-speaking country and be able to speak it in most everyday life situations'. The student mentioned that he was aiming to improve his conversational Chinese rather than memorising Chinese characters. He had a well-organised learning routine for practising listening and speaking (see Table 4.12) which contained the learning activities, durations, and his opinions of the learning activities. According to the

Table 4.11 Differences in the use of two memory strategies in relation to the learning goal of attaining a very high level of proficiency ($N = 23$)

Memory strategy	LLS item in the survey questionnaire	Learning context	Group mean		Asymp. Sig. (p)
			Yes (52%)	No (48%)	
Using mechanical techniques (Nation, 2001)	Use character cards to help memorise new Chinese words	Self-directed learning outside the online classes	2.92	3.45	.47
Placing new words into a context (Oxford, 1990)	When I am learning a new Chinese word, I put it in a sentence, so I can remember it		3.50	2.82	.22

Note: 'Yes' means 'chose this goal'; 'No' means 'did not choose this goal'.

Table 4.12 S8's daily Chinese-language-learning routine

Learning activity	Duration	S8's opinion
Watching children's videos, online Chinese courses on YouTube	15 minutes	Slow and clear voice in the children's videos was good for his understanding
Listening to MP3, podcasts, etc. in Chinese	15 minutes	Convenient for listening
Chatting with Chinese people in local shops for a coffee or lunch	Intermittent	Utilising Chinese language there; can hear Mandarin with different accents
Studying Chinese characters and words	30 minutes	Convenient and effective for memorising vocabulary
Completing coursework such as online quizzes, weekly exercises, video viewing, occasionally with a language partner	1–2 hours; adjustable	Fully follow the course requirements, complete them before attending online classes

Data source: recorded interview with S8, 2015.

interview with him, such a routine involved 10–12 hours of learning every week, and around 1–2 hours per day.

As shown in Table 4.12, S8's learning routine contained detailed schedules and he followed this routine for the whole study period. The decisions in relation to the learning activities in the routine underlined the fact that S8 expected to improve Chinese speaking through listening and understanding the conversations. This was also confirmed by the survey data when he reported, *'for me, speaking and listening are the most important for learning. I try to watch videos every day and I try to chat with Chinese speakers every day. Chinese requires daily practice, or I will quickly forget'* (Survey questionnaire part III, S8, 2015). When S8 talked about the most important aspects of his learning, he stressed that the learning routine was essential, and self-discipline was the key to his routine. He believed that such self-discipline was a learning habit that had been formed through his long working experience, and that completing tasks on time, and considering the details in presentations, was paramount.

The other interviewee, S15, had a learning goal of improving in all four skills (listening, speaking, reading, and writing) in order to achieve the highest language-proficiency level, with which his learning routine was well aligned. In a similar way to S8, the key feature of S15's learning routine was self-discipline, which was particularly valuable in helping him complete different learning activities. In responding to the open-ended survey question regarding the most useful LLSs that he had discovered so far in the course, he wrote *'Routines are important. As soon as a routine is broken it is difficult to get started again. No matter how tired or demotivated I am, I always try to do something. I have done a lot of work with flashcards[,] mainly the app, "StickyStudy". I constantly read books in Chinese and use HSK [Hànyǔ Shuǐpíng Kǎoshì] exams as motivation'* (Survey questionnaire part III, S15, 2015).

Compared with S8's learning routine, S15's routine appeared to be more flexible in terms of his study time arrangements but more multifarious in its learning content, which aligned well with his learning goal of improving in all four language skills. S15 claimed that he constantly changed learning activities to maintain his learning time and interest in learning, as shown in Excerpt 4.4.

Excerpt 4.4 Flexibility in S15's learning routine

S15: I want to do [what] one supposes [is supposed] to do, I just do it anyway, I just force myself to do it. And, I guess, you know if I don't want to do a chat from the book, then I'll do something, I'll do 10-minute flashcards, you know, I'll do something else. But – once I avoid it, maybe I instead do something else, maybe watch TV or play computer games or something, then I start to lose interest. So the answer is, I just force myself to do it. (00:20:20 in the recording, Interview, S15, 2015).

From Excerpt 4.4, it can be seen that S15's routine was flexible, and this helped prevent him from being distracted. According to the interview with him, he also prioritised the completion of the assessment tasks in his schedule. Once he completed the assessment tasks, he tried to find additional time to engage in those Chinese-learning activities that he was more interested in, such as reading a book written in Chinese.

Overall, these two interviewees' different routines and the metacognitive strategy use of '*Organising*' indicated that they tended to achieve more than the goals set for them by the online courses, such as passing *HSK* exams (S15), and understanding conversations in Pimsleur (a digital Mandarin course). This was possible due to their planning, decision-making with a priority schedule, self-discipline, and taking more control of the learning progress for online learning. It was also clear that when these two students developed their own thinking and learning processes, they took into account the effectiveness of the metacognitive strategies they used to achieve the learning goals they set. As a result, these two interviewees exhibited a strong sense of responsibility for their Chinese-language learning and had developed personal processes and techniques to promote their specific Chinese-language skills. These findings are consistent with Brown's (2007) idea of a 'locus of learning'. That is, language learners who expect to be successful in learning believe they have responsibilities and capabilities to control the learning process.

With regard to finding opportunities to practise Chinese skills, the interview data suggested that the learning goals were once again an influencing factor. This can be seen from the input from the interviewed students (S5, S8, S9, S10, S12, S14), who indicated that they used the metacognitive strategy of '*Seeking practice opportunities*', but did so in different ways. The interviewees (S5, S8, S10) who focused on improving conversational Chinese, and had Chinese-speaking people around them, would seek practice opportunities to engage in general conversations in Chinese as the easiest way to upgrade their real-life speaking skills. For example, S8, who lived in a Chinese-speaking country, chatted with Chinese people in local shops when having a coffee or lunch every day.

However, those interviewees (S14, S18) who wanted to achieve a high language-proficiency level and had Chinese-speaking people around them would purposely prepare conversational topics and arrange regular meetings with native Chinese speakers in order to improve their Chinese-speaking skills. For example, S18 lived in China. He attended an 'English corner' (an English-language-learning activity in China, which is commonly used by learners of English to practise oral English on a regular basis). He went equipped with his Chinese book, so that he could help Chinese people speak English there but also practise his Chinese with them.

Another student, S14, explained his interaction with native Chinese speakers in the interview (see Excerpt 4.5). S14 mentioned that he went to the university to meet a Chinese student once a week, evidencing that he regularly arranged this activity. These interview findings indicated that the learning goal was an influencing factor in guiding the students to take control of their language learning through the use of the metacognitive strategies of 'Organising' and 'Seeking practice opportunities'.

> **Excerpt 4.5 An example of 'Seeking practice opportunities' by S14**
>
> S14: I also go to Sydney Uni, there is a Chinese student, which I speak to her [with whom I speak], and it helps me. And I have a [Chinese] colleague, we go to lunch together and we practise Chinese. (00:06:43 in the recording, Interview, S14, 2015).

The learning goal 'I would like to attain a very high level of proficiency and be able to work as a translator/interpreter or teach Chinese' also influenced the survey respondents' social strategy use in the context of online class participation. Table 4.13 shows the different mean scores and Mann–Whitney U test results of the usage of the four social strategies by two groups of students in relation to the learning goal 'I would like to attain a very high level of proficiency and be able to work as a translator/interpreter or teach Chinese'. There is a significant difference for the questionnaire item 'I ask other students to correct me' between the 'Yes' and the 'No' groups of respondents ($p =.00; p <=.05$). This result indicated that the respondents who had no expectations ('No' group) of achieving a very high level of proficiency preferred to encourage other students (and the teacher, although not to a significant degree) to correct them. On the other hand, the 'Yes' group seemed to seek more than just corrections, as shown in the responses to other strategy items in Table 4.13. More specifically, the 'Yes' group tended to seek clarifications and verifications from the teacher more often and used text messages to ensure that their questions were correctly conveyed and their interactions were effective.

Table 4.13 Differences in the use of social strategies related to the goal of 'I would like to attain a very high level of proficiency and be able to work as a translator/interpreter or teach Chinese' ($N = 21$)

Social strategy	LLS item in the survey questionnaire	Group mean		Asymp. Sig. (p)
		Yes (48%)	No (52%)	
Netiquette (LLS specific to online learning)	I prefer keeping the webcam on to let the teacher and other students see me	2.45	2.90	.43
Asking for correction (Brown, 2007)	I ask the teacher to correct me	2.82	3.50	.36
	I ask other students to correct me	1.36	3.30	.00
Asking for clarification and verification (Oxford, 1990)	If I do not understand, I ask the teacher to explain/repeat	3.64	3.30	.44
	If I do not understand, I ask the other students to slow down, repeat, or clarify what was said	1.91	3.00	.25
	I ask the teacher to verify that I have understood or said something correctly	3.64	3.30	.42
Using the tools available to improve communication and interaction (LLS specific to online learning)	I type text messages for the purpose of effective communication	3.36	3.10	.49
	If I do not understand, I ask questions using the text chat	3.09	2.40	.37

Note: 'Yes' means 'chose this goal'; 'No' means 'did not choose this goal'.

In summary, this section confirmed that the learning goal 'I would like to attain a very high level of proficiency and be able to work as a translator/interpreter or teach Chinese' influenced how the participants used their memory, metacognitive, and social strategies. Both the quantitative data and the excerpts from interviews suggested that the participants who chose this learning goal focused on different learning activities compared with those of the 'No' group. Some interviewees (e.g., S14) preferred to memorise words and phrases in a context ('*Placing new words into a context*') rather than use flashcards ('*Using mechanical techniques*'). Most of the interviewees found various opportunities to practise Chinese listening, speaking, reading, and writing ('*Seeking practice opportunities*'; '*Organising*'). In the context of online classes, they expected to receive as much in the way of clarifications and feedback from their teachers as possible in order to verify their understanding, rather than asking for corrections from their peers.

4.3.3 Age and LLS use

As discussed in Section 2.6.5, researchers have already noted that age is an important learner characteristic in relation to language learners' strategy use (Cohen,

134 *Factors influencing LLS adoption*

1998; Krashen, 1982; Oxford, 1990, 1996). In order to examine whether the use of LLSs differed between the younger and older adult students in my study, the respondents were divided into two groups: those aged below 30 ($n = 7$) and those above 30 ($n = 16$). According to the results, age is likely to be a factor that affected the respondents' use of two affective strategies, three memory strategies, and one compensation strategy.

Firstly, the participants' affective-strategy use appeared to be influenced by age according to the hierarchical clustering analysis results, shown in a dendrogram in Figure 4.2. The horizontal axis of the dendrogram represents the distances or dissimilarities among the respondent-clusters for all the affective-strategy items considered in this project, whilst the vertical axis represents the respondent-clusters. Each joining of two respondent-clusters is represented on the graph by the merging of two horizontal lines into one horizontal line (from left to right). The horizontal position of the merge, shown by a short vertical bar, describes the distance (dissimilarity) between the two respondents' or the respondent-clusters' affective-strategy use.

The clustering analysis provides a broad order guide to the relationship between the reported use of affective strategies and age. Eleven students (S22, S33, S15, S10, S26, S18, S28, S14, S9, S5, S8) are grouped into one cluster at a distance of

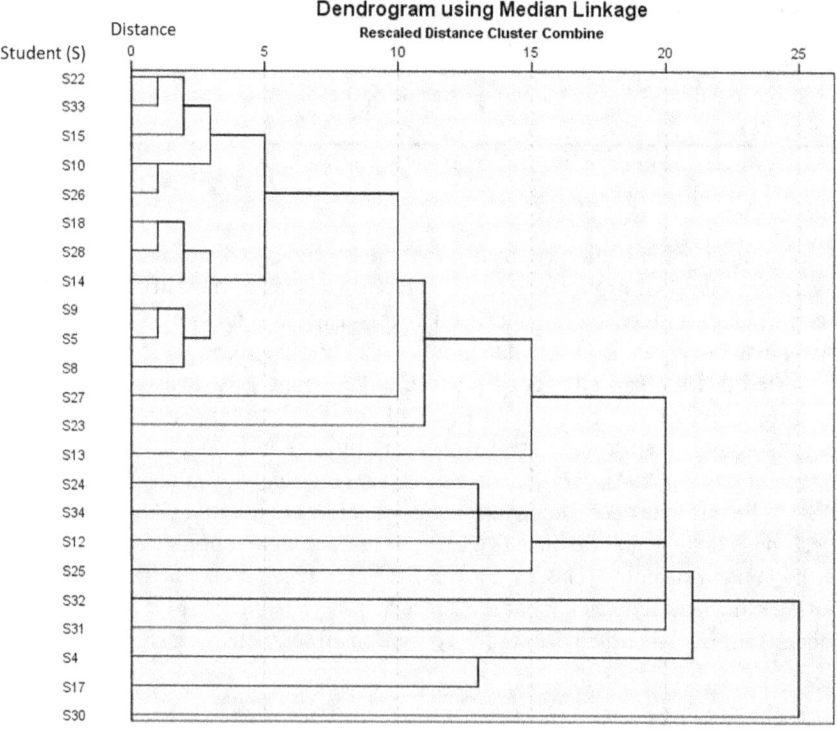

Figure 4.2 The dendrogram of a hierarchical clustering analysis showing the clusters from age and affective-strategy use

five. According to the background information in these eleven students' survey responses, nine of them were over 30 years old. According to the survey responses, these nine respondents gave a rating of 4 (Generally true of me) or 5 (Always or almost always true of me) for the affective strategies of *'Making positive statements'* and *'Taking risks wisely'*. These two affective strategies refer to the students encouraging themselves with positive statements and taking risks when interacting with others in the context of self-directed learning. These cluster analysis results indicated that age increase was likely to encourage adult students to adjust their emotions when they faced various learning difficulties.

The hierarchical clustering analysis results relating to the importance of the two affective strategies to older students can be further illustrated through the survey and the interview data provided by S15. He was a Chinese teacher in the UK who belonged to the older adult group and, as a Chinese-language learner in Britain, he had little access to native Chinese speakers. The survey data evidenced that he always encouraged himself. He applied a rating of 4 (Generally true of me) to the affective strategy of *'Making positive statements'* in his survey questionnaire responses. As a Mandarin teacher, he understood the importance of using affective strategies for Chinese-language learning. During the interview, he used a Chinese idiom to describe his determination as 愚公移山. The story behind this idiom is about a man who was determined to move the mountains that blocked his way to the outside world.

Excerpt 4.6 Understanding the importance of 'Making positive statements' by S15

S15: I think we are not good at seeing what we have achieved. I always do that with my students. I say, don't you think you have achieved anything? Very much! Look back to the first page of the book, where we started, months ago ... It's the numbers, one two three four. That's easy, everybody knows that. But you don't know them when you start, you have made progress, but you don't notice it, because it's so slow; and it's important to measure it yourself, the progress you've made. (00:33:44 in the recording, Interview, S15, 2015).

Excerpt 4.6, which in fact is not directly related to S15's self-encouragement, recalls his encouragement of his students. Nevertheless, it reflects his positive attitude towards language learning as an older adult in an online Chinese-learning course. In the interview, he also gave another example that showed his enjoyment of each step in the progress he was making in Chinese-language learning. Once, he found a small difference in the first strokes of the two Chinese characters, 干 and 千, which made him 'extremely happy'. As such, learning Chinese vocabulary for enjoyment was essential for him to transfer his Chinese vocabulary learning from

136 Factors influencing LLS adoption

his short-term memory to his long-term memory. This example indicated that S15 noticed the benefits of using affective strategies to maintain positive emotions for effective language learning.

Age also seems to be an influencing factor which affects the respondents' memory-strategy use according to the hierarchical clustering analysis results. The dendrogram in Figure 4.3 shows how similar the survey respondents' memory-strategy uses are in relation to the respondents' ages. S15, S34, S18, S5, S23, S8, S9, S10, S30, S28, S26 are grouped into a cluster at a distance of 12. These 11 survey respondents were all over 30 years of age and belonged to the older adult group. Moreover, most of them (nine of the 11) gave a *low* rating of 2 (Generally not true of me) to the memory strategy of '*Placing new words into a context*'. All of them favoured using the strategy of '*Using mechanical techniques*', as they gave a rating from 3 (Somewhat true of me) to 5 (Always or almost always true of me) in response to the relevant strategy questionnaire item.

The comparison of mean score results further explained the respondents' memory-strategy use in relation to their ages. Table 4.14 shows the Mann–Whitney U test results with the mean score comparisons of the three memory strategies between the younger and older groups of adult students. The older adult students employed the two memory strategies of '*Using mechanical techniques*' and '*Semantic*

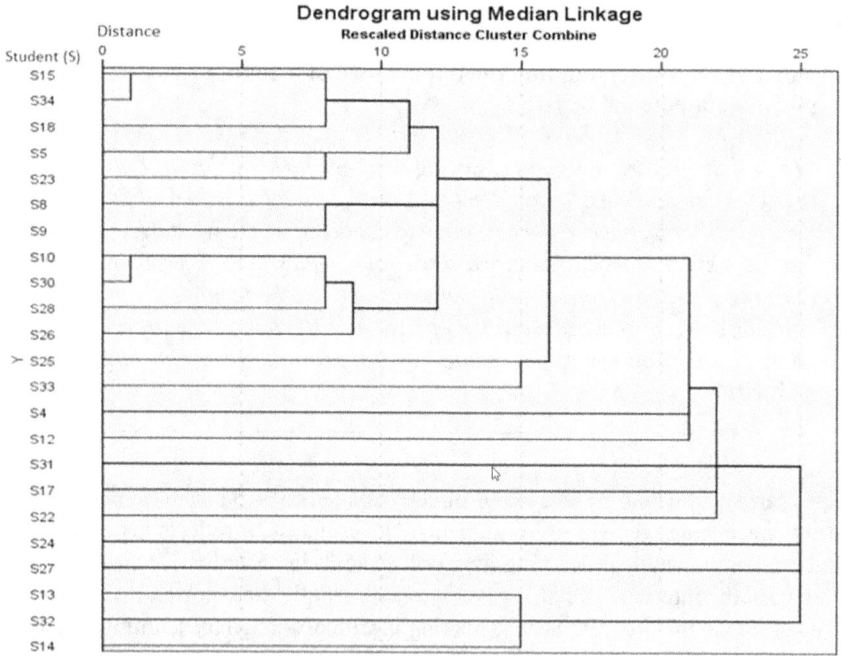

Figure 4.3 The dendrogram of a hierarchical clustering analysis showing the clusters from age and memory-strategy use

mapping' more frequently than the younger adult students. In other words, the older students preferred to use character cards and find associations between words to learn vocabulary. By contrast, the younger adult students preferred to memorise a new Chinese word in a sentence. These comparison results are near-marginal significant ($p = .10, .17$ and $.24$, respectively). The survey results of the use of '*Semantic mapping*' is also in line with Sepasdar and Soori (2014)'s finding that A. D. Cohen himself, as a Chinese-language learner (67 years old), frequently used this memory strategy as well.

Furthermore, one compensation strategy of '*Selecting the topic*' was also influenced by the students' age according to the Mann–Whitney U test results (Table 4.15). As mentioned in Section 3.2.6, overall, the survey respondents used this strategy with medium-frequency-range use ($Mdn = 3$). However, the results in Table 4.15 indicate that there are significant differences between the 'Younger' and 'Older' groups in terms of their compensation strategy use. The 'Younger' group used the strategy '*Selecting the topic*' less frequently than the 'Older' group ($p = .03$, $p <= .05$). A possible explanation of this result is that the older adult students had

Table 4.14 Differences in the use of three memory strategies in relation to age ($N = 23$)

Memory strategy	LLS item in the survey questionnaire	Group mean		Asymp. Sig. (p)
		Yes (30%)	No (70%)	
Using mechanical techniques (Cohen & Li, 2013)	Use character cards to help memorise new Chinese words	2.43	3.50	.10
Placing new words into a context (Oxford, 1990)	When I am learning a new Chinese word, I put it in a sentence, so I can remember it	3.71	2.94	.17
Semantic mapping (Oxford, 1990)	When I am learning a new Chinese word, I list words I know that are related to it and draw lines to show relationships	2.14	2.69	.24

Note: 'Yes' means 'younger adult students', < 30 years old; 'No' means 'older adult students', >= 30 years old.

Table 4.15 Significant difference in the use of one compensation strategy in relation to age ($N = 23$)

Compensation strategy	LLS item in the survey questionnaire	Group mean		Asymp. Sig. (p)
		Yes (30%)	No (70%)	
Selecting the topic (Oxford, 1990)	When speaking with other students, I tend to steer the conversation onto a topic for which I know the words	1.86	2.94	.03

Note: 'Yes' means 'younger adult students', < 30 years old; 'No' means 'older adult students', >= 30 years old.

more experience of engaging with conversation practices and, perhaps, more confidence in conversations, which might have made them readier to direct such conversations. This finding corroborated an idea in a study by Oxford (1990), who suggested that language learners with past learning experiences may have more strength in adopting compensation strategies at an older age.

The results on the learner characteristic of age are consistent with the general findings regarding the impact of age on LLS adoption from previous LLS studies (Cohen, 1998; Krashen, 1982; Oxford, 1996; Sepasdar & Soori, 2014). At the same time, the strategy-use differences between the 'Younger' and the 'Older' groups of students provide new evidence that age can be stratified as a factor for adult learners which influences their LLS use, especially in online Chinese learning. Echoing previous research, this research project confirmed that older adult participants had more learning experience in controlling their learning emotions, memorising words and phrases, and engaging in conversation practices. These older students used two affective strategies ('*Making positive statements*' and '*Taking risks wisely*'), two memory strategies ('*Using mechanical techniques*' and '*Semantic mapping*'), and one compensation strategy ('*Selecting the topic*') more frequently than the younger students. These results may, therefore, be used by language teachers to explicitly guide different age groups of adult students to use particular strategies.

4.3.4 Length of prior learning of Chinese and LLS use

Rather than asking the respondents about their levels of language proficiency, the survey question asked about the length of their prior learning of Chinese ('*How long have you been studying Chinese?*'). The 23 respondents were then classified according to whether their prior learning of Chinese had been for a longer or shorter period than six months, into two groups: the 'Yes' group (less experienced Chinese learners), which consisted of 13 respondents, and the 'No' group (more experienced Chinese learners), which contained 10 respondents.

The Mann–Whitney U test and the mean score comparison results, shown in Table 4.16, suggest that there is a significant difference ($p = .04$, $p <= .05$) between the less experienced and the more experienced Chinese learners. The 'No' group (more experienced group, $M = 4.23$, high high-frequency range of strategy use) used the strategy '*Repeating*' more frequently than the 'Yes' group (less experienced group, $M = 3.50$, low high-frequency range of strategy use) to imitate the tones that native Chinese speakers used. This result indicates that the experienced respondents believed that imitating native Chinese speakers' tones was of importance. Even though the less experienced students did not use the strategy so often, they still employed it with a mean in the high-frequency use range. Such a survey result also implies that these students were aware of the importance of tones in Chinese-language learning. For instance, S12 (an experienced student) reflected on the challenges she encountered during her collaboration with her language partner, and suggested her language partner should practise imitating native Chinese pronunciations to a greater extent, as shown in Excerpt 4.7.

Table 4.16 Significant difference in the use of one cognitive strategy in relation to the length of prior learning of Chinese ($N = 23$)

Cognitive strategy	LLS item in the survey questionnaire	Learning context	Group mean		Asymp. Sig. (p)
			Yes (57%)	No (43%)	
Repeating (Sepasdar & Soori, 2014)	I imitate the tones that native Chinese speakers use	Self-directed learning outside the online classes	3.50	4.23	.04

Note: 'Yes' means 'less experienced Chinese learners', < 6 months; 'No' means 'more experienced Chinese learners', >= 6 months.

Excerpt 4.7 S12's suggestion to her language partner of using 'Repeating'

S12: we practised our dialogue together, and I honestly couldn't understand anything he said ... so instead of trying to correct him, I got one of my friends (a Chinese friend), who recorded him [himself] doing the recording. So he completed the dialogue, and I sent it back to my language partner ... And I said to him, 'Perhaps you should practise following my friend's recording?' (00:35:02 in the recording, Interview, S12, 2015)

These two students failed their first assessed collaborative task, practising a role play (questions and answers), due to S12's language partner's inaccurate pronunciation. S12's friend (a native Chinese speaker) then made a recording of the language partner's part as a reference. By using the recording, her language partner improved his pronunciation, tones, intonation, and fluency in general.

There are two significant differences between the two groups of students in their use of two metacognitive strategies (see Table 4.17). The experienced respondents used the strategy '*Self-monitoring*' less frequently to highlight their errors when speaking Chinese ($p = .02$, $p <= .05$), and similarly the strategy '*Overviewing and linking with known material*', by reviewing the course-recommended online resources, was less used by this group ($p = .03$, $p <= .05$).

The mean score comparison results in Table 4.17 suggest that the less experienced group paid more attention to noticing their errors in Chinese speaking and reviewing recommended resources in self-directed learning than did the experienced respondents. One possible reason for this phenomenon might be that the experienced students might gradually start to use various other learning activities on top of the ones related to these metacognitive strategies as their language proficiency progresses. For instance, their learning experiences might make it easier for these students to learn from their peers' speaking errors, during assessment-task completion, and through online class participation. Similarly, the more experienced respondents might have discovered and chosen to actively access various

Table 4.17 Significant differences in the use of metacognitive strategies in relation to the length of prior learning of Chinese (N = 23)

Metacognitive strategy	LLS item in the survey questionnaire	Learning context	Group mean		Asymp. Sig. (p)
			Yes (57%)	No (43%)	
Self-monitoring (Oxford, 1990)	Try to notice my errors when speaking Chinese and to work out the reason for them	Self-directed learning outside the online classes	4.00	3.40	.02
Overviewing and linking with known material (Oxford, 1990)	Review the resources that are recommended in the online Chinese courses		3.54	2.60	.03

Note: 'Yes' means 'less experienced Chinese learners', < 6 months; 'No' means 'more experienced Chinese learners', >= 6 months.

online resources throughout their Chinese study, and therefore would not be limited to reviewing only the recommended learning resources ('*Overviewing and linking with known material*').

The interview results complement the survey results and suggest that the length of prior learning of Chinese also influenced the ways in which some participants used one social ('*Asking for correction*') and one cognitive strategy ('*Using resources for receiving and sending messages*'). In relation to learner experience, it was also interesting to note from the interview data that an experienced student, S15, used to seek immediate feedback on tones and pronunciation from native Chinese speakers, an approach related to the social strategy '*Asking for correction*'. However, he reported that, over time, he had gradually used this social strategy less and relied more on using an e-dictionary to help learn and improve his pronunciation and understanding of vocabulary, which is related to a cognitive strategy of '*Using resources for receiving and sending messages*'.

This transition suggests that the student became more confident in his Chinese pronunciation over time, and that the provision of standard pronunciation in tools like an e-dictionary also facilitated this transition. Furthermore, as he advanced from beginner to intermediate level, his shift of learning focus also contributed to this transition. He explained that he focused on pronouncing Chinese correctly when he was a beginner, but as he moved to the intermediate level, his focus shifted to expanding vocabulary, refining the meaning of known words, and learning more advanced grammatical patterns. However, these interview findings do not suggest that S15 might have used the social strategy '*Asking for correction*' less frequently, as he may have employed this strategy to ask for corrections with essay writing.

The use of the memory strategy '*Creating stories for memorising Chinese character writing*' was also, according to the interview results, influenced by the length of prior learning of Chinese. This strategy refers to learners memorising Chinese characters by creating stories reflecting the shapes of strokes and the meaning of the components in a Chinese character, such as using the story 'one person supports another person' to memorise '人 (which means "human being" in English)', and the story 'one person follows another person' to memorise '从 (which means "follow" in English)'. This example helps explain why some learners may learn '从' on the basis of the meaning and shape of '人'. Excerpt 3.4 provided a similar example of the memory-strategy use extracted from the interview data. However, these examples demonstrate that this memory strategy requires that the students accumulate enough vocabulary and knowledge of the language before they are able to use it more frequently. This is why the adoption of this strategy was only reported by the experienced group.

4.4 Summary

This chapter investigated the question of whether certain factors appear to influence learners' LLS use. Findings confirmed that these influencing factors involved some characteristics of the learning contexts (the asynchronous and synchronous environment; the categories of interactants with whom the learners interacted), and some characteristics of the individual learners (the learning motive of being able to communicate with Chinese-speaking friends or family; the goal of attaining a very high level of proficiency and thus being able to work as a translator/interpreter or teach Chinese; age; the amount of prior learning of Chinese). This chapter also sought to explore how and to what extent the students' use of LLSs differed relative to such influencing factors.

By applying Mann–Whitney U tests, a number of significant differences between groups of students were found in the participants' use of one compensation strategy, one social strategy, three cognitive strategies, and four metacognitive strategies, in relation to the four influencing factors of individual-learner characteristics. By employing mean score comparisons and hierarchical clustering analyses, some important (although sometimes not statistically significant) findings emerged from the students' relevant strategy use. The data analyses of the interviews and the observed data helped explain how the participants used LLSs and various learning tools differently in the three learning contexts and with different people. These data analyses also helped uncover the reasons behind the participants' LLS use and their opinions in relation to the effectiveness of different LLSs and learning tools.

References

Brown, H. D. (2007). *Teaching by principles: An interactive approach to language pedagogy* (3rd ed.). White Plains, NY: Pearson Education.

Cohen, A. D. (1998). *Strategies in learning and using a second language*. London, UK: Longman.

Cohen, A. D., & Li, P. (2013). Learning Mandarin in later life: Can old dogs learn new tricks? *Contemporary Foreign Language Studies, 396*(12), 5–14.

Han, J., & Lu, Q. (2018). A correlation study among achievement motivation, goal-setting and L2 learning strategy in EFL context. *English Language Teaching, 11*(2), 5–14. https://doi.org/10.5539/elt.v11n2p5

Hurd, S. (2008). Affective and strategy use in independent language learning. In S. Hurd & T. Lewis (Eds.), *Language learning strategies in independent settings* (pp. 218–236). Bristol, UK: Multilingual Mattters.

Krashen, S. D. (1982). *Principles and practice in second language acquisition.* Oxford, UK: Pergamon.

Matzen, L. E., & Benjamin, A. S. (2009). Remembering words not presented in sentences: How study context changes patterns of false memories. *Memory & Cognition, 37*(1), 52–64. https://doi.org/10.3758/MC.37.1.52

Nation, I. S. P. (2001). *Learning vocabulary in another language.* Cambridge, UK: Cambridge University Press.

Oxford, R. (1990). *Language learning strategies: What every teacher should know.* Boston, UK: Newbury House.

Oxford, R. (1996). Employing a questionnaire to assess the use of language learning strategies. *Applied Language Learning, 7*(1), 25–45.

Saito, R. (2005). Internet chat as collaborative CALL: Language learning strategies in an internet chat class. In B. Bourke, M. Parry, & Y. Watanabe (Eds.), *Innovative practice in Japanese language education* (pp. 55–64). Brisbane, Australia: Queensland University of Technology.

Sepasdar, M., & Soori, A. (2014). The impact of age on using language learning strategies. *International Journal of Education and Literacy Studies, 2*(3), 26–31. https://doi.org/10.7575/aiac.ijels.v.2n.3p.26

Soo, K.-S., & Bonk, C. J. (1998). *Interaction: What does it mean in online distance education?* Retrieved from https://eric.ed.gov/?id=ED428724

White, C. (1995). Autonomy and strategy use in distance foreign language learning. *System, 23*(2), 207–221.

5 Individual LLS reports on the interviewees

5.1 Student 5 (S5)

5.1.1 Background information, learning motives, goals, difficulties, and strengths

Table 5.1 Background information (S5)

Nationality	Australian
First language	English
Age range	Over 40
Course enrolled	Level 1 (CHN11), Study Period 3, 2015
Previous Chinese-language-learning experience	One year self-directed learning Pimsleur Digital Mandarin course
Study hours per week (including online tutorial time)	6 hours 40 minutes to 8 hours 40 minutes

Data source: recorded interview with S5.

Table 5.1 shows S5's background information. S5's first language was English and she lived in Australia. Although S5 enrolled in the beginners' class, she should be considered a lower-beginning-level student because she had learnt Chinese for a year by herself before joining the online Chinese course. This student chose the Pimsleur Digital Mandarin course as part of her self-directed learning materials. In the interview, she reported that she was on Phase 3 of Pimsleur, and the previous two phases had contained a total of 26 lessons.

The motives S5 declared in the survey questionnaire for learning Chinese were:

- To be able to communicate with Chinese-speaking friends or family members;
- As a courtesy for the two Chinese students living with her at the moment;
- For pleasure and interest;
- To improve her career prospects.

In the interview, S5 confirmed these motives and identified her learning goal as being able to hold a conversation in Chinese. She identified her learning strengths as Chinese-speaking and -writing skills. My observations of her performance in the online tutorials also revealed her strengths in pronunciation.

144 *Individual LLS reports on the interviewees*

5.1.2 *The key LLSs used by S5 and the tools used for these LLSs*

The qualitative data for S5 indicated the main contributor to her learning was a positive interest and attitude towards her Chinese learning, as well as more prior learning. Her use of LLSs indicated her awareness of the importance of selecting technological tools, building positive relationship with peers and her Chinese friends, and effective use of key LLSs.

This section mainly focuses on S5's six key LLSs. The data in Table 5.2 from S5's interview, survey, and observed data revealed her learning motives for LLS use, key LLSs, the contexts for her LLS use, the language-learning tools she adopted for the key LLSs, and related LLS categories in the three learning contexts. The interview data with S5 generally corroborated her survey responses in relation to the use of metacognitive, memory, and cognitive strategies. The interview data also highlighted S5's use of specific social strategies, and provided explanations of how and why she used these strategies.

Key LLSs in self-directed learning outside the online classes

The key LLSs that S5 used included '*Using mechanical techniques*', '*Repeating*', and '*Representing sounds in memory*', as shown in the following examples.

The way in which S5 used technological tools for vocabulary learning indicated she made extensive use of cognitive and memory strategies. She selected flashcard apps from a large range of choices to suit her needs for memorising vocabulary and practising pronunciation. For example, she used two flashcard apps: Short-Term Spoken Chinese (an app accompanying the textbook used in the course) and Pinyin Training (an app for mastering tones). Short-Term Spoken Chinese allowed her to review the vocabulary list in the textbook and imitate the pronunciation of those words, whilst the Pinyin Training app helped her improve her accuracy in Pinyin pronunciation.

When learning vocabulary and conversations, S5 stated that she generally preferred audio materials (Pimsleur Digital Mandarin course materials) (see Excerpt 5.1). She combined the cognitive strategy of '*Repeating*' with the memory strategy of '*Representing sounds in memory*'. This was driven by her learning goal of learning conversational Chinese.

Excerpt 5.1 Example of using the strategies of 'Repeating' (cognitive) and 'Representing sounds in memory' (memory) by S5

S5: I listened to those CDs... and you play it and it starts with little sections of – dialogues to listen to, and then it will ask you to repeat certain types of words, how do you say, 'good morning'... and then you get a chance to try to remember, they will model the correct pronunciation, and grammar. (00:01:50 in the recorded interview, S5, 2015)

Table 5.2 Reasons for LLS use, key LLSs, statements, language-learning tools, and related LLS categories in three learning contexts in S5's data

Self-directed learning outside the online classes

Reason for LLS use	Key LLS	Statement (paraphrased for brevity)	Data source (Usage)	Language-learning tool	LLS category
Memorising vocabulary in an effective way	Using mechanical techniques	Memorising words or characters by listening to sound files in flashcard apps over and over again	I	Flashcard app: Intelligent Flashcards STS Chinese; Pinyin Training	Memory
Improving accuracy of pronunciation in vocabulary and conversation	Repeating	Listening to recorded conversations many times	I	Digital Mandarin Language course Pimsleur	Cognitive
	Representing sounds in memory	Remembering phrases by listening to digital resources over and over again	I		Memory

Assessment-task completion (homework, speaking assignment)

Reason for LLS use	Key LLS	Statement (paraphrased for brevity)	Data source (Usage)	Language-learning tool	LLS category
Achieving success in the course	Using resources for receiving and sending messages	Searching online for the meaning of Chinese words	I, SII (H)	E-dictionary app: Google Translate	Cognitive
	Asking for correction	Asking Chinese friends to correct her pronunciation	I	WeChat: text and voice message	Social
	Repeating	Imitating pronunciation	I		Cognitive
	Representing sounds in memory	Remembering sentences by listening to voice messages over and over again	SII (H), I		Memory

Online class participation

Reason for LLS use	Key LLS	Statement (paraphrased for brevity)	Data source (Usage)	Language-learning tool	LLS category
Establishing Relationships with others	Using the tools and modes available to improve communication and interaction	Using emoticons and text chat to interact with others, such as praising other students' speaking, and answering other students' questions	OI	Blackboard: Emoticons (such as smiley face, LOL, and raised hand), text messages	Social

As presented in Excerpt 5.1, S5 used the CDs to help her listen, repeat, answer, and immediately self-check the pronunciations and grammar against the model sentences on the CD. These LLSs evidenced that she was aware of the importance of memorising vocabulary and conversations by rehearing the CDs.

Key LLSs in completing the speaking assignment

When asked how she used LLSs in completing the speaking assignment in the interview, S5 explained how she wrote a draft script. This student relied on using English to draft the script content first, and then translated it into Chinese. She had to check the e-dictionary, which is related to using the cognitive strategy '*Using resources for receiving and sending messages*'. This interviewee also described how she improved her accuracy in pronunciation and intonation by imitating native Chinese friends via WeChat (see Excerpt 5.2). She sent WeChat voice messages to ask two Chinese girls for corrections, and received voice messages back for her to imitate.

Excerpt 5.2 Example of using the strategies of 'Repeating' (cognitive) and 'Representing sounds in memory' (memory) via WeChat by S5

S5: They (the Chinese girls) would answer some questions on WeChat (voice messages) ... I could listen to the recording (voice messages) until I could understand it ... With using WeChat (voice messages), you can listen to it again, and I won't annoy anybody. (01:03:44 in the recording, Interview, S5, 2015)

From this excerpt, it is interesting to discover that using a learning tool (WeChat) may connect the social strategy of '*Asking for corrections*' with a cognitive strategy of '*Repeating*', and a memory strategy of '*Representing sound in memory*'. In other words, WeChat allowed S5 to employ these three LLSs in a creative way to prepare for the speaking assignment and improve her intonation and pronunciation. Additionally, she further explained that this method allowed her to repeat the voice messages without worrying about inconveniencing other people by asking them to repeat themselves.

Key LLSs in online tutorials

As S5 was familiar with Blackboard Collaborate, she could easily concentrate on general classroom interactions with the teacher whilst also communicating with other students using the text chat and emoticons embedded in Blackboard Collaborate. The observations showed that S5 used the text chat and emoticons in three ways to establish relationships with others: (1) responding to the tutor's questions, in English or in Chinese characters; (2) suggesting learning apps and learning materials to other students; and (3) interacting in a friendly or supportive way with other students. When she interacted with others, she:

- praised the other students' speech with emoticons;
- explained the class process using text chat to a student whose internet connection was unstable;
- alerted the classmates to poor audio quality via the text chat;
- helped the teacher to answer other students' questions via the text chat;
- showed other students how to listen to the other learning resources (e.g., the Pimsleur Digital Mandarin course) via the text chat.

Source: observed data from four online classes, S5, 2015

These learning behaviours suggested that S5 was aware that she was building positive and collaborative relationships with the teacher and her peers. Being accepted and valued may help online students feel they are an important part of an online class, which builds their self-esteem and effectively supports cooperation for collaborative language learning.

5.1.3 Summary of S5's LLS report

In summary, S5 was an autonomous learner because she chose appropriate LLSs and learning tools to achieve her learning goals and used those LLSs effectively. In particular, this student noticed the importance of accuracy in pronunciation and intonation for conversational Chinese. Additionally, her case is an example of the benefits to a student (in terms of achieving their goals) of selecting appropriate tools and using them effectively.

On the one side, she employed the memory strategy of '*Using mechanical techniques*' by using flashcard apps, and combined the cognitive strategy of '*Repeating*' and the memory strategy of '*Representing sound in memory*' by using the audio material on Pimsleur. Such tools increased the effectiveness of her strategy in memorising Chinese words and conversations as they promoted studying through active recall for rote memorisation. Representing sound may help students create a sound-based association between what is said in Pimsleur and already known vocabulary and conversations. On the other side, she imitated Chinese friends' WeChat voice messages to prepare for collaboration with her language partner. This type of action may enhance intelligibility during collaboration with a language partner in speaking practice. Lastly, she employed the social strategy of '*Using the tools and modes available to improve communication and interaction*' to establish relationships with other students and the teacher. This social strategy may help to develop positive relationships for collaboration with others in an online learning environment.

5.2 Student 18 (S18)

5.2.1 Background information, learning motives, goals, difficulties, and strengths

Similar to S5, S18 was an Australian English speaker, but he lived in China. This student worked as a full-time primary-school English teacher in a major city in Southwest China. The online Chinese course was an elective course for him as part of his bachelor's degree. Despite being busy, he achieved a high final grade in the online Chinese course. In the interview, he declared that he spent six to eight hours on Chinese learning every week and tried to master both Chinese characters and Pinyin (see Table 5.3).

Table 5.3 Background information (S18)

Nationality	Australian
First language	English
Age range	31–40
Course enrolled	Level 1 (CHN11), Study Period 3, 2015
Previous Chinese-language-learning experience	Had no prior study experience
Study hours per week (including online tutorial time)	6–8 hours

Data source: recorded interview with S18, 2015.

In the survey questionnaire, S18 declared two learning goals:

- I'd like to live and work in a Chinese-speaking country and be able to speak Chinese in most everyday life situations;
- I'd like to attain a high level of proficiency and be able to work as a translator/interpreter or teach Chinese.

This student confirmed his first learning goal regarding speaking Chinese during the interview. This learning goal reflected his current living environment, and coincided with his three learning motives as reported in the survey questionnaire:

- As an intellectual challenge;
- I hope to use it in my present or future work;
- To be able to communicate with Chinese-speaking friends or family.

In addition, in the interview this student stated that he regarded his strengths as speaking Chinese, and Chinese-character recognition. He reported that as a beginning Chinese-language learner, his difficulties were Chinese tones and Chinese-character writing.

S18 wanted to achieve a high level of proficiency and he put substantial effort into online Chinese learning. The Blackboard tracking data from the learner activities on the course site tended to confirm the cognitive effort this student put into studying the provided learning resources. S18's learning activities in Blackboard showed that he downloaded the course materials for self-directed learning (84% of his total hits), checked the announcements (6%), and visited the Discussion Board (3%). These data suggested that this student actively used the learning resources, although he did not participate in online classes at all. Therefore, it can be speculated that he employed cognitive strategies in using these learning resources.

The main learning aspects that emerged from the quantitative and qualitative data for S18 included his noticing the importance of reducing his learning anxiety in China, his belief in 'cross-training' (the term used by S18 to describe constantly making and using flashcards to learn vocabulary), his constant self-evaluation using the online recordings, and his initiative in practising Chinese with Chinese students.

5.2.2 The key LLSs used by S18 and the tools used for these LLSs

S18's interview and survey questionnaire data revealed that this student stressed the use of three metacognitive, one memory, and two affective strategies. Table 5.4 summarises his reasons for LLS use, key LLSs, statements, language-learning tools, and related strategy categories.

Key LLSs in self-directed learning outside the online classes

In order to make his learning more effective, S18 developed a weekly learning routine which related to the use of the metacognitive strategies '*Organising*' and '*Self-evaluating*'. During the interview, this student described three essential elements in the way he organised his weekly learning schedule: reviewing the previous lesson; learning a new lesson; and self-evaluating his learning results. He used tutorial recordings to check whether he was on the right track, thereby consistently using the metacognitive strategy of '*Self-evaluating*'. S18 also reported that Wednesday was the best day to start a week's cycle. This was because the video recordings of the Tuesday online tutorials became available on Wednesday every week. He normally downloaded the tutorial recording every Wednesday and then started to use the recording for self-learning. This was confirmed by the tracking data, which showed that during the whole study period, he spent the greatest number of hours engaging in activities on Wednesdays. As a result, this routine became effective in allowing him to control his learning.

In his learning routine, S18 valued using flashcards to memorise vocabulary, which was related to the memory strategy of '*Using mechanical techniques*'. S18 emphasised the personalisation that was possible when using the KTPict CE flashcard app, which was selected from many similar apps as it corresponded to his learning needs. Compared with other flashcard apps, he claimed that KTPict CE was the most effective tool. Firstly, it allowed him to build and edit his own glossary and thus, put all the new words from the textbook into the app. Secondly, the app showed Chinese characters, confirmed S18's spoken answers, and then provided

Table 5.4 Reasons, key LLSs, statements, language-learning tools, and related LLS category in one learning context in S18's data

Self-directed learning outside the online classes

Reason for LLS use	Key LLS	Statement (paraphrased for brevity)	Data source (Usage)	Language-learning tool	LLS category
Evaluating already learnt Chinese grammar and vocabulary	Organising	Developing a learning routine	I		Metacognitive
	Self-evaluating	Watching video recordings of online classes to check Chinese learning of words and grammar in each lesson of the textbook	SII (H) I	Video recordings: Blackboard tutorial recordings	
Memorising vocabulary in an effective way	Using mechanical techniques	Making flashcards and using them to memorise words	I	Home-made flashcards created using PowerPoint software; Flashcard app: KTPict CE	Memory
		Remembering words or characters by listening to flashcard apps repeatedly	SII (H) I		
Improving conversational Chinese	Seeking practice opportunities	Finding opportunities to talk with native Chinese speakers, such as taxi drivers, Chinese students in English corners	I		Metacognitive
	Taking steps to minimise anxiety when practising	Finding opportunities to talk with unknown native Chinese speakers to reduce speaking anxiety	I		Affective
	Taking risks wisely	Encouraging myself to take risks in Chinese learning	SII (H)		

the Pinyin and English versions of the Chinese characters for self-checking. This learning-tool-selection process showed how this personalised flashcard app met the student's vocabulary-learning requirements.

To practise Chinese speaking, S18 actively sought opportunities to converse with Chinese people, which related to the metacognitive strategy of '*Seeking practice opportunities*'. He attended English-practising corners, where he went equipped with his Chinese book, so that he could help Chinese people speak English there, but also practised his Chinese with them. Unlike other interviewees, S18 preferred to speak Chinese with unknown Chinese native speakers to reduce the stress of speaking Chinese, which related to affective strategies. I identified this strategy as an affective strategy since it helped the student to lower his anxiety (see Excerpt 5.3).

Excerpt 5.3 Example of using the strategy of 'Taking steps to minimise anxiety when practising' (affective) by S18

S18: If I'm getting a taxi, I can speak much better than to someone in my school, for example. Because I don't feel like there is any pressure on me. Or they (my colleagues) try to help me by correcting my words or anything [sic]. I'm not that self-conscious. That's a bit of [a] bad thing to be exposed to every day. (00:02:39, in the recording, Interview, S18, 2015)

This excerpt suggests that S18 tried to build a generally positive atmosphere when practising oral Chinese, which was related to the metacognitive strategy of '*Seeking practice opportunities*', as he consequently sought opportunities to practice Chinese with Chinese people who he did not know.

5.2.3 Summary of S18's LLS report

To sum up, S18 provides an excellent example of how a beginner can use various LLSs to study Chinese by taking advantage of the opportunities available to him whilst living in China. S18 chose to self-manage his LLSs, and his learning outcomes were mostly dependent on the strategies he adopted in the learning routine, such as using the metacognitive strategies of '*Seeking practice opportunities*', '*Organising*', *and* '*Self-evaluating*'. In addition to the use of metacognitive strategies in the routine, this student noticed the importance of sustained effort when employing memory strategies for vocabulary learning, such as '*Using mechanical technique*'. However, S18 acknowledged that speaking Chinese was difficult when living in China. Affecting factors for this were, for example, the fear of errors, social pressure, and local Chinese people's accents. This student recognised these problems and was aware of the need to use affective strategies to boost his self-confidence, such as '*Taking risks wisely*' and '*Taking steps to minimise anxiety when practising*'.

5.3 Student 8 (S8)

5.3.1 Background information, learning motives, goals, difficulties, and strengths

S8 achieved an excellent standard of performance in the course: he attended all online tutorials, completed all the assignments, and performed exceptionally well in the oral test. This interviewee's particular strength in Chinese learning appeared to be speaking Chinese. The recordings of his oral test, the speaking assignment, and the online tutorials suggested that he pronounced Chinese words correctly and had mastered the Chinese tones accurately. Table 5.5 shows S8's background information.

Table 5.5 Background information (S8)

Nationality	*Australian; British; American*
First language	English
Age range	Over 40
Course enrolled	Level 1 (CHN12), Study Period 3, 2015
Previous Chinese-language-learning experience	14 months self-learning Pimsleur Digital Mandarin course
Study hours per week (including online tutorial time)	10–12 hours

Data source: recorded interview with S8, 2015.

According to the interview, this student was currently working in a Chinese-speaking country, and he believed that he had benefited from working and living in Chinese-speaking countries with regard to his Chinese learning. For example, he had worked in China for nearly five months and travelled to 72 cities in China. When travelling to these cities he constantly sought opportunities to speak Chinese through different methods. For instance, talking with Chinese colleagues, ordering coffee and lunch in Chinese shops, chatting with Chinese taxi drivers, and occasionally chatting with Chinese friends through both audio and text chat on WeChat. He was willing to get in contact with Chinese people to assist with his language learning.

S8 studied Chinese because he needed to use Chinese in Chinese-speaking countries, and he also had a keen interest in Chinese culture. In the survey questionnaire, he selected four learning motives:

- For pleasure and interest;
- As an intellectual challenge;
- I hope to use it in my present or future work;
- To be able to communicate when visiting a Chinese-speaking country.

His learning goal expressed in the survey was: 'I'd like to live and work in a Chinese-speaking country and be able to speak it in most everyday life situations'. Although he achieved an excellent final result, he explained that getting a certificate from the online Chinese course was actually not meaningful for him as his goal was simply to master Chinese as a foreign language, especially conversational Chinese. Hence, S8 spent an enormous amount of time and effort on online Chinese learning, and studied using the learning materials provided by the online course. He reported in the survey questionnaire that he studied Chinese for 10–12 hours a week. The tracking data showed the hours he spent accessing the course materials in Blackboard alone amounted to over 71 hours across the study period. In other words, he spent nearly six hours a week on the online platform and accessed it every day, especially Mondays, Wednesdays, and Thursdays. S8 checked the content items in the online course frequently, and his number of hits for this reached 366, which was the highest number in his class and represented 81% of his total hits. These data suggest that he took the online Chinese course seriously, which also led to his employing relevant cognitive strategies.

The quantitative and qualitative data from S8 show us the benefits of the following: strong interest in learning Chinese, more prior learning, the self-discipline to his learning routine, seeking opportunities to communicate with Chinese people, building positive relationship with peers and his Chinese friends, and creating memory strategies to memorise Chinese characters.

5.3.2 The key LLSs used by S8 and the tools used for these LLSs

The key strategies used by S8 according to his interview data, survey questionnaire data, and additional data are presented in Table 5.6. It also shows his reasons for LLS use, key LLSs, statements, learning tools, and related LLS categories in two learning contexts.

S8 indicated that students needed to take responsibility for their own learning if they expected to be successful in their learning (see Excerpt 5.4). This was why he stressed the importance of self-teaching and full preparation before attending the online tutorials. He treated the student's role as that of a teacher who teaches themselves in online Chinese learning. Hence, this student developed a learning routine for self-teaching. In the routine, he was particularly aware of the importance of choosing learning resources for listening and speaking Chinese.

Excerpt 5.4 S8's understanding of the learner role in online Chinese learning

S8: this (the tutorial) is not a teaching environment, like a normal school class, this is an environment where all of what you do is as a teacher, what they learn during the week, so they come into the tutorial and they should have prepared their speech and you (the tutor) can correct them with what they were reading. If they come to the class and are unprepared, it will be absolutely useless, it will have no value whatsoever... It is indirective learning; it is absolutely indirect learning. You have to teach yourself to learn. (00:18:31 in the recording, Interview, S8, 2015)

Table 5.6 Reasons for LLS use, key LLSs, statements, language-learning tools, and related LLS categories in two learning contexts in S8's data

Self-directed learning outside the online classes

Reason for LLS use	Key LLS	Statement (paraphrased for brevity)	Data source (Usage)	Language-learning tool	LLS category
Improving conversational Chinese	Organising	Developing a learning routine	I		Metacognitive
	Seeking practice opportunities	Finding opportunities to talk with native Chinese speakers	SII (H)		
		Listening to MP3s and podcasts in Chinese	I	MP3: podcast in Chinese	
		Watching children's videos, online Chinese courses on YouTube	SII (H)	YouTube: short video of online Chinese lessons	
Expanding vocabulary by listening and imitating conversation	Repeating	Listening to recorded conversations many times	I	Digital Mandarin course Pimsleur	Cognitive
	Representing sounds in memory	Remembering phrases by listening to digital resources over and over again	I		Memory
Memorising vocabulary in an effective way	Creating stories to memorise Chinese-character writing	Memorising Chinese characters by creating stories reflecting the meaning of strokes in a Chinese character	I		Memory

Assessment-task completion (homework, speaking assignment)

Reason for LLS use	Key LLS	Statement (paraphrased for brevity)	Data source (Usage)	Language-learning tool	LLS category
Achieving success in the course	Cooperating with peers	Collaborating with a language partner to draft and practise a speaking assignment	I		Social
	Seeking feedback from native speakers	Seeking feedback on an initial written draft from Chinese teacher or friends	I		
	Asking for clarification or verification	Asking the teacher questions about homework	AD		
	Netiquette	Respecting my language partner's time when we work together	I	WeChat: images, emojis, text and voice messages	
	Using resources for receiving and sending messages	Collecting, selecting, and modifying conversations in a series of videos online	I		Cognitive
		Searching online for the meaning of Chinese words	SII (H)	E-dictionary app: Screwit	

Key LLSs in self-directed learning outside the online classes

S8 had a well-organised learning routine for self-learning, especially for practising listening and speaking (see Table 5.7). The routine contained the learning activities, durations, and his opinion of the learning activities. This routine involved 10–12 hours learning every week, around one to two hours per day.

This routine was based on a detailed schedule and it appears that S8 developed its use into a habit, since he followed the routine for the whole study period. Consequently, metacognitive strategies appeared to be significant for his learning, such as '*Organising*' and '*Seeking practice opportunities*'. Additionally, his decisions about what kinds of learning activities to engage in indicated that this student expected to expand his vocabulary through listening and understanding conversations.

S8 highlighted the importance of his learning routine and self-discipline as the key to that routine. He believed his self-discipline was a learning habit formed through his long working experience of completing high-quality work on time, and giving detailed presentations. When I inquired what learning resources attracted him and how he used these resources, he outlined his use of the Pimsleur Digital Mandarin course (a type of digital resource) and commented on it as being 'incredibly helpful', 'convenient', and 'surprisingly effective'. He claimed that he was an auditory rather than a visual learner and that was the reason he had used the Pimsleur course over 14 months. The CDs contained classroom conversations between a teacher and two or three students, which allowed S8 to pretend to be a student in the class and respond to the teacher's questions. He then repeatedly practised listening, imitating, and speaking Chinese using the CDs. These descriptions suggested that S8 noticed his learning style and then employed the cognitive strategies of '*Repeating*' and '*Representing sound in memory*'.

According to S8, the most difficult aspect of learning written Chinese characters was memorising them, as he often 'quickly forgot'. He commented on the fact that he could use the LLS '*Creating stories for memorising Chinese-character writing*' effectively; an example was shown in Excerpt 3.4 and discussed in Section 3.2.5.

Table 5.7 S8's daily Chinese-language-learning routine

Learning activity	Duration	S8's opinions
Watching children's videos, online Chinese courses on YouTube	15 minutes	Slow and clear speech in the children's videos was good for his understanding
Listening to MP3, podcasts, etc. in Chinese	15 minutes	Convenient for listening
Chatting with Chinese people in local shops for a coffee or lunch	Not clear	Utilising Chinese language there; can hear Mandarin with different accents
Studying Chinese characters and words	30 minutes	Convenient and effective for memorising vocabulary
Complete coursework such as online quizzes, weekly exercises, video viewing, occasionally with a language partner	1–2 hours; Adjustable	Fully follow the course requirements, complete them before attending online tutorials

Data source: recorded interview with S8, 2015.

156 Individual LLS reports on the interviewees

Key LLSs in completing the weekly homework and speaking assignment

'*Asking for clarification or verification*' was regarded by S8 as an efficient social strategy for completing the weekly homework, and it was one that he frequently used. This student used WeChat as a learning tool to send a combination of images, emojis, voice, and text messages. Figure 5.1 shows S8's process for asking for clarification and receiving immediate teacher feedback. This figure shows that the student sent an image message, two text messages, and a voice message to ask a question about an online quiz, and the teacher used two voice messages to answer his question. The use of multiple types of messages made the interaction efficient, as the student avoided the step of describing the question in words.

S8 achieved a high score in the speaking assignment and the oral test, both of which required him to collaborate with a language partner and related to the social strategy of '*Cooperating with peers*'. S8's learning behaviours can be gleaned from the interview and survey data regarding his successful collaboration with his peers.

On the one hand, S8 maintained strong relationships with others by using the social strategies of '*Netiquette*' and '*Asking for clarification or verification*'. He sought feedback on his initial written draft from a Chinese teacher. In addition, he did not mind actively communicating with other distance learners first rather than waiting for their invitations.

On the other hand, he revealed in the interview that relying on himself to complete the assignment and lowering his expectations of the language partner were essential for successful collaborative learning. These were illustrated by his use of affective strategies to discern negative attitudes and emotions. For instance, he experienced an incident at the end of the study period when his first language partner suddenly quit the course whilst they were preparing for the final oral test preparation. S8 kept working on his final oral test preparation until he found a second language partner.

When drafting the speaking assignment, S8 reported that he frequently employed the cognitive strategy of '*Using resources for receiving and sending messages*'. He used this strategy not only to search for information about Chinese words, but also when

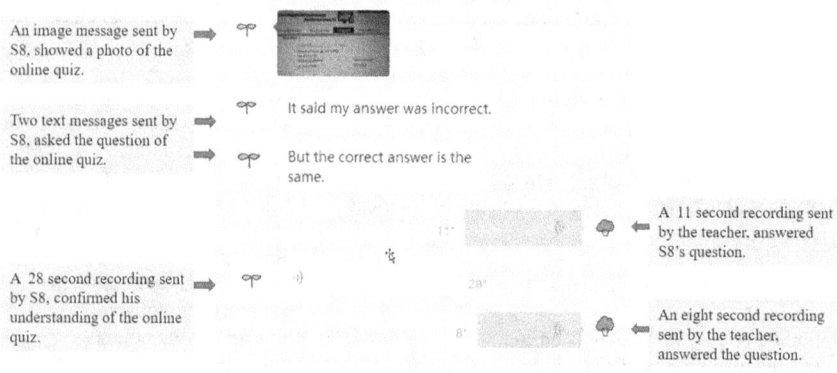

Figure 5.1 An example of using the social strategy of 'Asking for clarification or verification' via WeChat messages by S8

researching conversations in online Chinese videos when writing up his script for the speaking assignment. He listened to the conversations in these videos, collected some Chinese words, phrases, and word orders, and modified them for his own draft. The interview data evidenced that the student imitated Chinese speaking and writing from word level (e.g., pronunciation) to sentence level (e.g., phrases, sentence structure).

5.3.3 Summary of S8's LLS report

Overall, S8 was an autonomous distance-learning student who exhibited positive learning behaviour by developing a competent learning routine. This routine reflected his consideration that his learning style would benefit from structuring his study time and planning the learning activities. As an adult aged over 40, his success in online Chinese-language learning evidenced his strength in self-discipline when using the metacognitive strategies of '*Organising*' and '*Seeking practice opportunities*'. He also demonstrated excellent use of social strategies when collaborating with peers and teachers, such as '*Cooperating with peers*', '*Netiquette*', and '*Seeking feedback from native speakers*'. At the same time, the interactive learning tools (e.g., WeChat) enhanced his efficiency in using these social strategies. Finally, his use of cognitive and memory strategies for expanding vocabulary showed his cognitive effort and creativeness, such as '*Creating stories for memorising Chinese-character writing*' and '*Using resources for receiving and sending messages*'.

5.4 Student 9 (S9)

5.4.1 Background information, learning motives, goals, difficulties, and strengths

Whilst S9 was not studying Chinese in a Chinese-speaking country, the class observations showed that he made a significant improvement in accuracy in pronunciation. This interviewee attended seven out of the eight online tutorials, occasionally leaving early for personal reasons. As evidenced by his performance in the online tutorials, completion of all assessment tasks and frequent email exchanges with the tutor, he took Chinese learning seriously. Table 5.8 lists his background information.

Table 5.8 Background information (S9)

Nationality	Australian
First language	English
Age range	Over 40
Course enrolled	Level 1 (CHN12), Study Period 3, 2015
Previous Chinese-language-learning experience	Three-month online Chinese course in CHN11
Study hours per week (including online tutorial time)	4–6 hours

Data source: recorded interview with S9, 2015.

158 *Individual LLS reports on the interviewees*

This student reported five learning motives:

- For pleasure and interest;
- As an intellectual challenge;
- To be able to communicate with Chinese-speaking friends or family;
- To be able to communicate when visiting a Chinese-speaking country;
- Avoid dementia.

His main learning motive was to speak conversational Chinese in the interview. He was interested in travelling and wanted to learn six foreign languages offered by OUA in the coming years – Chinese, Japanese, Spanish, Italian, Indonesian, and an Aboriginal Australian language.

He had two learning goals, as follows:

- Get a taste of the language and culture;
- To be able to use Chinese for simple conversations and to obtain information when travelling in a Chinese-speaking country.

The main learning aspects that evolved from the quantitative and qualitative data for S9 included heavy reliance on the online Chinese courses, using fragmented time to learn Chinese, awareness of the importance of netiquette in online interaction, and constantly imitating native speakers' pronunciation.

5.4.2 The key LLSs used by S9 and the tools used for these LLSs

The interview and observed data demonstrated that this student employed metacognitive strategies to develop a learning routine and used social strategies to collaborate with his language partner. As shown in Table 5.9, he also employed cognitive strategies to help improve pronunciation and review vocabulary and grammar.

Key LLSs in self-directed learning outside the online classes

According to the interview data, S9 employed the metacognitive strategy of '*Organising*' to ensure that he completed all the assignment tasks on time. To be more specific, he listed all the deadlines of the assignments on his calendar and ticked them off one by one as he completed them. More importantly, if the deadline of the assessment task was close, he would sacrifice other commitments to complete the assessment.

Using fragmented time to learn Chinese was a special aspect of S9's learning routine, as he said in Excerpt 5.5. He could only focus on learning for 10 to 15 minutes at a time, but made sure to have two to three hours a day spent on learning Chinese.

Table 5.9 Reasons for LLS use, key LLSs, statements, language-learning tools, and related LLS categories in three learning contexts by S9

Self-directed learning outside the online classes

Reason for LLS use	Key LLS	Statement (paraphrased for brevity)	Data source (Usage)	Language-learning tool	LLS category
Achieving success in the course	Organising	Developing a learning routine	I SII (H)		Metacognitive
Memorising vocabulary in an effective way	Using mechanical techniques	Using fragmented time to learn Chinese Memorising words or characters by listening to sound files in flashcard apps over and over again	I SII (H) I	Flashcard app: Pleco, Google Translate, and Youdao	Memory

Assessment tasks completion (speaking assignment, oral test)

Reason for LLS use	Key LLS	Statement (paraphrased for brevity)	Data source (Usage)	Language-learning tool	LLS category
Achieving success in the course	Cooperat-ing with peers	Collaborating with a language partner to draft and practise a speaking assignment	I SII (H)	Blackboard Collaborate	Social
Establishing relationships with others	Netiquette	Responding quickly: responding to language partner's and tutor's emails within 24 hours	I	Email	

Online class participation

Reason for LLS use	Key LLS	Statement (paraphrased for brevity)	Data source (Usage)	Language-learning tool	LLS category
Reviewing already learnt Chinese vocabulary and grammar	Taking notes	Taking notes for updating lecture notes before and after online tutorials	I		Cognitive
Improving pronunciation	Repeating	Imitating the tutor's Chinese pronunciation, tones, and intonation	OI SII (H) I		

> **Excerpt 5.5 Using fragmented time for language learning (S9)**
>
> *S9: I've never been a student who can sit down thoroughly, and concentrate two hours on book work. I'm ten fifteen minutes, go away, do this, and ten fifteen minutes go away, come back. (00:15:06 in the recording, Interview, S9, 2015)*

Similar to other interviewees (S5, S18, S8), S9 reported using learning apps to search for and memorise vocabularies, which related to the strategies '*Using mechanical techniques*' (memory) and '*Using resources for receiving and sending messages*' (cognitive). He installed five apps (e.g., Pleco) with various functions to maximise his fragmented time for vocabulary learning. For example, to save time, instead of typing, S9 used the scanner function on the apps to record the Pinyin, the English meaning, and the pronunciation of the Chinese words for memorising.

Key LLSs in completing a speaking assignment and an oral test

In terms of his collaboration with his language partners for the speaking assignments, S9 was identified as a great language partner by his two classmates (Excerpt 5.6). They complimented him in the interviews as follows:

> **Excerpt 5.6 Language partners' comments to S9**
>
> *Language partner 1: S9 still wants to retain me as a language partner, even [though] I was very behind ... So yeah, I think he is very surprised. He did very well. (Data source: recorded interview, language partner 1, 2015)*
> *Language partner 2: S9 was really nice to work with, because he is ... if you say to him to do something, you know, he runs his business... if you say to him, can you do this, he says yes, and then he'll do it. So we have a good relationship. (Data source: recorded interview, language partner 2, 2015)*

This excerpt demonstrated that S9 was tolerant and willing to contribute to the collaboration processes. These can be seen as essential aspects of using the social strategy of '*Cooperating with peers*'. Also, S9 was aware of the importance of manners during the collaboration and used the strategy of '*Netiquette*', thus the excerpt evidenced the effect of the social-strategy use.

Email was the only channel S9 used to communicate with his language partners and the tutors outside class. The email correspondence between the tutor and S9 shows that he replied to his tutor's emails within 24 hours. This evidenced that he employed the social strategy of '*Netiquette*'. Consequently, it was his quick reactions and willingness to collaborate in learning that led his language partners to cooperate with him and feel obliged to keep up with him or offer help.

Key LLSs in online classes

Two key LLSs were found in S9's strategy use in online classes: the cognitive strategies of '*Taking notes*' and '*Repeating*'. Taking notes was seen by S9 as an important LLS and he liked to constantly update his notes before and after the online tutorials. In an email, he made a special request about note submission, wanting to add more notes into his lecture notes after the online classes for future reviewing. In addition, according to the observed data, S9 employed the cognitive strategy of '*Repeating*' to imitate the tutor's Chinese pronunciation; this was confirmed in the interview. As he was keen to improve his pronunciation by imitating a native speaker, this might be one important reason for the improvement of his pronunciation and intonation.

5.4.3 Summary of S9's LLS report

In short, S9's LLS adoption in his online Chinese learning suggested that he trusted the quality of the online Chinese course, preferred following the course instructions, and his LLS adoption therefore related to assessment-task completion and textbook learning. He continuously utilised cognitive and memory strategies to improve grammar, tones, pronunciation, and intonation whilst working on assessment tasks. The use of technological learning tools improved the efficiency of these strategies. He employed metacognitive strategies to develop a learning routine and adjusted it to better accommodate the way he learnt, such as by taking into account his short attention-span range of 10–15 minutes. During collaboration with his language partners, he was highly sociable and keen to learn from his peers, which demonstrated his use of social strategies.

5.5 Student 10 (S10)

5.5.1 Background information, learning motives, goals, difficulties, and strengths

S10 was different to other interviewees in terms of her ethnic background. She was a Philippines-born Chinese student who had migrated to Australia as a child, and she could speak four languages (see Table 5.10). After she moved to Australia, she started to learn English, and gradually mastered it for study and work. She had studied Mandarin from kindergarten until Year Four in the Philippines and then studied it again for four-to-five years at a weekend Chinese school in Australia starting when she was around nine or ten years old. She was able to speak Chinese with the standard tones of a native Chinese speaker. In the interview, she mentioned that she did not have enough time to study Chinese and seldom attended the online tutorials. In addition, she often flew overseas for work commitments, and therefore, this influenced her collaboration with her language partner and resulted in less use of LLSs.

S10 easily understood the tutor's instructions during the online tutorials and the oral test. However, she stated that the most difficult aspect of learning Chinese was

162 *Individual LLS reports on the interviewees*

Table 5.10 Background information (S10)

Nationality	Australian
Main language	Min Nan (a Chinese dialect); Bisaya (a Filipino dialect)
Foreign languages	English; Chinese
Age range	31–40
Course enrolled	Level 1 (CHN12), Study Period 3, 2015
Previous Chinese-language-learning experience	9–10 years
Study hours per week (including online tutorial time)	Up to 2 hours

Data source: recorded interview with S10, 2015.

listening, because she believed she could not answer the questions quickly enough. She decided to review Mandarin with the online Chinese courses, and mainly focused on Chinese speaking and simplified-Chinese-character recognition. In the survey questionnaire, she reported four motives for learning Chinese:

- Learn the Pinyin system;
- Communicate with family members;
- Learn simplified Chinese characters;
- Learn conversational Chinese.

She hoped to speak fluent Chinese to communicate with family members. She used to learn Chinese in traditional Chinese characters but she hoped she would also be able to recognise simplified Chinese characters. As she often travelled to Chinese-speaking countries, she noticed Mandarin and Chinese characters were widely used in these countries.

The main learning aspects arising from the quantitative and qualitative data for S10 included initiative in speaking Chinese at home, watching Chinese TV programmes, constant self-evaluation, and use of note-taking.

5.5.2 *The key LLSs used by S10 and the tools used for these LLSs*

Although S10's attendance was erratic, she spoke Chinese at home, and enjoyed watching Chinese TV programmes to improve her oral Chinese. She therefore had opportunities to use the relevant cognitive and social strategies. As shown in Table 5.11, she also employed a metacognitive strategy to evaluate her Chinese learning. Additionally, this student took notes of new words and grammar points, which was a learning behaviour derived from her past language-learning experience.

Key LLSs in self-directed learning outside the online classes

In the interview, S10 reported on her strategies for coping with difficulties in learning Chinese, which included making conscious efforts to maximise her exposure

Table 5.11 Reasons for LLS use, key LLSs, statements, language-learning tools, and related LLS categories in two learning contexts by S10

Self-directed learning outside the online classes

Reason for LLS use	Key LLS	Statement (paraphrased for brevity)	Data source (Usage)	Language-learning tool	LLS category
Improving listening and speaking	Practising naturalistically	Watching Chinese TV programmes and movies; speaking Chinese with family members	I	TV	Cognitive
	Self-evaluating	Evaluating Chinese by understanding Chinese TV programmes and script recognition	I	TV	Metacognitive

Assessment-task completion (speaking assignment, oral test)

| Achieving success in the course | Cooperating with peers | Completing writing and speaking assignments with a language partner | I | | Social |
| Establishing relationships with others | Cooperating with peers | Offering or giving corrections on the language partner's written draft | I | Word document | Social |

Online class participation

| Writing down grammar and vocabulary points | Taking notes | Writing notes on the textbook | I
SII (H) | | Cognitive |

164 *Individual LLS reports on the interviewees*

to Chinese. She talked with family members in Chinese and watched Chinese TV programmes and movies. The cognitive strategy '*Practising naturalistically*' relates to these activities. She received immediate feedback from family members, which helped her correct grammar errors in speaking. When talking about the TV programmes and movies, she said that she listened to the conversations on the TV shows, read through the Chinese subtitles, picked some sentences from the subtitles, and tried to understand the culture.

Through watching Chinese movies and interacting with family members, S10 also self-evaluated her Chinese learning, which related to the metacognitive strategy of '*Self-evaluating*', as shown in Excerpt 4.3. If she could understand the conversation in the movies or with her family, then she felt confident in her progress. S10 paid more attention to this type of practical evaluation than to just looking at her scores in the assessment tasks.

Key LLSs in completing the speaking assignment

S10 was a standout in the speaking assignment. When she cooperated with her language partner in completing the speaking assignment, she offered to help language partner, whose Chinese writing was not as good as hers. This related to the social strategy of '*Cooperating with peers*'. Hurd (2008) identified this strategy as an important collaborative strategy of '*Offering or giving corrections*', as it was the most frequently used strategy in Hurd and Lewis's research (2008). She corrected her language partner's initial draft, not only for the grammar errors but also problems with logic in Chinese writing.

Key LLSs in online classes

According to the interview data, when S10 attended the online classes, '*Taking notes*' was an essential strategy as it related to her previous learning experience. In class time, she focused on looking at the PowerPoint (PPT) slides and listening to the tutor speaking. To make sure her learning was more effective she wrote notes of the tones and example sentences. S10 explained that she used this strategy as a learning behaviour. Her Chinese teachers in the past had always encouraged her to write notes and review these notes to aid in language learning. From the online class observations, it appears that taking notes may have caused students to lose the thread of the conversations, making them hesitant to speak. However, if the student is an effective listener then this strength may help to mitigate the disadvantages of this strategy.

5.5.3 Summary of S10's LLS report

In summary, S10 had limited learning time but was still able to achieve her ideal result. This was because she already had a basic vocabulary foundation and benefited from the Chinese-speaking environment she lived in. Her LLS adoption in the online Chinese course was strongly influenced by her learning motives, her past language-learning experiences, and her current family environment. She liked to employ the strategy of '*Taking notes*', and also received corrections from family members. Additionally, S10's collaboration with her language partner and her offering to help with her partner's writing was another strategy that improved her Chinese-language learning, although improving her own learning may not have been an outcome she was conscious of. It is important that language partners in their collaborations distribute and negotiate their work according to their strengths and motives. This distribution may help them extend the value of collaboration rather than simply using it as a way to divide the work.

5.6 Student 12 (S12)

5.6.1 Background information, learning motives, goals, difficulties, and strengths

S12 was an Australian university student majoring in law. This student had previously successfully completed a one-month intensive Chinese-language course and CHN11, as presented in Table 5.12. She therefore had a foundation of vocabulary, which she mentioned in the interview: 'I think the new words in the textbook, many of the words, I – already knew'. At the time of the interview, she was studying in China for an exchange programme. She reported that she could not attend the online tutorials and download the video materials because of her poor internet connection. This also affected her weekly homework submission and the collaboration with her language partner.

Table 5.12 Background information (S12)

Nationality	Australian
First language	English
Age range	21–30
Course enrolled	Level 1 (CHN12), Study Period 3, 2015
Previous Chinese-language-learning experience	Four months learning Chinese followed by an intensive Chinese-language course and CHN11
Study hours per week (including online tutorial time)	Up to 2 hours

Data source: recorded interview with S12, 2015.

S12 reported four learning motives and two learning goals in the survey questionnaire. The four learning motives were:

- For pleasure and interest;
- To improve my career prospects;
- I hope to use it in my present or future work;
- To be able to communicate with Chinese-speaking friends or family.

166 *Individual LLS reports on the interviewees*

The two learning goals were:

- I'd like to live and work in a Chinese-speaking country and be able to speak it in most everyday life situations;
- I'd like to attain a very high level of proficiency and be able to work as a translator/interpreter or teach Chinese.

When talking about the difficulties of collaborating with her language partner, she pointed out that understanding the language partner's pronunciation and scheduling time to align with the language partner's availability were two such difficulties. The main learning aspects that stood out in the quantitative and qualitative data for S12 included a high level of learning goals, actively building Chinese friend circle, and strategy change from Australia to China.

5.6.2 *The key LLSs used by S12 and the tools used for these LLSs*

Table 5.13 shows S12's key LLSs, reasons for the strategies, statements, relevant tools, and related LLS categories. This interviewee employed metacognitive and social strategies to interact with her Chinese friends and to practise speaking Chinese in China.

Key LLSs in self-directed learning outside the online classes

Similar to most of the interviewees, S12 employed the memory strategy '*Using mechanical techniques*' and the cognitive strategy '*Using resources for sending and receiving messages*' by using the learning tool Pleco for self-learning. She used Pleco as an e-dictionary, to search for the meaning and pronunciation of new words as well as example sentences including them, and she used three input methods: Pinyin, finger writing, and English, depending on her knowledge of the new words. She liked to write the Chinese characters stroke by stroke as well as example sentences including the characters to review later. The interview and survey questionnaire data suggested that S12 tried to search for answers online and was keen to memorise vocabulary.

Her adoption of social strategies was unique among the interviewees because of the exchange programmes she had taken in China. Unlike other interviewees who lived in China, she had the opportunity to access a group of Chinese students and had actively built a friendship circle with them online using WeChat. Figure 5.2 shows an example of this type of interaction with a Chinese friend via WeChat.

During the interview, S12 shared her WeChat Moments with me and I saw that she posted personal photos and described them using sentences in English and Chinese. I identified this as the social strategy '*Using the tools and modes available to improve communication and interaction*', which is distinctly different from Oxford's social strategies. This strategy was one of the socio-environmental strategies identified by Hauck and Hampel (2008), in which students created opportunities

Table 5.13 Reasons for LLS use, key LLSs, statements, language-learning tools, and related LLS categories in two learning contexts in S12's data

Self-directed learning outside the online classes

Reason for LLS use	Key LLS	Statement (paraphrased for brevity)	Data source (Usage)	Language-learning tool	LLS category
Achieving success in the course	Seeking practice opportunities	Attending exchange programmes in China and chatting with lots of Chinese friends	I		Metacognitive
	Using resources for sending and receiving messages	Using the Pleco app as an e-dictionary to search for the meaning and pronunciation of Chinese words	SII (H)	E-dictionary and flashcard app: Pleco	Cognitive
	Using mechanical techniques	Memorising words or characters by listening to sound files from flashcard apps over and over again	I		Memory
Establishing relationships with others	Using the tools and modes available to improve communication and interaction	Sharing photos and comments on the photos in a private Chinese friend circle	I	WeChat moments	Social

Assessment-task completion (speaking assignment)

Reason for LLS use	Key LLS	Statement (paraphrased for brevity)	Data source (Usage)	Language-learning tool	LLS category
Achieving success in the course	Sharing Chinese friend resources with the language partner	Asking her language partner whether she can help them, such as by providing feedback on the language partner's pronunciation	I		Social
	Self-monitoring	Asking native Chinese speakers to provide feedback on her written draft	I		Metacognitive

168 *Individual LLS reports on the interviewees*

Figure 5.2 An example of an interaction with Chinese friends via WeChat Moments

to interact with Chinese friends. This interviewee observed her Chinese friends' interactive tool and then used it to virtually experience life in China and respond to comments in Chinese.

Key LLSs in completing the speaking assignment

According to the interview data, seeking feedback from native Chinese speakers was an essential step for S12 in completing the speaking assignment and the written assignment. This related to a metacognitive strategy of '*Self-monitoring*'. She asked her friends to provide initial feedback on her written drafts and to help script and record standard conversations for imitation.

However, she made a negative comment about her collaboration with her language partner. As Chinese is a tone language, she could not understand her language partner's Chinese pronunciation when he mispronounced tones during the speaking practice. In order to protect her language partner's self-esteem, she sent him a recording made by her Chinese friend for his own self-correction, as shown in Excerpt 5.7.

This strategy was identified as a social strategy of 'Sharing with other students' specific to online collaboration. This can be understood as an example of collaborative learning strategies as set out by Stickler and Lewis (2008), as it contributes to the achievements of both students. The result of S12's social strategy was that their

> **Excerpt 5.7 S12's suggestion to her language partner of using the cognitive strategy 'Repeating'**
>
> *S12: ... we practised our dialogue together, and I honestly couldn't understand anything he said... so instead of trying to correct him, I got one of my friends (a Chinese friend), who recorded him [himself] doing the recording. So he completed the dialogue, and I sent it back to my language partner... And I said to him, 'Perhaps you should practise following my friend's recording?' (00:35:02 in the recording, Interview, S12, 2015).*

performance in the speaking assignment and her language partner's pronunciation were improved. This strategy appeared to help them enhance their speaking practice and establish a better relationship during collaboration.

5.6.3 Summary of S12's LLS report

Summing up, S12 presents an example of how a student responded to environment change and LLS adoption after she had participated in an international exchange programme to China. Although the survey data indicated that she did not employ any social strategies in online classes, the interview data demonstrated that she used social strategies to interact with Chinese friends and her language partner. This change is mainly reflected in social-strategy adoption, as she tended to employ social strategies rather than cognitive strategies after her arrival in China. This change did not diminish the importance of Chinese to S12, however. The reason behind the strategy change relates to the role of Chinese in different language-learning environments. In Australia, Chinese was an academic subject for S12 and she needed to utilise cognitive strategies to cope with the exams. Whilst in China, she increased her Chinese vocabulary and socialised with Chinese university students to improve her spoken Chinese. The exchange programme provided opportunities to access local students, and she employed social strategies to solve communicative problems. More importantly, she actively built a friendship circle and immersed herself in both the real-life language environment and a virtual environment by using WeChat. This circle of friends positively increased the strength and frequency of her social-strategy adoption.

5.7 Student 13 (S13)

5.7.1 Background information, learning motives, goals, difficulties, and strengths

S13 lived in Korea and was the only interviewee who lived in a non-Chinese- or a non-English-speaking environment. This interviewee had studied at an Australian university for nearly four years in order to achieve a bachelor's degree in

170 *Individual LLS reports on the interviewees*

Table 5.14 Background information (S13)

Nationality	Korean
First language	Korean
Age range	31–40
Course enrolled	Level 1 (CHN12), Study Period 3, 2015
Previous Chinese-language-learning experience	Level 1 (CHN11)
Study hours per week (including online tutorial time)	Up to 2 hours

Data source: recorded interview with S13, 2015.

accounting. As an experienced online learner, he had completed CHN11, a prerequisite for CHN12, and was therefore familiar with Blackboard and the online course requirements (see Table 5.14).

The data seemed to suggest that S13 had low expectations about Chinese learning when he studied CHN12. He selected one learning motivation in the survey questionnaire, 'For pleasure and interest'. The learning goal was 'I'd like to be able to use Chinese for simple conversations and obtaining information when travelling in a Chinese-speaking country'. In the interview, S13 claimed that the main reason he was learning Chinese was for his future career. He would like to work overseas and might use Chinese for simple conversations when travelling in a Chinese-speaking country. However, he had a full-time job in Korea and was studying four courses at that time. Thus, he could only learn Chinese for two hours a week, and could not attend the online classes.

The main learning aspects derived from the quantitative and qualitative data for S13 included low tone accuracy, use of a learning routine, lack of Chinese-speaking environment, and limited use of strategies.

5.7.2 *The key LLSs used by S13 and the tools used for these LLSs*

As shown in Table 5.15, S13 used three key LLSs in self-directed learning outside the online classes, namely, '*Organising*', '*Using recourses for sending and receiving messages*', and '*Self-evaluating*'. The table also presents his reasons for strategy use, statements, language-learning tools, and related strategy categories in self-directed learning outside the online classes.

It is apparent from the table that very few key strategies were reported in the interview and survey questionnaire data. These data suggest that the student mainly focused on the assessment-task completion, tried to search for answers online, but did not use social strategies due to his isolated learning environment.

Key LLSs in self-directed learning outside the online classes

S13 had a strict learning routine based around the materials provided by the course and assessment-task completion. He gave a rating of 5 (always or almost always true

Table 5.15 Reasons for LLS use, key LLSs, statements, language-learning tools, and related LLS categories in one learning context in S13's data

Self-directed learning outside the online classes					
Reason for LLS use	Key LLS	Statement (paraphrased for brevity)	Data source (Usage)	Language-learning tool	LLS category
Achieving success in the course	Organising	Developing a learning routine	I SII (H)		Metacognitive
	Self-evaluating	Using the online quiz as the last step to review and evaluate his self-learning	I I	Online quiz	Cognitive
	Using resources to send and receive messages	Searching using online tools to solve learning problems, such as Google Translate, Google	I	Website: Google Translate, Google	Cognitive

of me) to the item 'developing a routine', which related to a metacognitive strategy of '*Organising*'. This strategy was manifested in the routine he developed. This meant that he tried to complete each lesson within a week and followed the same learning process step by step. Excerpt 5.8 shows an example of his learning routine.

> **Excerpt 5.8 Example of using the strategy of 'Organising' (metacognitive) by S13**
>
> *S13: My learning routine, for Chinese, – was – I firstly attempt to see the contents, the weekly contents, provided by professors, online, the material, and then, and next, I go to the online lecture (prerecorded mini-lecture videos), just recites [sic] the notes, just in front of the screen, when I was listening to the lectures, I wrote each of the important points, so it gives [them] step by step, that is easier to follow, you know. (00:22:50 in the recording, Interview, S13, 2015)*

It can be seen from the excerpt that his learning process and routine were all around new words and text learning, listening to the prerecorded mini-lecture videos, writing grammar points, and finally completing the weekly homework and online quizzes.

This student also used the metacognitive strategy of '*Self-evaluating*' in the online quizzes as the last step to evaluate his self-learning. The online tracking data evidenced that S13 submitted the weekly homework and online quizzes earlier than the other students. He explained that he was consciously ahead of the schedule for the purpose of self-checking and reviewing learning content using the online quizzes.

172 *Individual LLS reports on the interviewees*

As a distance student living in Korea, S13 relied on the internet to help him to solve learning problems using the cognitive strategy of '*Using resources for sending and receiving messages*'. Google on his computer and Google Translate on his smartphone were the main technological tools he used. A notable feature of employing this strategy was that this student used both English and Korean to search for the answers to his questions. He seemed to derive more benefit from using two languages than a single language when finding information whilst he was learning Chinese.

5.7.3 Summary of S13's LLS report

To sum up, S13's short-term learning goal (complete the course towards a degree) led to his strategy adoption. He employed metacognitive strategies to help him achieve this learning goal successfully, especially by following a weekly learning routine. However, if he expects to improve his conversational Chinese, as he indicated in his choice of learning goal in the survey, he might need to seek opportunities to use social strategies by interacting with peers and native Chinese speakers more. As Chinese is a tonal language, the correct pitch accent is essential to allow others to understand speakers. Therefore, practising with and receiving immediate feedback from native speakers could be more efficient in helping him attain his goal of speaking better Chinese.

5.8 Student 14 (S14)

5.8.1 Background information, learning motives, goals, difficulties, and strengths

S14 was a polyglot who could speak seven languages, and as such his profile was obviously less common than those other interviewees. His mother tongues were Italian and Hebrew, and Chinese was his seventh language. Although English was one of his foreign languages, he spoke it fluently and used it to learn Chinese and other subjects at university, to communicate with his language partner, and to work full-time as an online fraud investigator in Australia.

Most of the courses that S14 had chosen to study in Australia were related to Chinese historical, economic, and social contexts. He claimed that they had deepened his understanding and love of Chinese. Although these courses were taught in English, they would have improved his understanding of China and his interactions with Chinese people. Learning Chinese also involves learning Chinese culture more effectively. In the interview, he expressed his increasing feelings about how he liked Chinese because of his study of China-related subjects: '*I found it's interesting, the more you studied, the more you like it*'.

Table 5.16 presents S14's background information. He was an intermediate-level student, was awarded an excellent final grade for the course and received full marks on the weekly homework and the written assignment.

According to the survey responses, S14 reported that his learning goal was 'I'd like to attain a very high level of proficiency and be able to work as a translator/

Table 5.16 Background information (S14)

Nationality	Italian; Australian
First language	Italian; Hebrew
Foreign language	English; Chinese
Age range	31–40
Course enrolled	Level 2 (CHN222), Study Period 3, 2015
Previous Chinese-language-learning experience	2–3 years' self-learning
Study hours per week (including online tutorial time)	8–10 hours

Data source: recorded interview with S14, 2015.

interpreter or teach Chinese' and his learning motive was 'I hope to use it in my present or future work'. When asked about any difficult aspects of collaborating with a language partner, in both the survey and interview he reported that there were no difficulties with collaboration. However, he reported two difficulties in Chinese-language learning, one being listening, and the other memorising grammar points in the speaking assignment and the oral test.

This student was ambitious and keen to achieve a high final grade in all his subjects at university. Therefore, he normally worked eight hours a day and then studied for five hours in the evening. In the survey questionnaire, he reported that he studied Chinese 8–10 hours a week, which meant 1.6–2 hours a day. The tracking data demonstrated that he spent a significant amount of time on the online Chinese course site (about 125 hours) and focused on the provided resources and assessment-task completion. Additionally, he logged into his account 335 times throughout the study period and the top three items that he accessed were the provided learning resources (including audio and prerecorded mini-lecture videos; tutorial slides; videos for character writing; revision question documents; online quizzes), the weekly homework submission (journals), and his marks.

The main learning aspects that emerge from the quantitative and qualitative data for S14 included positive interest and attitude toward his Chinese learning, liking Chinese based on understanding culture and related subjects, an exceptionally long learning time, and effective use of strategies.

5.8.2 The key LLSs used by S14 and the tools used for these LLSs

This section presents S14's seven key LLSs as listed in Table 5.17. These strategies related to his metacognitive, cognitive, memory, and social-strategy use. His reasons for LLS use, statements, language-learning tools, and relevant LLS categories are also set out in the table.

The results suggested that S14 managed his learning time, memorised a large amount of vocabulary, and practised Chinese writing and speaking. He also actively employed social strategies to interact with his language partner and two Chinese friends.

174 *Individual LLS reports on the interviewees*

Table 5.17 Reasons for LLS use, key LLSs, statements, language-learning tools, and related LLS categories in two learning contexts in S14's data

Reason for LLS use	Key LLS	Statement (paraphrased for brevity)	Data source (Usage)	Language-learning tool	LLS category
Self-directed learning outside the online classes					
Achieving success in the course	Organising	Developing a learning routine	I		Metacognitive
Improving Chinese speaking	Seeking practice opportunities	Talking with a Chinese friend once a week, and chatting with Chinese colleagues frequently at lunchtime	SII (H) I		
Achieving success in the course	Taking notes	Taking notes of new words	I SII (H)	Notebook	Cognitive
Memorising vocabulary in an effective way	Using resources for receiving and sending messages	Searching online for the meaning of Chinese words	I SII (H)	Flashcard and e-dictionary app: Pleco	
	Using mechanical techniques	Memorising words or characters by listening to sound files on flashcard apps over and over again	I SII (H)		Memory
Online class participation					
Establishing relationships with others	Using the tool and modes available to improve communication and interaction	Using emoticons and texts chat to interact with others for language learning, such as praising the other students', speaking, and answering other students' questions	SII (H)	Emoticons (such as smiley face, LOL, and raised hand), text messages	Social
	Netiquette	Responding to tutor and students' questions quickly; keeping the webcam on	I		Social

Key LLSs in self-directed learning outside the online classes

In the interview, S14 described his daily routine, which related to the use of a metacognitive strategy '*Organising*'. His organising of self-learning was around the textbook content, exercises, and assignments. He could not calculate his exact learning time. However, he had a four-hour learning period for all the subjects he was studying, from 7 to 11 p.m. after dinner every day. The routine consisted of learning characters, words, and sentences in each lesson, memorising the new words, and taking notes of all related information on the words for later reviewing. After learning the words, he practised listening to the text, completed the exercises, watched prerecorded mini-lecture videos, and reviewed the grammar points.

The routine also included weekly speaking practice with his Chinese friends and daily practice with Chinese colleagues, which related to the metacognitive strategy of '*Seeking practice opportunities*'. He explained his interaction with the native Chinese speakers in the interview, as presented in Excerpt 4.5. It can be seen that S14 did not plan the conversations purposely for language learning. Indeed, he said that he would not turn his friends into his private tutors. This can also be understood as a cognitive strategy of '*Practising naturalistically*' which may have helped him improve his conversational Chinese through practising in a natural setting.

When talking about vocabulary learning, S14 introduced the sequence of his Chinese learning, which clearly articulated the cognitive strategy '*Using resources of receiving and sending messages*' and the memory strategies '*Using mechanical techniques*' and '*Taking notes*' by using the app Pleco. Finally, he took notes as shown in Figure 4.1, which consists of seven aspects of S14's note-taking. He:

- wrote Chinese characters, words, and Pinyin with tone marks;
- wrote the English meaning of the Chinese characters and words;
- made sentences using the Chinese characters and words;
- used different colours (pencil, black ink, and highlighter) to show the words and their meaning;
- highlighted important information about a word;
- noticed the homonyms of Chinese words; and
- learnt new characters through association.

Key LLSs in online tutorials

S14 attended all eight online tutorials during the whole study period and employed a significant amount of social strategies. The survey and observation data indicated that this student was sufficiently prepared in topic discussions and carefully answered the tutor's questions in online classes. He could remain focused and listen attentively to follow directions and was sometimes willing to answer the other students' questions. In responding to the survey questionnaire, he gave a rating of 5 (always or almost always true of me) to the survey item 'using the emoticons' which related to a social strategy of '*Using the tool and modes available to improve communication and interaction*'. In addition, he treated his classmates and the tutor with respect, which reflected the social strategy of '*Netiquette*'.

176 *Individual LLS reports on the interviewees*

5.8.3 Summary of S14's LLS report

In summary, S14 provides a case of 'no pain, no gain' according to his own understanding of language learning in the interview. This student mentioned the 'pain' was memorising vocabulary and as such, he was obliged to be more engaged. He therefore adopted a wide repertoire of cognitive and memory strategies in vocabulary memorising. Additionally, his strategy use evidenced that he was fully immersed in Chinese language-learning through choosing relevant Chinese subjects, memorising vocabulary, completing assessment tasks, and regularly interacting with others in Chinese. It was this engagement that achieved lasting learning. Of course, this only worked for him as he was so motivated to learn and had a high-level learning goal. As an intermediate-level student, he created opportunities to practise conversational Chinese with native speakers. These practices may have helped him combine already learnt Chinese vocabulary and grammar points in a real conversation.

5.9 Student 15 (S15)

5.9.1 Background information, learning motives, goals, difficulties, and strengths

S15 was a Mandarin and physics teacher (teaching a beginner-level Mandarin class) at a secondary school in Britain. He had studied Mandarin for nearly three years without attending any on-campus or private language-school classes. As a Chinese-language learner in Britain, he had little access to native Chinese speakers. S15 completed all the assessment tasks, and achieved a very high score in the final oral test. Additionally, he made excellent progress, and had moved through two levels (from level one to level four) in the Hànyǔ Shuǐpíng Kǎoshì (HSK) (Chinese proficiency) test within two years (the highest level of HSK is level six). Level four indicates that a student can understand and use 1,200 Chinese words and can communicate with native Chinese speakers fluently on a wide range of topics. Table 5.18 shows S15's background information.

Table 5.18 Background information (S15)

Nationality	British
First language	English
Foreign language	Chinese
Age	31–40
Course enrolled	Level 2 (CHN222), Study Period 3, 2015
Previous Chinese-language-learning experience	Three years self-learning
Study hours per week (including online tutorial time)	10–12 hours

Data source: recorded interview with S15, 2015.

S15's clear learning motives and ambitious goals led to excellent improvement in his performance. His motive was to achieve a high level of Chinese proficiency so that he could teach Chinese, which was his learning goal, and he had three language-learning motives:

- For pleasure and interest;
- I hope to use it in my present or future work;
- Pass HSK tests.

His learning goal was to be a proficient Chinese speaker and he consistently invested approximately two hours every weekday in Chinese learning. In the interview, he described his study period as lasting from 9 or 10 o'clock p.m. until 1 or 2 o'clock a.m. In addition to these specific learning hours, he also managed fragmented time to review Chinese words by using a flashcard app. His final grades and marks demonstrated positive linear relationships between his learning motives, goals, length of learning time, strategies, and performance.

When discussing the difficulties in online Chinese learning, he complained that the time difference between Britain and Australia was the sole difficult aspect of his collaboration with a language partner and he was unable to find a way to overcome this difficulty. This disadvantage limited his social-strategy use, as he seldom attended the online classes or collaborated with a language partner.

The main learning aspects that emerged from the quantitative and qualitative data for S15 included being a Chinese teacher in UK, lack of a Chinese-speaking environment, self-direction in Chinese learning, skilful use of the e-dictionary and Google Translate as learning tools, and use of strategies for reading novels.

5.9.2 The key LLSs used by S15 and the tools used for these LLSs

According to the interview data, S15 employed a wide repertoire of LLSs, with the exception that he used no social strategies. Table 5.19 shows his reasons for LLS use, key strategies, statements, relevant learning tools, and related LLS categories for self-directed learning.

Key LLSs in self-directed learning outside the online classes

S15's LLS adoption was aligned with his language-learning goals. He hoped to improve in all four skills (listening, speaking, reading, and writing) to achieve the highest language-proficiency level. The survey data showed that he believed in three essential aspects of self-learning: maintaining a learning routine, using flashcards, and reading books in Chinese. As a result, he employed relevant metacognitive, memory, and cognitive strategies in his self-learning. In responding to the open-ended survey question regarding the most useful LLS that he had discovered, he wrote the following (Excerpt 5.9):

Table 5.19 Reasons for LLS use, key LLSs, statements, language-learning tools, and related LLS categories in one learning context in S15's data

Self-directed learning outside the online classes

Reason for LLS use	Key LLS	Statement (paraphrased for brevity)	Data source (Usage)	Language-learning tool	LLS category
Improving Chinese proficiency	Organising	Developing a learning routine	I		Metacognitive
		Establishing a quiet study zone	SII (H)		
	Analysing contrastively	Reading novels in two versions, a Chinese and an English version	I	Printed books	
Memorising vocabulary	Using mechanical techniques	Using flashcard apps to memorise vocabulary	I	Flashcard app: StickyStudy	Memory
			SII (H)		
Learning vocabulary	Using resources for receiving and sending messages	Using the e-dictionary to search for the meaning and pronunciation of Chinese words	I	E-dictionary: TrainChinese	Cognitive
			SII (H)		
Developing confidence for self-learning	Making positive statements	Self-encouragement for continuous hard studying	I		Affective
			SII (H)		
Practising conversational Chinese	Self-monitoring	Recording one half of a conversation on a smartphone and then playing the other role by using the recording	I	Recorder on the smartphone	Metacognitive

> **Excerpt 5.9 'Organising' (metacognitive) as the most useful strategy reported by S15**
>
> S15: Routines are important. As soon as a routine is broken it is difficult to get started again. No matter how tired or demotivated I am, I always try to do something. I have done a lot of work with flashcards mainly the app 'StickyStudy'. I constantly read books in Chinese and use HSK exams as motivation. (Data source: survey questionnaire III, S15, 2015)

The student emphasised using the metacognitive strategy of '*Organising*' as he had a learning routine. Similar to S8, the key feature of S15's learning routine was self-discipline and it was particularly valuable to help him complete learning activities, such as using flashcards, and preparing for the HSK exam.

Another feature of S15's learning routine, unlike that of S8, was to be flexible. S15 claimed that he constantly changed learning activities to maintain his learning time and his interest in learning, as shown in Excerpt 4.4. From the excerpt, it can be seen that S15's routine even relieved a certain level of learning anxiety, and this helped prevent him from being distracted by playing games. In addition to the two features discussed above, the third feature of S15's routine was to prioritise the completion of the assessment tasks in the schedule. Once he completed the assessment tasks he tried to find extra time to engage in Chinese-learning activities he was more interested in, such as reading a book written in Chinese. He admitted that this flexible approach had developed after he had enrolled in the online Chinese course. This change demonstrated that the course produced influences on the student's learning routine.

In all learning activities, memorising words by using the flashcard app was highly recommended by S15; this related to the memory strategy '*Using mechanical techniques*'. Previously, he had made thousands of paper cards when he first started to learn Chinese and played with them all the time for memory recall of Chinese words, for example by reordering them, picking a selection to read over, or choosing them randomly for self-testing. He had then installed a flashcard app on his smartphone, which was called StickyStudy. This app helped him to visualise Chinese words efficiently as he was able to memorise them and recall any information related to the Chinese words, such as pronunciation, tones, and even the writing order of a Chinese character. Another app recommended by S15 was an e-dictionary called TrainChinese, which related to the cognitive strategy of '*Using resources for receiving and sending messages*'. Noticeably, this student reported inputting Chinese characters into the e-dictionary using his finger on the screen. He then explained that the purpose of using this input technique was to improve his Chinese-character writing.

As a teacher, S15 understood the meaning of using affective strategies in Chinese-language learning and he always encouraged himself. He applied a rating of 4 to the affective strategy of '*Making positive statements*' in the survey questionnaire responses. He used a Chinese idiom to describe his determination: 愚公移山. He also gave an example of his self-encouragement, showing his enjoyment of each step in the progress he was making in his Chinese-language learning.

180 *Individual LLS reports on the interviewees*

Once, he found a small difference in the first strokes of two Chinese characters, 干 and 千, which made him extremely happy.

What was interesting in the interview data was that S15 used limited social strategies in the online learning, compared to his previous experiences. When he was a beginner, he used to seek immediate feedback about tones and pronunciation from native Chinese speakers. After the cumulative vocabulary and grammar learning, he focused on vocabulary expansion, refining the meaning of known words, and learning more advanced grammatical patterns. These learning activities produced an impact on his social-strategy adoption as he could rely on checking other resources, such as websites, to overcome the disadvantage of the lack of interactions with native Chinese speakers. In order to remedy the problem of a lack of a language partner, S15 employed a metacognitive strategy of '*Self-monitoring*' to practise and memorise Chinese dialogues and complete the speaking assignments. After preparing the script for a two-role conversation, he recorded one half of the conversation on his smartphone and left some gaps in the recording, and then he played the other role using the recording until he had memorised it.

5.9.3 Summary of S15's LLS report

In brief, S15's LLS adoption demonstrates how an autonomous student learns a language. The five features of his LLS use were that he:

- had specific short-term and clear long-term learning goals;
- was effective in employing metacognitive strategies to manage learning;
- emphasised practising and memorising using cognitive and memory strategies;
- used affective strategies to maintain positive emotions;
- created ways to act two roles to memorise conversations.

Instead of treating Chinese-language learning as deliberate learning with the specific aim of learning vocabulary or grammar points, he was willing to spend enormous amounts of time using Chinese in his favourite learning activities. This deliberate learning may have assisted him in learning grammar rules, but the learning activities were also 'cramming' language knowledge into his short-term memory and thus made the vocabulary and grammar points easier to forget. As such, the activity of reading books in Chinese for enjoyment was essential for him to transfer Chinese content from his short-term memory to his long-term memory. Moreover, this student's achievements suggested that distance students may create LLSs in an unfavourable language environment through balancing the LLSs.

5.10 Student 17 (S17)

5.10.1 Background information, learning motives, goals, difficulties, and strengths

S17 had been learning Chinese for a long time (see Table 5.20), as Chinese was now one of her family languages. She was originally from South Africa and had lived in Taiwan and mainland China for almost four years. After that, she immigrated to

Table 5.20 Background information (S17)

Nationality	South Africa; Australia
First language	Afrikaans
Foreign language	English; Chinese
Age	31–40
Course enrolled	Level 2 (CHN222), Study Period 3, 2015
Previous Chinese-language-learning experience	Two years of Chinese-language learning with two private tutors
Study hours per week (including online tutorial time)	2–4 hours

Data source: recorded interview with S17, 2015.

Australia for nine years with her husband, an Australian Chinese man whose dominant language was English. The student recalled her Chinese-learning experiences and how she had learnt at least 3000 Chinese characters in the one year she had spent studying with a private tutor in Taiwan. She then studied with a different private tutor for another year in mainland China. The difference was that she had studied more than eight hours a week in Taiwan, but just a few hours a week in mainland China. She explained that in mainland China, she had to use more Chinese than in Taiwan because people there spoke little English. Table 5.20 presents her background information.

From observations of the online tutorials, S17's strength was Chinese speaking and she spoke Chinese with clear articulation. This strength was also reflected in her collaboration with her language partner in completing the speaking assignment and the oral test. They both declared that they were a pair of complementary partners as her language partner was good at writing in Chinese. The interview and survey data showed that S17 was satisfied with the cooperation with her language partner and she reported no difficult aspects of the collaboration. Additionally, she attended all eight online tutorials, submitted all the weekly homework, and completed all the assessment tasks.

Similar to S10 but unlike the other interviewees, S17 only used the online course to maintain her Chinese-language proficiency as she hadn't studied Chinese over the last seven years. According to the survey data, an important motive for her to keep learning Chinese was that she hoped to mainly use Chinese to communicate with Chinese-speaking family members. In the interview, she expressed her expectation of reviewing the vocabulary that she had learnt before and achieving a high language-proficiency level.

The main learning aspects that arose from the quantitative and qualitative data for S17 included long-term Chinese-language-learning experience, speaking Chinese at home, building positive relationship with one's language partner, limited learning time, and developing a learning routine.

5.10.2 *The key LLSs used by S17 and the tools used for these LLSs*

The collected data showed that S17 valued metacognitive, social, and cognitive strategies. Moreover, the survey result explained that S17 had a greater preference for using metacognitive strategies than the other LLSs. The interview data indicated that she used cognitive and social strategies, as shown in Table 5.21.

182 Individual LLS reports on the interviewees

Table 5.21 Reasons for LLS use, key LLSs, statements, language-learning tools, and related LLS categories in two learning situations in S17's data

Self-directed learning outside the online classes

Reason for LLS use	Key LLS	Statement (paraphrased for brevity)	Data source (Usage)	Language-learning tool	LLS category
Improving conversational Chinese	Organising	Developing a learning routine	I		Metacognitive
	Practising naturalistically	Talking with family members in Chinese	SII (H) I		Cognitive

Assessment-task completion (speaking assignment)

Reason for LLS use	Key LLS	Statement (paraphrased for brevity)	Data source (Usage)	Language-learning tool	LLS category
Achieving success in the course	Organising	Scheduling meeting time	I		Metacognitive
		Distributing work with a language partner	I		
	Cooperating with peers	Discussing a written draft with a language partner	I		Social
Building positive and collaborative relationships with others	Using the tools and modes available to improve communication and interaction	Using different contact tools to interact with different groups of people	I	Email, WhatsApp, WeChat	Social

Key LLSs in self-directed learning outside the online classes

As she had a limited amount of time every week to spend on her learning, S17 felt stressed and emphasised that time management was important to balance family, work, and her Chinese-language learning. Therefore, according to the survey data and the interview data, she utilised the metacognitive strategy of '*Organising*'. Similar to S8 and S14, she confirmed that self-discipline was the key to successful Chinese learning (see Excerpt 5.10).

Excerpt 5.10 Self-discipline is the key to successful Chinese-language learning (S17)

S17: My week is pretty structured; so you know, I just suppose it is the discipline, not distracted by the other things, you know, so I have set time that I have to do the certain things, and – I make sure that I do these things. (00:39:27 in the recording, Interview, S17, 2015)

S17 had adapted to her Chinese-speaking environment at home, and therefore benefited from this (see Excerpt 4.1). She also employed a cognitive strategy of '*Practising naturalistically*' which reflects that she tried to actively use the language and adapt to the speaking environment. She provided two examples of understanding new words and then using those new words immediately in an everyday conversation. The following example (Excerpt 5.11) was about the Chinese word, 磨叽 <to nag>.

Excerpt 5.11 Example of using the strategy of 'Practising naturalistically' (cognitive) by S17

S17: But if I hear a new word, I just put it into a conversation. For example, my mother-in-law is nagging me, so I asked my husband how to say nagging. S17: 磨叽, 磨叽, 唠叨 <to nag, to nag, to rattle >, I'll tell my mother-in-law with 别磨叽我, <do not nag me, do not nag me>. You know, Chinese mother always pest [sic] you, have to do this, you have to do that, that kind of things? (00:18:44 in the recording, Interview, S17, 2015)

Another example, shown in Excerpt 4.2, was about the Chinese word, 毛病 <problem>. These examples demonstrate how S17 shifted Chinese from her short-term memory to her long-term memory in daily conversations. She had only just learnt how to say these two Chinese words, but later in the textbook, or when the teacher introduced examples of these words, she reinforced her understanding of these two words and recognised the characters.

Key LLSs in completing the speaking assignment

S17 illustrated an example of successful collaborative learning with her language partner. Both of them agreed that they were happy to study with each other. The most successful aspect of the collaboration was that they built an effective relationship which positively influenced their language learning and assignment completion. S17 complimented her language partner, as shown in Excerpt 5.12. It seemed that her language partner worked hard, which motivated S17 to complete the assessment tasks.

> **Excerpt 5.12 Comments on S17's language partner**
>
> *S17: He is the only language partner, I don't think there is any problem to cooperate with him, because he's very motivated. You know, because he's motivated, you don't want to let him down ... he works very hard and I don't drag him down, it seems [a] team element come[s] through it. (00:40:22 in the recording, Interview, S17, 2015)*

When discussing their productive collaboration in completing the speaking assignment, S17 described their collaboration as it related to two strategies. One was the metacognitive strategy of '*Organising*', as they negotiated meeting times and the distribution of work. The other was the social strategy of '*Cooperating with peers*', as they negotiated writing content. S17 described the collaboration in Excerpt 5.13, from which we can see that both learners obtained feedback from each other. This strategy was similar to the collaborative strategy of '*Offering and giving corrections*' Stickler and Lewis (2008).

> **Excerpt 5.13 Example of the strategy of 'Cooperating with peers' (Social) by S17**
>
> *S17: So we both, we basically chat about our work and then, you know, if something [is] wrong, we'll ask questions, [once] we [each] thought the other [had made] mistakes, so [there was] a drop of our grades ... but initially, I wrote two scenes, and he wrote two scenes, he sent [it] to me or I sent [it] to him. And then, we kind of question the others' work. (00:26:27 in the recording, Interview, S17, 2015)*

When talking about the communication tools (email, WhatsApp, WeChat) for interacting with others in the interview, S17 had a metacognition of how to select these tools wisely and how these multiple tools consequently influenced her metacognitive- and social-strategy adoption. In other words, when she considered how to interact with others, communication tools were considered as a social gesture. Email was seen as a professional tool used to save time and show respect, whilst social apps such as WhatsApp and WeChat were seen as a personal tool to reduce communicative anxiety. The two social apps were similar, but she used them to interact with different people. WhatsApp was used to talk with friends in Western countries, and WeChat was used to talk to her parents-in-law in Chinese. She normally negotiated a meeting time with her language partner using email but used WeChat to discuss the assessment tasks. This is also seen as a socio-environmental strategy, '*Using the tools and modes available to improve communication and interaction*', in Hauck and Hampel (2008).

5.10.3 Summary of S17's LLS report

In summary, S17 presents an excellent example of a mature, experienced language learner, who had little anxiety about Chinese learning and was goal-oriented to fulfil particular needs and demands such as communicating with family members, and reinforcing her Chinese learning. The online Chinese course and assessment tasks were not challenging enough for S17 because of her strong foundation, which was built on previous Chinese learning, especially vocabulary learning. Hence, she seldom employed memory strategies, but stressed the use of metacognitive, cognitive, and social strategies to complete assessment tasks and improve her Chinese speaking. However, she succeeded in achieving her short-term learning goal, which was to reinforce her vocabulary. Also, her maturity extended to her communicative capability in collaborative learning with her language partner. They developed a positive relationship and this promoted their positive attitude towards the assessment-task completion, for which they used various metacognitive and social strategies, such as '*Organising*' and '*Cooperating with peers*'.

References

Hauck, M., & Hampel, R. (2008). Strategies for online learning environments. In S. Hurd & T. Lewis (Eds.), *Language learning strategies in independent settings* (pp. 283–302). Bristol, UK: Multilingual Matters.

Hurd, S. (2008). Affective and strategy use in independent language learning. In S. Hurd & T. Lewis (Eds.), *Language learning strategies in independent settings* (pp. 218–236). Bristol, UK: Multilingual Mattters.

Hurd, S., & Lewis, T. (Eds.). (2008). *Language learning strategies in independent settings*. Bristol, UK: Multilingual Mattters.

Stickler, U., & Lewis, T. (2008). Collaborative language learning strategies in an email tandem exchange. In S. Hurd & T. Lewis (Eds.), *Language learning strategies in independent settings* (pp. 237–261). Bristol, UK: Multilingual Matters.

6 Discussion and recommendations for online Chinese learning

6.1 Introduction

This chapter focuses on synthesising and further interpreting the results relating to the most significant and unique aspects of LLS use in online language learning in general, and online Chinese-language learning in particular. The discussion in this chapter, as well as recommendations and suggestions for both language teachers and learners, are organised in reference to the three learning contexts in Sections 6.2 to 6.4:

- Self-directed learning outside online classes (asynchronous environment);
- Assessment-task completion outside online classes (asynchronous environment); and
- Online class participation (synchronous environment).

Section 6.5 discusses two important observations that can be made on the basis of this research project, namely the importance of technology in LLS use and the complexity surrounding LLS classification and adoption.

6.2 Key findings and recommendations in regard to LLS use in self-directed learning outside online classes

In their self-directed learning, the participants had flexibility in managing and controlling their learning activities, and they therefore employed a wide repertoire of LLSs in respect of Oxford's (1990) six strategy categories. This section focuses on five of these. Compensation strategies are not discussed as there were limited data collected in the context of self-directed learning.

6.2.1 Affective strategies

The participants employed five affective strategies, all of which were used in the context of self-directed learning. Of these, two strategies '*Taking risks wisely*' and '*Making positive statements*' were heavily used by the participants, and the strategies '*Discussing your feelings with someone else*' and '*Taking steps to minimise anxiety when practising*' were found to have been used in ways that were different from those shown in previous LLS research. There was no evidence from the data collected in this project to show that the participants employed the other affective strategies identified by Oxford (1990).

'Taking risks wisely' and 'Making positive statements'

The findings in Section 3.2.2 demonstrated that the participants heavily relied on using two affective strategies, *'Taking risks wisely'* and *'Making positive statements'*, when encountering learning difficulties and maintaining positive learning motivation. However, it should be noted that these two strategies were only used by the participants when studying alone as opposed to in their interactions with others (see Section 4.2.2). There are three key factors that influenced their use of the two strategies, as shown in Sections 3.2.2 and 4.3.3.

The first and most important factor found in the interview results is related to the specific online learning environment. The learning difficulties associated with the online environment are: the lack of immediate support from teachers compared with that found in the face-to-face classroom situation; the task of scheduling collaborations with a language partner, which was often difficult and inefficient due to time-zone differences and lack of face-to-face contact; and the feeling of being isolated from other course members. The interview data from S15 suggested that a lack of immediate support from teachers might have led students to use the strategy *'Taking risks wisely'* during conversations with native Chinese speakers. When encountering other learning difficulties, such as feeling slow in achieving learning progress and having no clear picture of the learning journey towards their learning goals, participants' responses indicated that they used the strategy *'Making positive statements'* as a way of maintaining their learning motivation in independent learning.

However, this pattern in the use of affective strategies contrasts with that of on-campus students. On-campus students have previously been found to rank the two affective strategies as low-frequency-range use (ranked 46th and 50th in a 50-LLS questionnaire) (Hong-Nam & Leavell, 2006). In fact, W. Jiang and Wu (2016) found the whole affective-strategy category to have the lowest use by on-campus students among Oxford's six strategy categories; the authors identified this as potentially attributable to ease of access to teachers and peers, which favours the use of social rather than affective strategies. Such differences suggest that it was the online environment, rather than the target language, which caused the high frequency of use of the two affective strategies.

The second influencing factor in the use of these two affective strategies is the difficulties that some of these participants faced in understanding native speakers' accents when communicating with them. For instance, one interviewee who lived in a western Chinese city and another interviewee who lived in a northern one both experienced the difficulty of understanding Mandarin spoken with different accents. Therefore, they had to push themselves to take risks in conversations even though they knew they might make mistakes (*'Taking risks wisely'*), and to encourage themselves (*'Making positive statements'*) to continuously engage with others in such a language environment. Previous research has stressed that generally,

Chinese-language learners often face specific difficulties related to listening comprehension (e.g., distinguishing tones in listening; recognising words by their sounds) which, when combined with language learners' own weaknesses in expression (i.e., errors of lexis, grammar, and pronunciation) (B. Hu, 2010; X. Jin, 2019), may lead to learning anxieties. Accent plays a particularly important role in listening comprehension, as Chinese is a tonal language. Slight differences in pronunciation, tones, and intonations often make it difficult for a learner to understand a conversation.

Moreover, the different geographical locations in which distance students study (as discussed in Section 1.3.2) mean that they could be exposed to different Chinese dialects. When they are exposed to a dialect other than Mandarin, they often have to deal with this challenge by themselves because of a lack of immediate access to their teachers and peers. This, coupled with being isolated from other course members, considerably increases their learning anxiety.

The interview data showed that the participants who lived, or had used to live, in a Chinese-speaking country (S8, S10, S12, S18) felt anxious when listening to Chinese people with strong accents, a fast pace of speech, or unfamiliar vocabulary. This situation could be exacerbated in cases where Chinese-speaking people believe they are speaking standard Mandarin and do not realise that their accents are influenced by their local dialects. In other words, the standard Mandarin accent learnt by students in an online Chinese programme, and the accents they actually experience, could be different. Indeed, these types of differences in accents were reported to be a source of anxiety for participants (S8, S10, S12, S18), as they increased the difficulty that they had in communicating with native speakers, leading to a need to more frequently use the two affective strategies of '*Taking risks wisely*' and '*Making positive statements*'.

The third factor influencing the use of these two strategies is the learner characteristic of age. The hierarchical clustering analysis results (presented in Section 4.3.3) suggest that the older adult participants appeared to take more risks when speaking Chinese ('*Taking risks wisely*') and to encourage themselves more frequently to study hard in Chinese learning ('*Making positive statements*'). The fact that older adults were better able to overcome learning difficulties through adjustments of their emotions in self-directed learning was also confirmed by the interview data, as shown in Section 4.3.3. Previous studies have demonstrated that from primary, secondary, and high school to university students, the older the students are, the more affective strategies they use (M.-L. Chen, 2014; Sepasdar & Soori, 2014). However, there has been no comparison in the literature on how affective strategies are used by different adult age groups, such as the one in the current project between the younger adult group (< 30 years old) and the older adult group ($> = 30$ years old). The findings on the employment of these two affective strategies relate specifically to different *adult*-age-group students, which can be used to guide the promotion of the two affective strategies for different adult-age language learners.

'*Discussing your feelings with someone else*'

When encountering the learning difficulties mentioned earlier in this section, the participants also employed the affective strategy '*Discussing your feelings with someone else'*. This strategy was used in a different way to its use in Oxford's (1990) original proposition, as technology was used to express the online students' feelings. For example, the participant S36 used the Discussion Board to express her feelings about Chinese-language learning (Section 3.3.1). The Discussion Board was deliberately provided for students as a place where they could socialise online without the supervision of the teachers, and it helped to create an online environment in which students could share experiences and offer advice and support.

There are two advantages in using this strategy with such a technology. On the one hand, it is easier for online students who prefer communicating via text to vocal or face-to-face mode to express their feelings, and this is especially the case for shy, introverted, and reticent students (Suler, 2004; Q. Wang & Woo, 2006). On the other hand, students can receive responses that are more relevant to their learning from peers through the discussions than they could from friends and family members. As these peers have a similar background and/or first language, face the same assessment tasks, and have similar issues in using the online learning environments, such interactions are more relevant and meaningful as online students can discuss issues and collaboratively search for and share solutions to problems they encounter in their learning (Woo & Reeves, 2008).

The descriptive analysis showed that the respondents employed '*Discussing your feelings with someone else*' in medium-frequency-range use (Section 3.2.2). However, the responses to this strategy diverged among the respondents, with some students choosing to discuss their feelings with others and other students preferring not to. The lack of opportunities to access peers and external interactants seemed to contribute to the pattern of this strategy's use. Although being isolated is a common phenomenon in online environments (Croft et al., 2010; Hurd, 2007), the participants did have opportunities to use this affective strategy by involving external interactants (family members, colleagues, and friends).

However, swiftly building social relationships with peers was not easy for some of the participants because of the lack of interaction among them, and they therefore hesitated to share their feelings with others on the Discussion Board. Indeed, some interviewees (S17, S18) claimed that they 'don't [didn't] know them (other course members) very well', which affected their rate of use of, as well as the type of comments they posted, on the Discussion Board. A reluctance to post comments in online forums when this is not part of an assessment task is not uncommon (Woo & Reeves, 2008). Earlier research also suggested that online students can be concerned about security issues, and can fear negative feedback in an online environment (Lai & Gu, 2011; S. Wang & Heffernan, 2010). However, this did not appear as a concern in the participants' posts within the courses (e.g., Discussion Board).

'Taking steps to minimise anxiety when practising'

This research found one affective strategy, '*Taking steps to minimise anxiety when practising*', which is not included in those affective strategies already defined by Oxford and other researchers. This strategy refers to online students who choose specific learning activities and groups of Chinese-speaking people to interact with in order to reduce their speaking anxiety. The learning activities in this project in which this strategy was discovered included watching children's TV programmes in Chinese, reading books in parallel-text versions, using flashcards when feeling tired, and talking to native speakers in Chinese. Overall, the interviewees (S5, S8, S14, S17, S18) reported that these learning activities gave them a sense of immersion in Chinese learning, kept them engaged with learning activities, maintained their learning motivation, and strengthened their learning confidence.

The case (S18) in which strangers, such as taxi drivers and unfamiliar Chinese students, were preferred as interactants for practice shows an interesting and effective way to reduce speaking anxiety (Section 3.2.2). This result is different from those found in earlier studies, which suggested students felt anxious when talking with unfamiliar native speakers (Regan, 1998; Regan et al., 2009). Self-esteem played an important role here, as the participant explained that he felt embarrassed when his colleagues and friends corrected his speaking mistakes. A similar self-esteem issue was described in Hurd and Xiao (2010, p. 194). Obviously, these learners feel it is less embarrassing to make errors and mistakes in front of random strangers, as it is unlikely that they will encounter them again. This result also indicates that this strategy may not be applicable to everyone, as each individual student's self-esteem is different.

'*Taking steps to minimise anxiety when practising*' is particularly important for online students as they need to autonomously find practice opportunities and maintain learning motivation. Compared to other affective strategies, the use of this affective strategy often involves practising the target language in natural settings, and learners need to consider the match between the difficulty level of the practice and their own level of language-learning proficiency. Talking with strangers may increase learners' confidence level and consequently motivate them to progress with their language studies.

The difficulty of maintaining positive motivation for distance students in language learning has been frequently pointed out by researchers (Bosmans & Hurd, 2016; Bown & White, 2010; White, 2014), whilst '*Taking steps to minimise anxiety when practising*' provides a practical solution to address that difficulty. It is worth noting that this strategy may not suit all online students as, firstly, not everyone has opportunities to access native Chinese speakers, and secondly, students need to reach a certain proficiency level before they can engage in meaningful conversations with native speakers.

Recommendations

In online language learning, affective strategies play an important role in building learner confidence and the strategy use is aligned with learner autonomy (Hurd, 2008; White, 1995). The following recommendations are proposed based on the literature and the findings from this book:

1. Language teachers could adopt a more proactive role in helping students deal with language-learning difficulties (e.g., difficulties in Chinese-character learning and Chinese speaking) by using the strategy '*Discussing your feelings with*

someone else', as some online students are not willing to openly share their anxiety with other students and teachers. For instance, teachers may privately email students who are reluctant to participate in online discussions and encourage them to share their good ideas about language learning and their learning experiences. Teachers could also take advantage of the course forum and post common learning difficulties (e.g., speaking errors from anonymised previous Chinese-language learners' recordings) experienced by other learners and encourage students to discuss their own. More importantly, during such discussions, teachers can offer specific solutions to address specific learning difficulties. These activities may facilitate meaningful interactions and enable teachers to understand the problems and hurdles that students are facing in a timely fashion.

2. Both online forums and social media apps (e.g., WeChat, Facebook) can be used within an online course to encourage the use of the affective strategy *'Discussing your feelings with someone else'*. Social media apps enable students to share their feelings in a timely and more casual way.
3. Since younger adult students seem to be less likely to use the strategies *'Taking risks wisely'* and *'Making positive statements'*, language teachers could prepare motivational quotes and messages for these students and suggest that distance students print them out and leave them on their desks. This idea aligns with that of White (2006), who suggested that teachers should help online students develop a sense of belonging, and help them maintain optimism in their online language learning.
4. Some online students may feel embarrassed talking to people they know, such as Chinese friends and colleagues, as in the case of S18. These students can be encouraged to use the affective strategy *'Taking steps to minimise anxiety when practising'*. They can apply it not only in real life but also in an online environment, with methods such as finding and chatting with native Chinese speakers who want to learn their native language as a foreign language. Students can be creative in designing these 'steps' to minimise their anxiety, and benefit from incorporating different exercises, such as speaking in front of a mirror; ordering food in a Chinese restaurant; reading novels in parallel-text versions (English and Chinese); and watching Chinese movies with or without English or Chinese subtitles.
5. To reduce learners' anxiety and increase their confidence and motivation, teachers should encourage students to actively engage in interaction in the target language with other language learners and native speakers. Such interaction can be conducted face to face or via social media apps such as WeChat and WhatsApp. As J. S. Lee and Chen Hsieh (Lee & Hsieh, 2019) pointed out, online activities that facilitate students' language output (e.g., interaction with someone online) are more effective than those learning activities that only provide input (e.g., listening to a song or watching movies or dramas in the target language) in terms of helping improve learner confidence and motivation.
6. Due to the greater importance of affective strategies for online students (in comparison with on-campus students), online students should be encouraged to explore other affective strategies whilst considering their effectiveness to their

individual selves, such as '*Using music*', '*Using laughter*', '*Using progressive relaxation, deep breathing, or meditation*', and '*Listening to your body*'. This suggestion echoes those of researchers who recommend that distance students use a wide repertoire of affective strategies when dealing with language-learning difficulties (Hurd & Xiao, 2010).
7. Learning anxiety frequently appeared in the data collected in this research project. As a countermeasure, teachers may consider sending an online anxiety checklist to students to enable them to measure their levels of anxiety at the early stages of and during online courses. The results of the checklist could be used by online students to identify whether they need to seek support from teachers, and by teachers to better support online students.

6.2.2 Cognitive strategies

As summarised in Section 3.2.3, the participants applied a number of cognitive strategies to different learning activities in self-directed learning, such as learning new words and phrases, practising pronunciation, taking notes, and summarising grammar points. The survey results revealed that the participants primarily employed two cognitive strategies, '*Using resources for receiving and sending messages*' and '*Repeating*'. They employed these two strategies to understand or interpret input and to find words or expressions to use the most frequently, and their use depended heavily on digital resources (e.g., CD recordings) and language-learning tools (e.g., e-dictionaries).

'*Using resources for receiving and sending messages*'

The cognitive strategy '*Using resources for receiving and sending messages*' was employed by the participants with a high-frequency range. In this project, the strategy was used in a different way to that defined by Oxford (1990), as the 'resources' used by the participants were mostly digital and they relied on the internet, contrasting with the 'print and non-print resources' in Oxford (1990). One particular use of this strategy, according to the interview and observed data, was the participants' checking of information relevant to new Chinese words via e-dictionaries or websites, such as example sentences and the meaning, pronunciation, and stroke-writing sequence of Chinese characters.

The data, in particular the interview data, in this project have confirmed that the associated language-learning tools are particularly important to online students because of their lack of interaction with teachers and difficulty in getting support for self-directed learning. Unlike on-campus students, who have more opportunities to consult with their teachers in classrooms about the meaning of new words, online students need to rely on themselves to study new words through the use of the various language-learning tools available to them. The interviewees (S12, S13, S15) mentioned they used this strategy frequently whenever they had difficulties in working out the meaning of unfamiliar words or phrases when reading and writing in self-directed learning.

Nearly all interviewees claimed that the use of e-dictionaries and websites was efficient in supporting them to complete various learning activities, and this finding aligns with a wealth of studies in the literature showing the efficiency and popularity of using online learning resources and tools (Alharbi, 2016; Huang, Chern, & Lin, 2009; L. Jin & Deifell, 2013; Klapper, 2008; Liu et al., 2019; McAlpine & Myles, 2003). Students often select online resources and tools which they can adapt to address their individual learning goals and needs (Liu et al., 2019). However, most participants in this project appeared to lack selection strategies in choosing appropriate online resources and tools to aid their learning, or randomly selected resources or learning tools and stuck to them in self-directed learning. These random choices may have affected their learning efficiency, as different learning needs require students to select different online resources or learning tools for effective learning (Alharbi, 2016; Klapper, 2008).

For example, Pleco (an English–Chinese e-dictionary) on smartphones was reported to have been randomly chosen by two interviewees (S5 and S8) as a way to help them with their Chinese reading comprehension. However, using a pop-up dictionary (e.g., a dictionary which gives the meaning of a word when it is double-clicked or selected on a webpage) could be more effective than Pleco when reading a passage on a computer, as it immediately provides basic information relating to the word on the screen, and such an immediate explanation may help reduce extraneous cognitive load by providing information relating to a word when reading (Liu et al., 2019). This example clearly indicates that there is a need to guide online students in selecting and using appropriate language-learning tools.

There are two possible reasons for the participants' random use of just a few language-learning tools, which may have impacted the effective use of the strategy '*Using resources for receiving and sending messages*'. The first is that there are a wealth of online learning tools and resources as technological developments progress and this makes it difficult for both teachers and learners to remain up-to-date with such tools. For instance, in 2015, Google Translate started to offer users a function whereby, if they simply focused their mobile phone cameras on written text, the corresponding translation and its readout would be instantly available to them. Prior to this, users usually would have needed to either type or copy the text into Google Translate (Johnson, 2019). As the number of technological tools and their updates increases, teachers may find that they have limited time to review and learn the use and benefits of these tools. As not all language-learning tools provide the same level of quality and effectiveness for language learning, lack of knowledge about these tools makes it challenging for teachers to suggest, and students to choose, the most suitable ones for effective learning.

The other reason is that the participants lacked awareness of the importance of discussion with their peers about effective tools for coping with various learning activities. Most of the time, they invested their efforts into searching for and testing different tools and resources as they studied alone, but they seldomly communicated their findings with other students. For instance, some interviewees used Short-Term Spoken Chinese (an app accompanying the textbook used in the courses) to review and test themselves on new words in the textbook. However, other interviewees in the same course did not even notice the existence of this app for vocabulary learning. Despite online students' discovery and use of such language-learning tools for self-directed learning, an obvious gap in the sharing of this information exists, which can be bridged by improved communications and discussions among online students.

'Repeating'

The participants' second-most-frequently-used strategy was that of '*Repeating*'. The strategy use by the participants in this research involved a variety of digital tools, such as flashcard apps, CD recordings, and WeChat voice messages. Technology, in this case, is instrumental not only in increasing the use frequency of this strategy, but also in improving its effectiveness in supporting language learning (see Section 3.2.3).

The findings from this research show that digital resources and tools allowed the participants to listen to and repeat what they heard as many times as and whenever they needed, rendering this cognitive strategy one of high-frequency-range use. This research result contrasts with this strategy's use by on-campus students who have previously been found to rank this cognitive strategy as medium-frequency-range use (Hong-Nam & Leavell, 2006). The result also differs from online students' use in Xiao and Hurd's study (2007), in which the online students rated '*Repeating*' at medium-frequency-range use. Such differences further underline the important role of technology in the high-frequency use of '*Repeating*'.

The importance of '*Repeating*' is further supported by the Mann–Whitney U test results, which revealed that the longer the students had studied Chinese, the more frequently they used this strategy (see Section 4.3.4). The findings concur with those from the literature on Chinese-language learning in emphasising the importance of accuracy (e.g., Chu et al., 2015). By contrast, English-language learners rated '*Repeating*' as a low-frequency-range use strategy (ranked 13th of 16 cognitive strategies) (Xiao & Hurd, 2007). '*Repeating*' as a strategy in Chinese-language learning is especially important for distance students, as they have limited opportunities to practise pronunciation and achieve accuracy and fluency with teachers in the classroom (Klapper, 2008).

Although the use of '*Repeating*' was in the high-frequency range, some interviewees' pronunciations and tones were still problematic, according to the observations. Simply using the strategy to imitate native speakers' pronunciation offers no guarantee as to the accuracy of the repeats. This argument also extends to achieving accuracy in writing Chinese characters. A key element beyond '*Repeating*' is immediate feedback, which is often absent in self-directed learning without the support of technology. The lack of immediate feedback from teachers to guide students in self-directed learning could also contribute to the accuracy issue (Truman, 2008).

Electronic feedback, which is provided 'just in time', is a solution proposed by Guichon et al. (2012). By using electronic feedback, online Chinese students may be able to check their errors and mistakes in speaking and Chinese-character writing. Students may be able to immediately correct their mistakes and analyse the reasons for them without waiting until they attend an online class. For instance, students can use a voice-input method to check whether their pronunciation can be recognised by a mobile e-dictionary tool (e.g., Google Translate) or a smart speaker. Similarly, they can also check their character writing by using built-in camera recognition or handwriting input methods when using e-dictionaries or Google Translate. This is similar to the use of a spell checker to help correct spelling errors (Lawley, 2016).

Recommendations

Whilst vocabulary and conversation learning with digital resources is not a novel way of transforming language learning with technology, such tools allow learners to enhance their learning efficiency, especially with the increased availability of learning tools and resources over the internet. However, a clear gap exists, both in this research project and in the literature, when it comes to highlighting how online students require explicit guidance in selecting the most effective resource and tools to support their language learning. Consequently:

1. It is recommended that teachers more actively guide students to assess the capabilities of technology in learning tools and digital resources for effective strategy use. For example, teachers may direct students towards: identifying the most appropriate types of e-dictionary to use; discussing and evaluating the strengths and the weaknesses of different functionalities in these e-dictionaries; and encouraging students to share their experiences of e-dictionary use with their peers.
2. These discussions should ideally begin at the early stages of the students' studies. These early discussions will help students find the appropriate technological tools to suit their different language levels and learning needs. In this process, a teacher could be an important facilitator in terms of directing students to the most suitable tools that will meet their needs and increase their language-learning efficiency through the development of cognitive-strategy use. If this happens, students will better understand the most appropriate tools to be used in a given situation and thus avoid distractions and consequent loss of study motivation.
3. As accuracy in pronunciation is particularly important in Chinese-language learning, it is recommended that distance language learners seek electronic feedback beyond simply using the strategy of '*Repeating*'. Students can apply the examples enumerated earlier or be creative in exploring further use cases and share their use experience with their peers.
4. More broadly, learners can utilise technologies to improve their Chinese speaking. Shi and Stickler (2019) suggested three types of technological tools for achievng this aim. First, tone recognition software such as NewPepper could be used for improving Chinese pronouciation and tones. Second, to facilitate online synchronous classroom interaction, the Elluminate programme may be

useful; thirdly, accessing authentic communication can be achieved through the use of software such as Skype. Language learners may discuss their options with teachers and select the most appropriate tools with which to develop their speaking skills.
5. In conjunction with the strategy of '*Repeating*', online Chinese-language learners are encouraged to use the cognitive strategy '*Formally practising with sounds and writing systems*'. A recent study demonstrated that successful Chinese-language learners are particularly aware of using this strategy and frequently employ it to practise the sounds of Chinese and write notes and messages in Chinese (Chu et al., 2015).

6.2.3 Social strategies

The participants in this research employed a number of social strategies in self-directed learning in order to interact with various people for the purposes of socialising, asking questions regarding assessment tasks, solving technological problems, and finding a language partner for completing related assessment items (see Sections 3.2.4 and 3.3.1). This section focuses on the use of one social strategy in order to interact with native Chinese speakers for socialising. The use of other social strategies when interacting with teachers and peers in self-directed learning is similar to the use of social strategies in the context of assessment-task completion, and these will be discussed in Section 6.3.2.

'Using the tools available to improve communication and interaction'

Specifically, the participants mainly used one social strategy, '*Using the tools available to improve communication and interaction*', to interact with native Chinese speakers, as shown in Section 4.2.2. This strategy refers to students' use of particular functionalities of communication tools to enhance social relations. It is a specific strategy for online language learning found in this research project and it is distinctly different from those social strategies already defined by Oxford (1990) and other researchers. These tools include email, WeChat, and WhatsApp. Among them, WeChat, the most popular instant-messaging app in Chinese-speaking communities (Wu, 2018), exemplifies how technology can be used as a communication tool to build friendship circles with Chinese friends.

There are clear benefits from using this strategy based on the observed and the interview data. Students can take advantage of the availability of Chinese native speakers for conversations in Chinese using social network software such as WeChat. This type of engagement in conversations in the target language is supported by previous studies that have reported on the various benefits of interacting with native speakers for foreign-language learning (Kaan & Chun, 2018; Mahfouz & Ihmeideh, 2009). In these casual conversations, it is likely that students, on the one hand, engage in the negotiation of meaning when interacting with native speakers. Such interactions promote learners' foreign-language development through requiring them to continuously adjust their language output, consequently improving their communicative competence and intercultural understanding (Tudini, 2003). On the other hand, native speakers could also help language learners improve their language proficiency by demonstrating the correct expressions and pointing out errors in voice and text messages because they have knowledge of the target-language culture and speak the language fluently (Maranto & Barton, 2010).

Language learners who frequently imitate Chinese friends' voice messages on WeChat can quickly adjust to native speakers' accents, reuse the syntactic structures they encounter (Kaan & Chun, 2018), increase their understanding of the culture, and even be more motivated to continue their learning (S. Wang, 2019). The findings on using WeChat in this project corroborate those in previous studies, which showed that such interactions help enhance language learners' communicative competence (Bosch, 2009; H.-I. Chen, 2013; Maranto & Barton, 2010), even for beginning-level students, who can benefit from practising Chinese expressions when using WeChat (L. Jin, 2018).

More broadly, the interactive social network nature of WeChat helped the students build a social network and foster their language learning at a distance. Their social network included not only Chinese-speaking friends, but also language teachers and peers. Building social relationships via communication tools is a part of online language learning (Hauck & Hampel, 2008); it is particularly important for distance students as it reduces the feeling of being isolated, expands their access to native-language speakers, and increases communicative opportunities. Social networks encourage students' interaction with others and the related communication tools allow them to foster their learning skills (Derakhshan & Hasanabbasi, 2015).

However, it is not always easy for distance students to use this strategy because of variations in their level of opportunity to access native Chinese speakers. For students in Chinese-speaking countries, it will self-evidently be relatively easy for them to make friends with Chinese native speakers and consequently build a network via social network software such as WeChat. However, this might not be the case for students in non-Chinese-speaking countries.

Recommendations

Given the benefits of using the tools available to improve communication and interaction, as discussed earlier in this section, it is recommended that:

1. Online language students should be encouraged to actively seek opportunities to interact with native Chinese speakers, taking advantage (where possible) of both their physical locations and online communication tools such as social media apps. Apps such as WeChat often provide a rich synchronous environment supported by video and/or audio conferencing, and instant text or audio chat functions, thereby allowing learners to have immediate conversations in Chinese with native speakers. Language chat platforms provide another useful language-learning community that can be found by simply searching for 'chat platforms for Chinese learners'. By using these communication tools and

platforms, online students may be able to improve their Chinese characters or Pinyin typing skills and writing skills through text chatting and listening, and their speaking skills through video and audio conferencing. They can also receive immediate feedback from native Chinese speakers.

2. Language teachers could add guest sessions into online Chinese courses where native Chinese speakers are invited to visit an online group through WeChat groups or synchronous sessions. This would be particularly valuable for those distance students who have limited exposure to an authentic Chinese-speaking environment. To improve the effectiveness of such encounters, teachers could also help students prepare vocabulary and possible questions to use when interacting with the online guests. This would also be a perfect occasion for students to adopt the strategy of '*Using the tools available to improve communication and interaction*' as the student can make use of the in-built features (e.g., text chat, video, and audio functions) in the synchronous environment to interact with such native speakers.

6.2.4 Memory strategies

A total of five memory strategies were identified in Section 3.2.5, which were all used by the participants when they studied alone. This section mainly focuses on four of them, namely '*Creating stories to memorise Chinese-character writing*'; '*Representing sounds in memory*'; '*Placing new words into a context*'; and '*Using mechanical techniques*'. Among these four strategies, all of which reflected how the online participants memorised new words and phrases, '*Creating stories to memorise Chinese-character writing*' is specific to Chinese-language learning. In using these memory strategies, the participants' language-learning tool selection, as reported by the interviewee S8, played a crucial role and helped them learn vocabulary, as the effectiveness of the use of these memory strategies was related to the selected tools. The fifth memory strategy, '*Semantic mapping*', is not discussed in this section due to its low frequency of use.

'Creating stories to memorise Chinese-character writing'

This strategy refers to creating idiosyncratic stories about Chinese characters using the learner's knowledge of radicals as cues (see Section 3.2.5). This knowledge facilitates Chinese-character recognition and memorisation (Shen, 2005; Xu et al., 2014), as radicals often provide a rough idea of the meaning of a character. However, learners cannot memorise a phonetic-semantic compound character just by guessing the meaning of the radicals in the character. Since more than 90% of Chinese characters are semantic-phonetic compounds with a radical and a phonetic component (Y. Hu, 2011), this memory strategy is particularly important to Chinese-language learners in Chinese-character learning.

However, the strategy '*Creating stories to memorise Chinese-character writing*', as a more 'intellectual memory strategy' (Xiao & Hurd, 2007, p. 157), was only used by one participant in this research project. Here, the term 'intellectual memory strategies' (e.g., '*Placing new words into a context*' and '*Semantic mapping*') is used to refer to strategies that are more effective than mechanical memory strategies (e.g., '*Representing sounds in memory*') (Xiao & Hurd, 2007, p. 157). On the other hand, more than 40% of the respondents relied on using mechanical memory strategies ('*Using mechanical techniques*') according to the survey results. In self-directed learning, adult students might be expected to use more intellectual memory strategies as they would normally have a wider knowledge base and a more developed intelligence than younger language learners (Xiao & Hurd, 2007).

Indeed, most of the interviewed students claimed that they felt challenged by the following aspects: memorising character writing; dealing with the large number of homophones in Chinese; remembering the pronunciation of characters; and understanding the meaning of those characters. Two interviewees had even given up learning Chinese-character writing and were focusing instead on learning to recognise Chinese characters and their pronunciations. These results are consistent with the findings of previous studies, which summarised the difficulties of memorising Chinese characters and emphasised the importance of employing specific memory strategies through which English speakers can learn Chinese characters (Grenfell & Harris, 2015; Hayes, 1988; X. Jiang & Zhao, 2001; Kan et al., 2018; Shen, 2005). These results reveal a clear need to make online students more aware of the wide range of uses that the repertoire of memory strategies can be used for in Chinese-character learning.

Language teachers can play an essential role in facilitating Chinese-character learning by using the strategy '*Creating stories to memorise Chinese-character writing*'. Beginner-level students need to be equipped with an initial knowledge of Chinese orthography features (i.e., radical knowledge, graphemics, semantics, and phonetics) before they can increase the use of this memory strategy (see Section 3.2.5). Language teachers could help address this need by guiding beginners to initially learn a small number of different radical-containing compound characters (Xu et al., 2014), and also provide clear instructions and concrete examples to demonstrate how Chinese orthography features can be used to help with memorising these Chinese characters. This small number of characters should thus form the core vocabulary to be learnt in their learning resources, such as the textbook (Xu et al., 2014), rather than the 1,000 most common Chinese characters (Loach & Wang, 2016). By learning a small number of characters related to their learning resources, online students can efficiently use the resultant knowledge of radicals to assist them in creating stories to memorise characters in their self-directed learning.

'Representing sounds in mind' and 'Using mechanical techniques'

The participants used the two strategies '*Representing sounds in mind*' and '*Using mechanical techniques*' concurrently when they were using digital resources. Whilst the use of the two memory strategies was expected, the times at which they were used were impacted by the schedules of the online students. The former strategy refers to students remembering a new word according to its sound, whilst the latter refers to remembering a new word by using tangible techniques, such as flashcards (Oxford, 1990). The ways in which these two strategies were used differed from the usages defined by Oxford (1990), as digital resources and tools expanded the ways in which these two strategies were used. The participants (S5, S8, S14, S18) reported that the technological tools and digital resources they had used were effective and that a variety of learning activities were enabled by these tools and digital resources.

The accessibility, portability, and ubiquity of the technological tools and resources prompted online students to use them as a vocabulary and conversation learning tool in their fragmented time, based on the interviewed data provided by S5, S8, S14, S15, S17, and S18. The use of fragmented time is especially important to online students because they can arrange their learning schedules more flexibly with the support of technology. Therefore, online students may use such mechanical memory strategies via technology to complement other memory strategies in order to learn vocabulary and short conversations, and in particular to review the previously learnt material, at times when the period available for study is very short (Xiao & Hurd, 2007).

'Placing new words into a context' and 'Using mechanical techniques'

'*Placing new words into a context*' refers to memorising new words in a context, such as in a sentence, whilst '*Using mechanical techniques*' refers to remembering a new word by using tangible techniques (Oxford, 1990). The respondents reported that they used these two memory strategies with a medium-frequency-range usage, but their use frequencies varied quite significantly in self-directed learning. About a third of the respondents barely used or never used these two strategies, whilst a similar percentage of respondents always used them. Similar findings have also been reported for on-campus English-language learners (Hong-Nam & Leavell, 2006). These results suggest that the online environment and the Chinese language might not be the influencing factors of the use of these two strategies.

Age was found to be a factor that affected online students' use of '*Placing new words into a context*' and '*Using mechanical techniques*', according to the hierarchical clustering analysis results (see Sections 4.3.2 and 4.3.3). The respondents who were younger adult students seemed to be more willing to spend time on finding associations between words and grouping words ('*Placing new words into a context*') but were less reliant on using flashcards to memorise words ('*Using mechanical techniques*'). These results in terms of age can explain, at least to a certain extent, why the older students in the interviews reported that they were frustrated by the challenge of memorising new Chinese words (which they 'quickly forgot') and understanding the meaning of words when carrying out listening activities; hence their need for more affective-strategy use, as discussed in Section 6.2.1.

Importantly, there is very little research in the literature on the relationship between adult age groups and memory-strategy use in language learning. M.-L. Chen (2014) found that with the increase of age, language learners' memory-strategy use increases. However, her study only compared the differences among primary, secondary, and university students, and did not segment the university students into different adult age groups. It is generally believed that memory peaks between the ages of 16 and 23, and decreases thereafter (Lyu & Xu, 2019). The results of the use of these two memory strategies in relation to age in this project suggest that not all memory strategies are used in the same way by different age groups of adult students.

There are two likely reasons for the different use of the two strategies. One is that older adults are less likely to employ a memory strategy if the strategy is perceived as difficult to use (Lineweaver et al., 2019). In language learning, '*Placing new words into a context*' is seen as one of the 'complex' strategies for vocabulary learning and memorising, whilst '*Using mechanical techniques*' is seen as one of the 'simple' strategies (Nation, 2001). The other reason is that older adults tend to use external aids, such as notes, to help them memorise information (Lineweaver et al., 2019). Given the importance of using both 'simple' and 'complex' strategies, as highlighted by Nation (2001), language teachers should recommend different memory strategies to different age groups correspondingly.

Recommendations

Memorising vocabulary and conversations using digital resources and language-learning tools allows online students to take advantage of technology to enhance their effectiveness in memory-strategy use. It is recommended that language teachers support online students' memory-strategy use in self-directed learning by pointing out a number of ways in which they could use such strategies:

1. When selecting language-learning apps for memorising vocabulary and phrases by using mechanical memory strategies ('*Representing sounds in mind*' and '*Using mechanical techniques*'), learners should consider testing themselves immediately after memorising new words as Li and Tong (2019) found that these tests were found to significantly improve memory recall. The employment of the metacognitive strategy '*Self-evaluating*' can help learners review vocabulary and enhance the effectiveness of their memory-strategy use.
2. As age influences the use of memory strategies ('*Placing new words into a context*' and '*Using mechanical techniques*'), teachers should particularly encourage older adult learners to be aware of the effectiveness of using fragmented time for learning, and spending more time on memorising words by analysing their associations, such as using the complex strategies '*Creating stories to memorise Chinese-character writing*', '*Placing new words into a context*', and comparing characters to spot similarities and differences in shape.
3. To better use the strategy '*Creating stories to memorise Chinese-character writing*' in online learning, language teachers may direct learners to good-quality YouTube videos on learning Chinese characters to help them create amusing and interesting stories, thus turning memorising characters from a burden into a fun activity. This recommendation echoes the research on Chinese-character learning by Shen (2005) and Grenfell and Harris (2015).

6.2.5 Metacognitive strategies

The findings in Section 3.2.7 demonstrated that the participants employed a total of six metacognitive strategies in the three learning contexts, and that all these strategies were used in self-directed learning. This section discusses five of the six metacognitive strategies, the exception being the strategy '*Self-evaluation*', as there were limited data collected for this strategy in self-directed learning.

'Organising'; 'Seeking practice opportunities'; 'Overviewing and linking with known material'; 'Self-monitoring'

As expected, the statistical analyses demonstrated that the questionnaire respondents were heavy users of four particular metacognitive strategies when it came to arranging a comfortable learning environment ('*Organising*'); planning one's time and learning activities ('*Organising*'); seeking opportunities for speaking Chinese ('*Seeking practice opportunities*'); reviewing learning resources ('*Overviewing and linking with known material*'), and noticing errors when speaking Chinese ('*Self-monitoring*'). There were two prominent factors that influenced how the online students used these four strategies, according to the research findings presented in Sections 3.2.7 and 4.3.

The first prominent factor is related to the flipped-classroom approach adopted by the online courses. The flipped-classroom approach encourages the students to gain an initial exposure to the provided learning materials (e.g., prerecorded mini-lecture videos), and requires them to arrange their self-paced learning prior to attending online classes. The learning routines developed by students such as S8, S14, and S17 exemplified how they employed the four strategies in coping with mastering these provided learning resources as part of their self-directed learning. In their learning routines, these students watched the prerecorded mini-lecture videos prior to the online classes, and then arranged the appropriate time and environment in which to complete their assessment items, which are identical to the learning activities described in flipped-language courses (Shih & Huang, 2019), by employing the strategy '*Organising*'. The students also actively sought opportunities (e.g., reading novels, speaking with native Chinese friends) to practise language-learning skills ('*Seeking practice opportunities*'); reviewed the provided learning resources ('*Overviewing and linking with known material*'); and monitored their own comprehension of the video lectures ('*Self-monitoring*') through the completion of the online quizzes relating to the video lectures.

The high-frequency-range use of these metacognitive strategies within the flipped-classroom approach contrasts with their use by students in an online course with a non-flipped-classroom approach. In the latter course, these metacognitive strategies were used at medium-frequency range for planning schedules ('*Organising*'), seeking speaking opportunities ('*Seeking practice opportunities*'), and self-monitoring learning progress ('*Self-monitoring*') (Solak & Cakir, 2015). These differences confirm that the flipped-classroom approach may lead language learners to increase their use of planning and monitoring strategies (Van Vliet et al., 2015). These results were anticipated as, in a flipped-classroom approach, online students are expected to actively take responsibility for their own learning and manage the learning process through self-directed learning (Chiang, 2017; Hung, 2015).

The other prominent factor found in the interview results is related to the students' learning goals. These goals refer to the learners' targets for engaging in online Chinese courses. Self-efficacy is an aspect of learning goals which refers to students' belief in their ability to organise and execute language learning. The interviewees arranged different learning activities in their learning routines based on the different learning goals they aspired to achieve. These learning activities assisted in developing their specific Chinese-language skills, as positive relationships exist between learners' self-efficacy, goal setting, and metacognitive-strategy use (Han & Lu, 2018; J. Wang et al., 2009; Yantraprakorn et al., 2018). Self-discipline, emphasised by both S8 and S15 as a powerful key to their learning routines, helped them in the online courses. Teachers may need to consider individual students' learning goals in order to better support them in developing practical learning plans.

'Preparing questions for attending online classes'

A rather unexpected survey result from this research was that the participants did not use the strategy '*Preparing questions for attending online classes*' as frequently as anticipated (Section 3.2.7). This strategy refers to preparing questions in advance to ask others in the online classes. It is a specific strategy for flipped-classroom learning added to the survey questionnaire, and is distinctly different from those metacognitive strategies already defined by Oxford (1990) and other researchers. Students might apply this strategy to learn from the course-provided materials each week before attending the online classes, as required by the flipped-classroom approach.

This approach emphasises 'interactive, collaborative, and hands-on active learning through the application of the content to problem solving activities' (Y. Wang & Qi, 2018, p. 50) in online classes. These activities require students to be fully prepared for the online classes by mastering the basic contents and bringing their questions to class in order to seek answers. Online students should consider 'task values' in self-directed learning, and this approach as part of their use of the strategy '*Preparing questions for attending online classes*' may help increase their critical thinking and consequently promote learning quality (Van Vliet et al., 2015, p. 1). Here, the task value refers to students' perception of the provided course materials in relation to 'interest, importance and utility' (Van Vliet et al., 2015, p. 1), and use of this strategy would improve their effectiveness in interacting with teachers and peers in the online classes.

There are two factors contributing to the less-than-expected usage of this strategy. The first is that attending online classes was not compulsory for the students and therefore some students lacked the motivation to prepare the questions every week. Instead, these students emailed the teachers to ask such questions or relied on online resources to find answers (see the cognitive strategy '*Using resources for receiving and sending messages*' in Section 6.2.2). The second factor is that some students did not fully appreciate the importance of learning before classes or the associated benefits of using this cognitive strategy according to the classroom observation. An implication of this is that language teachers could play a more active role in stressing the importance of the flipped-classroom approach and in raising students' awareness of the benefits of using this metacognitive strategy more consciously.

Recommendations

According to the findings of this project, metacognitive strategies are an important factor impacting the success of online students' achievements in self-directed learning. This is especially true of effective implementation of the flipped-classroom approach.

1. More individualised training and support should be provided to help language learners develop metacognitive strategies that suit individual learners' learning goals and learning needs. This should be done at the earliest stage of the students' online learning. For example, a simple survey could be conducted with online students at the beginning of their learning in order to better understand their learning goals and needs. Over time, teachers also need to constantly examine the strengths and weaknesses of each student's learning skills (listening, speaking, reading, and writing) in relation to their own goals, and suggest learning activities and aspects of the course that they should focus on. This will enable individual students to make meaningful decisions based on their learning needs, adopt the metacognitive strategies (e.g., '*Organising*' and '*Seeking practice opportunities*'), and incorporate these strategies into their self-directed learning, such as developing a better personal language-learning routine.
2. Although online quizzes were used in the courses to serve as a self-evaluation and self-monitoring mechanism to check students' understanding of the lecture videos, the existing online-quiz tool only allows yes-or-no answers. Therefore, this research suggests that more detailed and immediate feedback should be provided through multiple channels, such as in the online classes, through short video or audio recordings, via social media such as WeChat. Such feedback might encourage online students to use the strategy '*Preparing questions for attending online classes*' and help improve their effective use of the strategies '*Self-evaluation*' and '*Self-monitoring*' to evaluate their learning progress and learn from their errors.

6.2.6 Summary

This section has discussed the use of LLSs and their relationships to various influencing factors in the context of self-directed learning outside the online classes. From the discussion, four key features have emerged in relation to the use of different LLS categories and the associated influencing factors, and their implications are as follows:

1. Affective strategies are affected by three influencing factors: the online specific environment, individual learner characteristics (i.e., age), and the language environment which the individual students can access. Therefore, students need to be encouraged to appreciate the importance of this strategy category, and to try

to expand its usage when appropriate. At the same time, they need to consider those influencing factors as useful in helping build learner confidence and maintaining positive motivation in independent learning.
2. Metacognitive strategies are influenced by two prominent factors: the flipped-classroom approach adopted by online courses, and individual learner characteristics (i.e., self-esteem and learning goals). Therefore, these factors require the students to use effective metacognitive strategies to coordinate their learning.
3. Technology use was found to be a notable factor which influenced the effectiveness of the students' use of cognitive, memory, and social strategies. Teachers may assist students by selecting the most effective language-learning and communication tools to support their employment of these three strategy categories.
4. Memory strategies are influenced by the specific features of Chinese characters and individual learner characteristics (i.e., language-proficiency level and age), and technology plays a crucial role in facilitating the effective use of this strategy category.

In summary, the discussion in this section advances our understanding of students' LLS use in the context of self-directed learning. Firstly, self-directed learning, an important part of online learning, facilitates the employment of a distinctive set of LLSs which reflect students' autonomous learning. In particular, the asynchronous environment allows language learners to have more time and greater opportunities to employ a wider range of LLSs. Secondly, technology plays an important role in enhancing the effectiveness of LLSs. Thirdly, Chinese-language learning influences students' LLS use, especially in relation to memory strategies. Students therefore not only need to develop an awareness of LLSs in self-directed learning, but also to acquire sufficient knowledge about the tools and digital resources that facilitate language learning. Teachers need to provide appropriate strategy training in order to guide students in practising suitable LLSs, which enable them to cope with self-directed learning, rather than leaving language learners on their own to undertake the selection and use of LLSs.

6.3 Key findings and recommendations in regard to LLS use in assessment-task completion

In assessment-task completion, the participants had to collaborate with their language partners outside the classes. They employed 13 LLSs in respect of Oxford's (1990) five strategy categories: namely cognitive, social, memory, compensation, and metacognitive strategies. This section offers further discussion on the key features of participants' use of cognitive, social, and compensation strategies. Memory and metacognitive strategies are not included because of their low frequency of use in this learning context.

6.3.1 Cognitive strategies

The participants used four cognitive strategies when they studied alone and collaborated with others to complete assessment tasks (Section 3.2.3). Most cognitive-strategy use in this learning context is similar to the use in self-directed learning, such as searching online for the meaning of Chinese words ('*Using resources for receiving and sending messages*'); reading aloud ('*Formally practising with sounds and writing systems*'); and imitating native speakers' pronunciation ('*Repeating*'). Therefore, this section only focuses on one cognitive strategy specific to collaborative learning in this learning context, '*Learning from other students' written work*'.

A somewhat unexpected survey result from this research was that the online students did not use the strategy '*Learning from other students' written work*' as frequently as expected (low-frequency-range use) in completing a writing assignment as a form of collaborative learning (Section 3.2.3). This strategy allows the students to enhance their own writing by commenting on the written work of other students (language partners and other peers) and vice versa, and thus it is distinctly different from those cognitive strategies already defined by Oxford and other researchers. The questionnaire respondents reported using it at a low-frequency range.

Collaborative writing is a valuable aid to language learners as it encourages them to scaffold each other's performance and focus on grammatical accuracy, lexis, and discourse through learning from each other (Elola & Oskoz, 2010; Storch, 2002). For online students, this strategy is important, as spending more time using relevant cognitive strategies to revise writing drafts (e.g., replacing or rearranging the content of a written draft whilst noticing its content and linguistic accuracy) may help them, as independent learners, improve the content and the linguistic accuracy of their own writing (Bloom, 2008; De Silva, 2015; Kessler & Bikowski, 2010). In completing their written assignments, the students were required to collaboratively write an essay or design a webpage in Chinese. This is a process in which they were required to share ideas and opinions, check for accuracy, and provide feedback on their peers' work whilst working with their language partners and other peers.

The interview data revealed that some students were either not confident enough to provide corrections and comments because of their low language-proficiency levels, or were inclined to protect their language partner's self-esteem. These might, therefore, be the reasons that led to the low-frequency-range use of this strategy. However, unlike the results in this project, advanced-level online students in the study by Kessler and Bikowski (2010) were motivated whilst participating in a wiki-based collaborative writing task and performed five main actions as part of the collaboration: adding new information, deleting information, clarifying/elaborating on information, synthesising information, and adding web links. Potentially because of their higher language-proficiency level, they appeared to be motivated to join the discussions and were sufficiently confident to provide comments, unlike the participants in this project.

Although the survey results indicated that the employment of the strategy '*Learning from other students' written work*' was low, the students still benefited from the online collaborative writing process according to the results of the content analysis of their written drafts and the interviews. These students corrected their partner's grammar and errors (e.g., missing words), and even the structure of a written draft. These results are similar to the description in Elola and Oskoz (2010), which showed that learners' corrections to their language partners' essays focused on grammar, vocabulary, and sentence structure. In this project, the essay-structure correction only happened with S10, as her writing proficiency was much higher than that of her language partner.

This result differs from that of L. Lee (2010), who found that learners corrected each other's overall structure of writing. However, in Lee's (2010) study, all the participants were on-campus students and had taken part in a brief training on how to use Wikispaces before they started the online collaborative writing element of their course. More importantly, the instructor designed three essay-writing tasks with four clear steps (drafting, revising, editing, and publishing), and provided guidelines and grading criteria to the participants explaining how to contribute to the writing process during their collaboration. In contrast, the participants in this project did not receive specific training in the wiki platform and strategy training for collaboration, although a scaffolding of task stages was offered on their wiki page to guide their writing process.

Recommendations

Learning from a language partner's writing ('*Learning from other students' written work*') could be valuable to online students as it requires them to undertake a process of critical thinking in relation to the written work of their peers, and consequently improve both their own writing skills and those of their fellow students. To better use this strategy, students should be provided with a checklist in the form of questions to be used when providing feedback on their peers' writing. This checklist might include questions such as:

1. Are there inaccurate words and phrases in your language partner's written work?
2. Does your language partner employ appropriate punctuation conventions?
3. Is your language partner's writing interesting? Could you add anything to make it more interesting?
4. Are your language partner's ideas clear? How can you clarify the unclear ones?

By responding to these questions, students may be able to identify both strong and weak aspects of their language partners' drafts and learn from them.

6.3.2 Social strategies

The findings in Sections 3.2.4 and 3.3.1 revealed that the participants employed the most (seven) social strategies when completing assessment tasks, in comparison to other activities. These students employed these social strategies to discuss and negotiate ideas, share information and resources, and coordinate their collaborations. Most of these social strategies are specific to online or collaborative language learning, indicating that the students created such strategies to support their online interactions in collaborative learning. This section discusses four social strategies that are specific to the collaboration in assessment-task completion as follows.

'Netiquette'; 'Sharing with other students'; 'Negotiating with other students';
'Using tools available to improve communication and interaction'

These four strategies are grouped together as a subcategory, 'Collaborating with others'; and they are distinctly different from Oxford's subcategory of 'Cooperating with others' due to the differences between collaborative learning and cooperative learning, as discussed in Section 3.3.1. The participants employed these social strategies for effective communication in collaboration. These results support Oxford's (2017) description of LLS use, in which learners often combine strategies into a strategy cluster to meet a learning need.

The participants' resultant use of a number of LLSs in combination, such as those under 'Collaborating with others', is actually a common approach used by learners when completing a learning task or conducting a learning activity. LLS scholars call such a combination of LLSs a 'strategy cluster' (Cohen et al., 2002, p. 38) or a 'strategy chain' (Oxford, 2011, p. 188). For example, the participants in this research used these social strategies in a sequence: they first sent greetings to each other (*'Netiquette'*), then began to discuss the requirements of the assignments (*'Sharing with other students'*), and followed this by a discussion of work distribution (*'Negotiating with other students'*). The sequence and the types of LLSs are predictable when students are facing a learning activity or a collaborative learning task.

The interviews and the observed data suggest that there are two main motives behind the use of the four social strategies: namely, to achieve the collaborative learning required by the assessment design in the courses, and a desire for good learning outcomes. The assessment design clearly required the students to collaborate with a language partner in these courses. During the collaboration, the students expected to build positive social relationships with others. However, a key challenge in online collaboration is that it is not as easy for the students to build friendships as it would be for classroom students (Le et al., 2018). As a way of overcoming this challenge, the students used the four 'Collaborating with others' strategies to build positive social relationships among peers and teachers. For example, according to the observed data, the participants used the strategy *'Netiquette'* to send greetings and introduce themselves in the Discussion Board to find a suitable language partner.

By doing so, these students constructed personal identities and formed online social networks. This was partly necessitated by the fact that in online collaboration students need to make themselves visible by sending personal information (Harrison & Thomas, 2009), and continuously need to compensate for the infrequency of interactions inherent in distance learning (Hauck & Hampel, 2008). In this sense, the use of the four strategies helps foster a sense of social presence, as these strategies satisfy the two key factors, (i.e., intimacy and immediacy) of such social presence as defined by Short et al. (1976). The use of the four strategies (see Table 3.1) also reflects that the students were able to establish a sense of support for each other through their collaboration. Previous studies have already highlighted that positive correlations exist between social presence, collaborative learning, and overall satisfaction in online environments (Reio & Crim, 2013; So & Brush, 2008).

The other reason for using the four strategies relates to the students' expectation of good learning outcomes, such as the desire to meet or exceed the assessment-task requirements, which in turn fostered the use of collaborative strategies. For example, to satisfy the requirements of a speaking assessment task, two students shared their understanding of the requirements of word choices and word limits first ('*Sharing with other students*'), and then negotiated work distribution, set due dates, discussed meeting times and digital places, and selected communication and learning tools ('*Negotiating with other students*'). They further decided to exchange more information (English meaning, Chinese characters, and Pinyin) in the written drafts by WeChat in order to achieve a better understanding of each other's writing (Section 3.3.1). These observed data reflect that these students adopted a combination of strategies in their writing process and their expectations of achieving a high score were facilitated by a better 'control' of their collaboration through their use of these social strategies. Such controls refer to a sequential process in collaboration, which requires students to organise their collaboration step by step. This process needs to be explicit and visible to all students involved in the completion of the particular task, and they should be encouraged to use both verbal and non-verbal means (emojis, icons, picture, video) to aid communication in the use of these strategies.

However, according to the interview data and the analysis of students' written drafts, most of the online students did not discuss a detailed writing plan and explain their corrections after they had exchanged their written drafts. These results suggested that they did not sufficiently use the social strategy '*Negotiating with other students*' in order to plan a working schedule and provide clear explanations. Students need to take control of their learning when collaborating with others in order to cope with challenges, such as planning and setting goals, and monitoring progress towards the learning goals (Winne & Hadwin, 1998). Negotiating and sharing learning plans is also important to online collaboration as students are required to work together in order to surmount challenges that surface during the collaboration (Hadwin et al., 2018). In parallel, providing each other with clear explanations of their understanding of assessment-task requirements (e.g., word limit) and of the written draft content during a collaboration will benefit students and help them to achieve a successful collaboration. Such explanations reflect the reality that students share responsibility within a collaborative interaction in order to ensure the quality of collaboration (De Wever et al., 2015).

The four strategies in 'Collaborating with others' benefit online students in three ways during collaboration. Firstly, students can build friendships ('*Netiquette*') and are motivated to try harder in their collaborative tasks by using these strategies, such as being more careful to follow the assignment requirements ('*Sharing with other students*' and '*Negotiating with other students*') and writing with more care (e.g., avoid only writing conversations in Pinyin without tones). Secondly, students can gather useful information (e.g., information on effective learning tools and skills) by using the LLSs ('*Sharing with other students*' and '*Using tools available* to improve communication and interaction'). Thirdly, students can improve their language-learning proficiency through practising, sharing, and negotiating with their language partners ('*Sharing with other students*' and '*Negotiating with other students*'). Additionally, students are expected to provide and receive feedback during assessment-task completion (Chang & Windeatt, 2016; L. Lee, 2002), which essentially addresses the 'lurker' phenomenon discussed in Section 2.1.2 (Barnes, 2000; Murday et al., 2008).

Recommendations

In view of the importance of employing the four social strategies for successful online and distance learning, it is recommended that students should be made more aware of the usefulness of applying these strategies in collaboration, and to achieve this, language teachers could guide online students' collaborative social strategy use in a number of ways:

1. In the early stage of online courses, teachers could help students to develop awareness and promote the use of these social strategies by arranging for students to discuss a collaborative writing plan in online classes, which could contain (1) a brief outline of the content that will be covered in their written draft; (2) the responsibilities of each student; (3) a schedule for the completion of different drafts; (4) a list of effective language-learning and communication tools that they might use; (5) the process they will adopt for editing, reviewing, and providing feedback to meet the requirements.
2. As building interaction online presents many challenges, it is important for teachers to help learners develop sound netiquette from the start of their collaboration. For example, teachers could regularly remind students of the need to respond to their collaborators promptly as well as offering encouraging and constructive comments on others' work.
3. Given the benefits of using '*Netiquette*' to improve communication in collaboration, it is recommended that students should use a checklist to see if their online behaviour is appropriate in that environment. This checklist could include suggested online behaviour in general ('Quick guide to good netiquette', 2019); in email interaction ('Digital literacy: computer skills, netiquette and internet safety', 2019), and in online discussions (Goldberg, 2014; Pappas, 2015).

6.3.3 Compensation strategies

The findings in Table 3.1 revealed that the participants employed one compensation strategy, '*Providing extra clarification to others in writing for better understanding*', when collaborating with others in assessment-task completion. This strategy refers to cases in which the students provided more information (e.g., Pinyin, tones, Chinese characters, and English translation) in the written drafts to help both partners gain a better understanding of each other's writing and speaking. This strategy is specific to collaborative Chinese-language learning found in this research, and is not included among those compensation strategies proposed by Oxford and other researchers.

Two main factors contributed to the use of '*Providing extra clarification to others in writing for better understanding*'. The first one is related to the difficulties specific to the Chinese language, such as distinguishing between homophones and overcoming the learner's own weakness in expression (i.e., errors of lexis, grammar, and pronunciation) (B. Hu, 2010; X. Jin, 2019). Providing extra clarification helps Chinese learners be less reliant on other compensation strategies such as '*Guessing meaning*', '*Using linguistic clues*', and '*Paraphrasing*' in reading during online collaboration (Shakarami et al., 2017).

The other factor is related to collaborative learning. During collaboration, students can use this strategy to compensate for the lack of linguistic clues (i.e., pronunciation and tones) in writing and speaking. This is similar to the situation described in Le et al. (2018), in which a participant reported the difficulties of providing elaborate explanations to group members. As Birnholtz et al. (2013) pointed out, a key issue in collaborative writing is the need to provide sufficient information to enable writers to better understand and coordinate each other's efforts, which could be addressed by the strategy '*Providing extra clarification to others in writing for better understanding*'. Students need to carefully consider not only their own writing behaviours, such as only using Pinyin to write Chinese sentences, but also how these behaviours might affect others' understanding during collaboration.

Recommendations

Given that the strategy of '*Providing extra clarification to others in writing for better understanding*' and the associated technology used for realising this strategy enhance the effectiveness of online collaboration, we recommend using the following two examples of the use of this LLS as a starting point:

1. Technology has great potential to support the use of this strategy. For example, students can use, and should be made aware of the potential of using, tracked changes in their editing and should add comments as necessary when they collaborate with their peers for writing tasks, and this could be supplemented by the process of negotiating meeting times to explain each other's editing (e.g., through a WeChat meeting).
2. Students are encouraged to expand the use of this strategy in Chinese-language learning when they complete other forms of collaborative assessment tasks, such as drafting a speaking assignment or a role play.

6.3.4 Summary

This section discussed online students' use of cognitive, social, and compensation strategies and their relationship with a number of influencing factors in the learning context of assessment-task completion. Three key features relating to the differences and similarities among the use of the three strategy categories, in terms of influencing factors and their implications, can be summarised as follows:

1. Collaborative learning emerged as the prominent factor which affected the LLS adoption in all three strategy categories. The participants used social strategies to build positive relationships with peers; compensation strategies to facilitate a better understanding of each other's input; and cognitive strategies to learn from each other.
2. An individual learner characteristic (i.e., language-proficiency level) was found to be the influencing factor which impacted the effective use of cognitive strategies. Low proficiency levels led the students to be conservative in using cognitive strategies in collaborative assessment-task completion, such as giving comments and feedback to others.
3. The specific features of the Chinese language (i.e., Chinese characters, pronunciation, and tones) were found to be an influencing factor in respect of the students' use of compensation strategies.

On the whole, the participants noticed the importance of considering their language partners' feelings and of understanding, and took on their responsibilities in the collaboration to successfully complete assessment tasks. Teachers should incorporate strategy training in the three strategy categories specifically for collaborative tasks, as students will benefit from knowing how and when to use them, and consequently improve the effectiveness of their collaborations.

6.4 Key findings and recommendations in regard to LLS use in online class participation

The participants employed nine LLSs in respect to three of Oxford's (1990) strategy categories in the online classes, namely cognitive, social, and compensation strategies. This section focuses on the use of cognitive and social strategies.

6.4.1 Cognitive strategies

In the online classes, the participants employed four cognitive strategies to search for information online, take notes, imitate teachers' pronunciation, and compare sounds between English and Chinese (Sections 3.2.3 and 3.3.2). This section focuses on one cognitive strategy ('*Analysing contrastively*') as it was the only one that was specifically employed in the online classes. Whilst the other three cognitive strategies were also used, they have been discussed in the context of self-directed learning. More importantly, the strategy '*Analysing contrastively*' has been shown to be a 'very useful' strategy to language learners in an interactive learning environment (Bull & Ma, 2001), such as the online classes in this project.

The strategy '*Analysing contrastively*' originally referred to language learners comparing elements (sounds, vocabulary, grammar) of the target language with elements of their own language in order to determine similarities and differences

(Bull & Ma, 2001; Oxford, 1990). In the online class context, the participants used this strategy to compare English and Chinese pronunciation (Section 3.3.2). They used cross-linguistic similarities between English and Chinese to improve the accuracy of their pronunciation in Chinese. Indeed, their emphasis on accuracy matches the finding by Skehan (2009) that, whilst language learners' LLS use on different learning tasks varied in terms of degree of fluency, accuracy, and complexity, they prioritised accuracy overall in their language learning.

A similar emphasis was also found in the participants' use of this strategy in the self-directed learning context. However, in self-directed learning, it was used to compare the shapes and meanings of the characters containing identical components (e.g., 子 and 于). These comparisons are conducted within one language, which is different from Oxford's (1990) '*Analysing contrastively*' between languages. Use of such a strategy can effectively help enhance Chinese learners' ability to make informed semantic decisions in vocabulary learning and it can be used at different proficiency levels (Shen & Xu, 2015).

As this strategy use was derived from the observed data, it was not possible to determine its usage frequency. However, other researchers have reported that both on-campus and online students used this strategy at a medium-frequency range in order to focus on similarities between the target language and the students' first language (Griffiths, 2003; Hong-Nam & Leavell, 2006; Rokoszewska, 2012; Solak & Cakir, 2015). In other words, previous studies did not seem to support a proposition that learning environment was an influencing factor in the use of this strategy. However, findings from this research indicate that students used this strategy differently in different learning contexts. For example, in self-directed learning the participants employed it to compare the shapes of Chinese characters, whilst in online classes they compared sounds, as the asynchronous environment obviously allowed them to have more time and relevant resources to apply the strategy. In the online classes, the participants used it to compare sounds because they could receive immediate feedback from the teacher on the accuracy of their pronunciation.

This strategy deserves greater attention for two reasons. The first reason is that, within a flipped-classroom approach, in-class learning activities focus on high-frequency cognitive activities involving active learning, peer learning, and problem-solving (McNally, 2017). Online students are therefore expected to use these complex cognitive strategies to compare, analyse, and discuss learning contents within a flipped classroom (Chiang, 2017). From this perspective, they need to realise that cognitive strategies can be used in a different way in self-directed learning and online classes.

The second reason is that students' first languages are often different, and they should therefore be encouraged to take responsibility for finding the similarities and differences between their first languages and the Chinese language. For example, six of the ten interviewees in this project had English as their first language whilst the other four did not. Hence, teachers may not be able to illustrate these similarities and differences using English as a lingua franca. For instance, the vowel 'ü' in Pinyin is similar to the umlaut 'ü' in German or the French 'u'; however, this sound cannot be found in English.

Recommendations

As online students will benefit from using the LLS '*Analysing contrastively*' to promote quality Chinese learning, not only in respect of pronunciation but also Chinese-character learning, they should consciously make use of this strategy to compare the similarities and dissimilarities between the Chinese language and their own language, and within the Chinese language for a deeper understanding of the target language. Other cognitive strategies, such as '*Taking notes*' and '*Highlighting*', can be used in online classes to support the use of '*Analysing contrastively*'. Teachers should also encourage students to discuss these similarities and dissimilarities and to critique responses made by other students in online classes. Students should also take advantage of the online classroom environment (e.g., the platform functions and the availability of the teacher), and employ additional cognitive strategies such as '*Formally practising with sounds and writing system*' to support their language learning.

6.4.2 Social strategies

A total of four social strategies were identified in Section 3.3.2, which were all used by the participants in the online classes. This section primarily focuses on two of them, '*Asking for correction*' and '*Using tools available to improve communication and interaction*', which were employed by the online students to interact with their teachers and peers for effective collaboration. The tools they adopted played an essential role in facilitating the use of these strategies. The use of the other two social strategies in interacting with teachers and peers in online class participation is similar to the use of social strategies in the learning context of assessment-task completion, which was discussed in Section 6.3.2.

'Asking for correction'

As anticipated, the participants employed the strategy '*Asking for correction*' to ask their teachers and peers to correct them during collaboration in online classes. The survey data demonstrated that the respondents rated this strategy at a medium-frequency range of use, which matches the results reported in online language-learning research, such as Solak and Cakir (2015). However, the use frequency of this strategy by online students is different from that of on-campus students, who have been previously found to have used the strategy '*Asking for correction*' less frequently (low-frequency-range use) (Griffiths, 2003; Hong-Nam & Leavell, 2006). This difference in strategy use between online and on-campus students reflects the online students' 'psychological sense of loss' at not being able to receive immediate feedback from teachers and a wish to interact directly in a synchronous environment (Perveen, 2016, p. 34). There are two key factors that influenced the online students' use of this strategy.

The first influencing factor in respect of the use of '*Asking for correction*' is related to the categories of interactants with whom the students interacted. In the online classes, the students were keen to ask for the teachers' correction directly (high-frequency-range strategy use), thereby relying on the synchronicity and immediacy of such a learning context, whilst they were less likely to ask other students for correction (low-frequency-range strategy use). The interview data and the observed data suggested that the online students valued the synchronous interactions with their teachers in the online environment and expected to receive more professional feedback on their Chinese speaking from their teachers. This finding is consistent with Perveen (2016), who reported that online language learners expected to improve speaking skills in a synchronous environment. The interview data and the observed data in this project indicated that *some* beginner-level students often repeated the teachers' pronunciation, expecting the teacher to provide immediate feedback on their pronunciation, which was an indirect use of '*Asking for correction*'.

The second influencing factor in the students' use of '*Asking for correction*' is related to the learning goal of 'I would like to attain a very high level of proficiency and be able to work as a translator/interpreter or teach Chinese'. The participants who chose this learning goal used the '*Asking for correction*' strategy more frequently (medium-frequency-range use) than those students who did not choose the learning goal (low-frequency-range use). This finding aligns with previous research which showed that motivated language learners favoured the use of this social strategy (Griffiths, 2003; Hong-Nam & Leavell, 2006), and in this research, the students who had this learning goal expected to receive as much clarification and feedback from their teachers as possible in order to verify their understanding and pronunciation of Chinese.

'Using the tools available to improve communication and interaction'

The participants employed the strategy '*Using the tools available to improve communication and interaction*' to interact with teachers and peers in the online classes (Section 3.3.2). This strategy was discussed earlier as a social strategy of 'Collaborating with others' when the online students worked with their language partners. In the online classes, this strategy was used differently by the students as its use involved more interactants and technological tools than in the assessment-task completion. In the online classes, the students needed to collaborate with more interactants, including teachers and peers. The use of technological tools here mainly refers to the participants' use of the Collaborate classroom-interface elements (built-in functions), such as the whiteboard, the hand-raising icon, the Participants panel or the use of texts, emojis, and emoticons in the Chat panel. These tools played a central role in sustaining an interactive and communicative learning environment in the online class as they supported teachers and students in their interactions with one another orally, visually, and in text.

Previous studies have already demonstrated similar use of this strategy. Examples can be found in highlighting and underlining words for correction in emails, 'Using symbols for correction' (Stickler & Lewis, 2008, p. 243), and 'Using the tools and modes available to improve communication and interaction' (Hauck &

Hampel, 2008, p. 296). However, these studies discussed this strategy use in an asynchronous environment, such as an email-writing collaboration or a blog activity. The current project found that this strategy was also applied in the synchronous environment, but in different ways and for different purposes. As anticipated, the online students used their voices to effectively communicate with each other. They also typed texts in Chinese and English, and sent emoticons and emojis, as an asynchronous way of interacting in the synchronous environment, in order to increase their opportunities to participate in learning activities, supplement their synchronous interaction, and improve the effectiveness of their collaborative learning. By using various forms of interaction (oral, visual, or textual) to work with a learning content (e.g., discussing a sentence structure), students achieve a more effective interaction with teachers and peers and facilitate knowledge acquisition (Politis & Politis, 2016). This strategy is therefore essential to online students, as through it they can share their answers and evaluate their peers' answers simultaneously.

The observed data revealed that some participants frequently used emoticons and emojis in their text messages ('*Using the tools available to improve communication and interaction*') when collaborating with others, such as praising peers' answers by using an emoji of a thumbs-up, or ending a question with an emoji of a smiley face. This strategy use is particularly important to students in online classes for one main reason. That is, the comparatively limited duration of the online classes in the synchronous environment means that the students have less time to interact with others than in the asynchronous environment. Thus, as a way of improving the effectiveness of their interactions, students often use emoticons and emojis to reflect their 'electronic personalities' and generally add charm to their text messages in an efficient and effective way (LaPointe et al., 2004; Rodrigues et al., 2018). The use of such tools can also create a positive atmosphere, leading to smoother and more effective interactions in online classes – an example being the sending of a broken-heart emoji to highlight the problem of occasional internet lag. In a sense, this also helps develop the social strategy '*Netiquette*' by showing diplomacy, patience, and sensitivity (e.g., using an emoji of a smiley face to soften the tone of a message). It also facilitates the use of the social strategy '*Negotiating with other students*' by showing effective responses, cooperation, and hindsight (Ebner, 2017).

The size of online classes also impacts the frequency of this strategy use, according to the observed data. In this research, when there were more than ten students in a class, this strategy was employed more frequently to send texts, emoticons, and emojis via the Chat panel than was the case in a smaller-sized class. Teachers in smaller-sized classes were able to concentrate on an individual student's performance, provide immediate and targeted support to students, and increase teacher–student interactions (Z. Chen & Yeung, 2015; Handal et al., 2013). The students in such small online classes rarely sent text messages. On the other hand, the students in larger-sized classes tended to asynchronously engage with the language-learning process by, for example, responding to the teachers' questions, typing questions, praising other students, and solving occasional internet issues.

Recommendations

As there is a limited amount of time available in online classes, students may need to improve the use of the two social strategies in order to enhance their communicative efficiency. This can be achieved in a number of ways.

1. Although the strategy '*Asking for correction*' is important to students, they should consider reducing this strategy use in online classes. Instead, they could consider using the strategy '*Asking for correction*' more frequently in self-directed learning, especially via electronic feedback, as discussed in Section 6.2.2, in order to more effectively utilise the time available in online classes.
2. Language teachers should be tolerant of the errors in students' pronunciation (i.e., not correct every mistake) in a synchronous environment. Instead, they should encourage students to take risks to develop their spoken fluency (Lewis, 2011) by allowing them to finish speaking notwithstanding their minor grammar errors.
3. To improve the use of the strategy '*Using the tools available to improve communication and interaction*', teachers should create clear written instructions, illustrated by high-quality screenshots of the functions available within online classes. Students will then be able to refer to these instructions whenever they need to. Video tutorials can also be created to explain how and when to use these functions and thereby facilitate synchronous and asynchronous interactions. The use of these tools could also be practised at the beginning of an online course.
4. Students in larger-sized classes should be encouraged to use a range of communication forms (oral, visual, written) via the technological tools which are available in online classes in order to achieve effective communication with their peers and teachers.

6.4.3 Summary

In summary, this section has mainly discussed the participants' use of cognitive and social strategies in the context of online class participation. Three key features that influenced their cognitive and social strategies, and their implications, are as follows:

1. The synchronous environment provided the participants with less time to interact with others than did the asynchronous environment. Thus, the synchronous nature of the online class required the students to use cognitive and social strategies effectively in order to participate in learning activities and interact collaboratively with others. The students therefore needed to develop an awareness of the optimal use of cognitive and social strategies, as well as sound knowledge of the technological tools available in online classes.
2. In online collaboration, as the participants needed to effectively interact with teachers and peers, their social strategies were consequently influenced by

218 *Discussion and recommendations for online Chinese learning*

different categories of interactants. When taking part in online classes they usually preferred to ask teachers for corrections rather than to ask their peers, due to the synchronicity and immediacy of that learning context.

3. Individual student characteristics (e.g., the learning goal of attaining a very high level of proficiency) appeared to be a factor that influenced their use of the metacognitive strategies.

The size of online classes also impacted students' use of social strategies. When using relevant social strategies, students in smaller classes used synchronous interactions more frequently than those in larger classes. Although the online students noticed the importance of using cognitive and social strategies to participate in online learning activities, seek immediate feedback, and employ the built-in tools in the synchronous environment, they should be more frequently encouraged and trained to use the complex cognitive strategies to compare, analyse, and discuss the answers offered by teachers and other students in online classes (Chiang, 2017) (e.g., '*Analysing contrastively*'). Teachers should also consider the size of their class when deciding whether to use asynchronous or synchronous interactions in online class participation. It is also recommended that language teachers conduct cognitive-strategy training specifically for high-level cognitive activities that involving active learning, peer learning, and problem-solving (McNally, 2017).

6.5 Two important observations from this research project

Based on the data analyses in earlier chapters, and the discussion presented thus far in this chapter, two important observations could be drawn from this research project. One is that the participants' LLS use was significantly influenced by the wealth of technologies available to them, and the other relates to the complexity of LLS classification.

6.5.1 The importance of technology in LLS use

The term 'technology' here refers to the various technological tools and digital learning resources that the online students used to support their LLS use. Technology played an indispensable role in the participants' LLS use in online Chinese learning in a number of ways (see Table 3.1). First of all, technology supported the participants' language learning by reducing learner anxiety in online forums (affective), helping them study online learning resources (cognitive), facilitating online collaboration (social and compensation), memorising vocabulary (memory), and organising and evaluating online language learning (metacognitive). These findings reveal that technology supported the use of LLSs that promote more effective foreign-language learning (cf. Griffiths & Oxford, 2014).

Secondly, technology improved the participants' use of their memory and metacognitive strategy in an autonomous learning process. For example, some participants relied on a quiz-based tool (e.g., Quizlet) to memorise Chinese-character writing, whilst others listened to digital learning resources (e.g., Pimsleur) in their use of memory strategies. By using such technology, students can access a large volume of information that their teachers are not able to provide in a timely fashion (Gilakjani, 2017), maximise the deep learning of learning resources, promote recall of already learnt knowledge (Scott & Beadle, 2016), and control their own learning process (Gilakjani & Sabouri, 2014).

Thirdly, the application of new technological tools highlighted the need to enrich and expand on Oxford's LLS definitions. This project demonstrated the specifics of the participants' decisions in relation to LLSs and technology and how they utilised technology in online learning activities and online collaboration. Example strategies included '*Using resources for receiving and sending messages*', '*Repeating*', '*Representing sounds in mind*', and '*Using mechanical techniques*', all of which were discussed earlier in this chapter. Oxford's (1990) LLS definition did not encompass these aspects, as most of these technological tools and resources did not exist in 1990. Oxford's (2017) recent LLS definition treated technology as a part of teaching and learning, and placed it alongside the concept of self-regulation. By considering technology use as part of their LLS use, students may approach online learning resources and engage in collaborative learning activities in more than one way and therefore make their learning more effective.

Fourthly, the importance of technology is also reflected through the development of specific LLSs that address the needs of online language learning, such as the strategies of '*Netiquette*' and '*Using the tools available to improve communication and interaction*'. Therefore, these strategies expand online learners' LLS repertoire.

LLS researchers and educational instructors should appreciate the importance of technology from three perspectives. The first is that LLS researchers should note that not all language-learning tools are equally effective. Secondly, taking into account the embeddedness of technology and the richness of the available learning tools, LLS researchers need suitable instruments to investigate LLSs in online language learning (Zhou & Wei, 2018). Lastly, technology cannot guarantee that all learners' LLS use is equally effective. This research has revealed that when technology was used appropriately, it facilitated students' LLS use and improved their learning. This suggests that teachers could help language learners improve by integrating technology with LLS use (Zhou & Wei, 2018).

6.5.2 The complexity of LLS classification

The earlier chapters proved that it is challenging to classify some LLSs into single categories. These LLSs were '*Netiquette*'; '*Negotiating with other students*'; '*Using the tools available to improve communication and interaction*'; and '*Providing extra clarification to others in writing for better understanding*'.

A good example of this is the classification of '*Providing extra clarification to others in writing for better understanding*' as a compensation strategy. As illustrated in the discussion in Section 4.2.1, a participant used highlighting, bold letters, and colours to highlight important information in a collaborative written draft in Microsoft Word, and did so for two purposes: in order to help the language partner notice the grammatical corrections in their collaboration (social), and to practise speaking as part of self-directed learning (cognitive). Therefore, this strategy could also be classified as a social or cognitive strategy. A similar picture was described in Cohen et al. (2002), when a learner (Sam) used the cognitive strategy of practising ways to introduce himself in the target language just before attending a job interview. As Sam felt anxious before meeting the interviewer, then such practices could also be considered as a kind of affective strategy. This book embraced suggestions from previous studies, such as Hurd (2008), and classified such strategies by function (Cohen et al., 2002), to highlight the most important feature of these behaviours/actions. Thus, '*Providing extra clarification to others in writing for better understanding*' was only classified as a compensation strategy.

Two aspects of the complexity of LLS classification were found in this research. On the one hand, the abundant availability of technological tools sometimes increased the complexity of understanding learners' LLS use, such as '*Providing extra clarification to others in writing for better understanding*'. For instance, in Figure 3.2, the use of highlighting resulted in the participants' applying two LLSs simultaneously. The participants highlighted important information in a written draft, which meant that they used both '*Using tools available to improve communication and interaction*' (social) and '*Highlighting*' (cognitive) at the same time. On the other hand, collaborative learning promoted the complexity of LLS classification. This reflects the fact that the participants needed to consider their language partner's role when applying LLSs in collaboration.

The observations from this research project are consistent with those of LLS scholars such as Stickler and Lewis (2008) and Park and Kim (2011). They identified new LLSs associated with online language learning, and pointed out that, whilst the current LLS categories as set out by Oxford (1990) and the Strategy Inventory for Language Learning (SILL) can help classify LLSs, they need to be modified to suit different studies. The findings in this book aligned with their observations in that it identified the need to use new LLSs as well as using existing LLS classifications and the SILL.

6.6 Summary

The discussions in this chapter were designed to facilitate a deeper understanding of the key findings relating to why the participants used different types of LLSs in different ways in the three learning contexts: self-directed learning outside the online classes; assessment-task completion; and online class participation.

Overall, this research has identified four prominent characteristics of LLS use by the participants. Firstly, self-directed learning witnessed the adoption of the greatest number of distinct LLSs (from among those considered in this project), with assessment-task completion coming second, and online class participation last. Secondly, affective strategies were only used in one context (self-directed learning), whilst memory and metacognitive strategies were used in two learning contexts (self-directed learning and assessment-task completion), and cognitive, social, and compensation strategies were used in all three contexts. Thirdly, technology (online learning resources, communication tools, and language-learning tools) that could help enhance the effectiveness of LLSs was used differently, in order to suit learner needs, in the three different learning contexts. All these results revealed that students were aware of their responsibilities in relation to the use of LLSs and technology in different learning contexts. Fourthly, clusters of LLSs (e.g., 'Collaborating with others') were commonly used in all learning contexts. This finding supports Oxford's (2017) description of LLS use, according to which learners often combine LLSs in various ways to meet learning needs.

The factors that influence online students' LLS use are multifaceted and complex in nature, and include the different learning contexts, the interactants, the technology, the individual learner characteristics, and the specific features of the Chinese language.

This research therefore advances our understanding of LLS adoption in online language learning in many ways. Firstly, it has discovered nine non-SILL LLSs which are specific to online learning, Chinese-language learning, flipped-classroom learning, or collaborative learning. The technology used, learning environments, and course and task design (flipped-classroom learning and collaborative learning) were found to directly contribute to the emergence of these nine strategies.

Secondly, findings from this research have demonstrated that a total of 14 of Oxford's LLSs were used differently from their originally proposed use, and these differences were attributed to the involvement of technology. For example, the 'resources' in '*Using resources for receiving and sending messages*' in this research are mostly digital and reliant on the internet, and hence are different from the 'print and non-print resources' in Oxford (1990).

Thirdly, this research has revealed the complexity of LLS classification and adoption as shown in the case of potential multiple categorisations of one strategy, and the concurrent use of multiple strategies in completing one learning task.

Finally, this book has given recommendations regarding LLS training and LLS use for language teachers and language learners. Teachers may consider using different kinds of LLS training to support online students' LLS adoption in accordance with the special learning needs imposed by different learning contexts. For example, in self-directed learning, teachers could support online students by: raising their awareness of the use of a wider repertoire of affective strategies; helping students develop metacognitive strategies to effectively manage their self-paced learning; developing their use of social strategies to access native speakers; and providing training in memory strategies for effective vocabulary learning. For collaborative assessment-task completion, teachers could promote the use of cognitive and social strategies specific to the challenges of collaboration among students. For online class participation, teachers may incorporate systematic instruction on how the technological tools in the synchronous classroom can be effectively employed to support the use of cognitive and social strategies and thereby cope with the challenges associated with synchronous learning.

References

Alharbi, M. A. (2016). Using different types of dictionaries for improving EFL reading comprehension and vocabulary learning. *JALT CALL Journal, 12*(2), 123.

Barnes, S. (2000). What does electronic conferencing afford distance education? *Distance Education, 21*(2), 236–247. https://doi.org/10.1080/0158791000210203

Birnholtz, J., Steinhardt, S., & Pavese, A. (2013). Write here, write now! An experimental study of group maintenance in collaborative writing. In *Proceedings of the SIGCHI Conference on Human Factors in Computing Systems* (pp. 961–970). ACM.

Bloom, M. (2008). Second language composition in independent settings: Supporting the writing process with cognitive strategies. In S. Hurd & T. Lewis (Eds.), *Language learning strategies in independent settings* (pp. 103–118). Bristol, UK: Multilingual Matters.

Bosch, T. E. (2009). Using online social networking for teaching and learning: Facebook use at the University of Cape Town. *Communicatio: South African Journal for Communication Theory and Research, 35*(2), 185–200.

Bosmans, D., & Hurd, S. (2016). Phonological attainment and foreign language anxiety in distance language learning: A quantitative approach. *Distance Education, 37*(3), 287–301. https://doi.org/10.1080/01587919.2016.1233049

Bown, J., & White, C. J. (2010). Affect in a self-regulatory framework for language learning. *System, 38*(3), 432–443. https://doi.org/10.1016/j.system.2010.03.016

Bull, S., & Ma, Y. (2001). Raising learner awareness of language learning strategies in situations of limited resources. *Interactive Learning Environments, 9*(2), 171–200. https://doi.org/10.1076/ilee.9.2.171.7439

Chang, H., & Windeatt, S. (2016). Developing collaborative learning practices in an online language course. *Computer Assisted Language Learning, 29*(8), 1271–1286. https://doi.org/10.1080/09588221.2016.1274331

Chen, H.-I. (2013). Identity practices of multilingual writers in social networking spaces. *Language Learning and Technology, 17*(2), 143–170.

Chen, M.-L. (2014). Age differences in the use of language learning strategies. *English Language Teaching, 7*(2). https://doi.org/10.5539/elt.v7n2p144

Chen, Z., & Yeung, A. S. (2015). Self-efficacy in teaching Chinese as a foreign language in Australian schools. *Australian Journal of Teacher Education, 40*(8), 23–42. https://doi.org/10.14221/ajte.2015v40n8.2

Chiang, T. H.-C. (2017). Analysis of learning behavior in a flipped programing classroom adopting problem-solving strategies. *Interactive Learning Environments, 25*(2), 189–202. https://doi.org/10.1080/10494820.2016.1276084

Chu, W.-H., Lin, D.-Y., Chen, T.-Y., Tsai, P.-S., & Wang, C.-H. (2015). The relationships between ambiguity tolerance, learning strategies, and learning Chinese as a second language. *System, 49*, 1–16. https://doi.org/10.1016/j.system.2014.10.015

Cohen, A. D., Oxford, R., & Chi, J. C. (2002). Language strategy use survey. In A. D. Cohen & S. J. Weaver (Eds.), *Style and strategies based instruction: A teachers' guide* (pp. 68–74). Minneapolis, MN: University of Minnesota Center for Advanced Research on Language Acquisition.

Croft, N., Dalton, A., & Grant, M. (2010). Overcoming isolation in distance learning: Building a learning community through time and space. *Journal for Education in the Built Environment, 5*(1), 27–64. https://doi.org/10.11120/jebe.2010.05010027

De Silva, R. (2015). Writing strategy instruction: Its impact on writing in a second language for academic purposes. *Language Teaching Research, 19*(3), 301–323. https://doi.org/10.1177/1362168814541738

De Wever, B., Hämäläinen, R., Voet, M., & Gielen, M. (2015). A wiki task for first-year university students: The effect of scripting students' collaboration. *The Internet and Higher Education*, *25*, 37–44. https://doi.org/10.1016/j.iheduc.2014.12.002

Derakhshan, A., & Hasanabbasi, S. (2015). Social networks for language learning. *Theory and Practice in Language Studies*, *5*(5), 1090–1095. https://doi.org/10.17507/tpls.0505.25

Digital literacy: Computer skills, netiquette and internet safety. (2019). *Netiquette for emails and social media.* Retrieved from https://bowvalleycollege.libguides.com/c.php?g=10214&p=52001

Ebner, N. (2017). Negotiation is changing. *Journal of Dispute Resolution*, *2017*(1), 99.

Elola, I., & Oskoz, A. (2010). Collaborative writing: Fostering foreign language and writing conventions development. *Language Learning and Technology*, *14*(3), 51–71.

Gilakjani, A. P. (2017). A review of the literature on the integration of technology into the learning and teaching of English language skills. *International Journal of English Linguistics*, *7*(5), 95–106.

Gilakjani, A. P., & Sabouri, N. B. (2014). Role of Iranian EFL teachers about using pronunciation power software in the instruction of English pronunciation. *English Language Teaching*, *7*(1), 139.

Goldberg, C. (2014). 15 rules of netiquette for online Discussion Boards. *Touro College.* Retrieved from http://blogs.onlineeducation.touro.edu/15-rules-netiquette-online-discussion-boards/

Grenfell, M., & Harris, V. (2015). Memorisation strategies and the adolescent learner of Mandarin Chinese as a foreign language. *Linguistics and Education*, *31*, 1–13. https://doi.org/10.1016/j.linged.2015.04.002

Griffiths, C. (2003). Patterns of language learning strategy use. *System*, *31*(3), 367–383.

Griffiths, C., & Oxford, R. (2014). The twenty-first century landscape of language learning strategies: Introduction to this special issue. *System*, *43*, 1–10.

Guichon, N., Bétrancourt, M., & Prié, Y. (2012). Managing written and oral negative feedback in a synchronous online teaching situation. *Computer Assisted Language Learning*, *25*(2), 181–197.

Hadwin, A. F., Bakhtiar, A., & Miller, M. (2018). Challenges in online collaboration: effects of scripting shared task perceptions. *International Journal of Computer-Supported Collaborative Learning*, *13*(3), 301–329. https://doi.org/10.1007/s11412-018-9279-9

Han, J., & Lu, Q. (2018). A correlation study among achievement motivation, goal-setting and L2 learning strategy in EFL context. *English Language Teaching*, *11*(2), 5–14. https://doi.org/10.5539/elt.v11n2p5

Handal, B., Maher, M., & Watson, K. (2013). From large to small classes: A classroom window. *Australasian Canadian Studies*, *31*(1/2), 53–72.

Harrison, R., & Thomas, M. (2009). Identity in online communities: Social networking sites and language learning. *International Journal of Emerging Technologies and Society*, *7*(2), 109.

Hauck, M., & Hampel, R. (2008). Strategies for online learning environments. In S. Hurd & T. Lewis (Eds.), *Language learning strategies in independent settings* (pp. 283–302). Bristol, UK: Multilingual Matters.

Hayes, E. B. (1988). Encoding strategies used by native and non-native readers of Chinese Mandarin. *The Modern Language Journal*, *72*(2), 188–195. https://doi.org/10.1111/j.1540-4781.1988.tb04181.x

Hong-Nam, K., & Leavell, A. G. (2006). Language learning strategy use of ESL students in an intensive English learning context. *System*, *34*(3), 399–415.

Hu, B. (2010). The challenges of Chinese: A preliminary study of UK learners' perceptions of difficulty. *The Language Learning Journal*, *38*(1), 99–118. https://doi.org/10.1080/09571731003620721

Hu, Y. (2011). *Mordern Chinese* (7th ed.). Shanghai, China: Shanghai Educational Publishing House.

Huang, H.-C., Chern, C.-L., & Lin, C.-C. (2009). EFL learners' use of online reading strategies and comprehension of texts: An exploratory study. *Computers & Education*, *52*(1), 13–26. https://doi.org/10.1016/j.compedu.2008.06.003

Hung, H.-T. (2015). Flipping the classroom for English language learners to foster active learning. *Computer Assisted Language Learning*, *28*(1), 81–96. https://doi.org/10.1080/09588221.2014.967701

Hurd, S. (2007). Anxiety and non-anxiety in a distance language learning environment: The distance factor as a modifying influence. *System*, *35*(4), 487–508. https://doi.org/10.1016/j.system.2007.05.001

Hurd, S. (2008). Affective and strategy use in independent language learning. In S. Hurd & T. Lewis (Eds.), *Language learning strategies in independent settings* (pp. 218–236). Bristol, UK: Multilingual Mattters.

Hurd, S., & Xiao, J. (2010). Anxiety and affective control among distance language learners in China and the UK. *RELC Journal*, *41*(2), 183–200. https://doi.org/10.1177/0033688210373640

Jiang, W., & Wu, Q. (2016). A comparative study on learning strategies used by Australian CFL and Chinese EFL learners. *Chinese as a Second Language Research*, *5*(2). https://doi.org/10.1515/caslar-2016-0009

Jiang, X., & Zhao, G. (2001). A survey on the strategies for learning Chinese characters among CSL beginners (初级阶段外国留学生汉字学习). *China Academic Journal*, *2001*(4), 10–17.

Jin, L. (2018). Digital affordances on WeChat: learning Chinese as a second language. *Computer Assisted Language Learning*, *31*(1–2), 27–52. https://doi.org/10.1080/09588221.2017.1376687

Jin, L., & Deifell, E. (2013). Foreign language learners' use and perception of online dictionaries: A survey study. *Journal of Online Learning and Teaching*, *9*(4), 515.

Jin, X. (2019). A case study of communication difficulties between a Chinese advanced learner and native speakers. *Journal of Language Teaching and Research*, *10*(1), 114–125. https://doi.org/10.17507/jltr.1001.13

Johnson, K. (2019). Google Translate's camera can now automatically detect languages. *Venture Beat*. Retrieved from https://venturebeat.com/2019/07/10/google-translates-camera-can-now-automatically-detect-languages/

Kaan, E., & Chun, E. (2018). Priming and adaptation in native speakers and second-language learners. *Bilingualism*, *21*(2), 228–242. https://doi.org/10.1017/S1366728916001231

Kan, Q., Owen, N., & Bax, S. (2018). Researching mobile-assisted Chinese-character learning strategies among adult distance learners. *Innovation in Language Learning and Teaching*, *12*(1), 56–71. https://doi.org/10.1080/17501229.2018.1418633

Kessler, G., & Bikowski, D. (2010). Developing collaborative autonomous learning abilities in computer mediated language learning: Attention to meaning among students in wiki space. *Computer Assisted Language Learning*, *23*(1), 41–58. https://doi.org/10.1080/09588220903467335

Klapper, J. (2008). Deliberate and incidental: Vocabulary learning strategies in independent second language learning. In S. Hurd & T. Lewis (Eds.), *Language Learning strategies in independent settings* (pp. 159–178). Bristol, UK: Multilingual Matters.

Lai, C., & Gu, M. (2011). Self-regulated out-of-class language learning with technology. *Computer Assisted Language Learning, 24*(4), 317–335. https://doi.org/10.1080/0958 8221.2011.568417

LaPointe, D. K., Greysen, K. R. B., & Barrett, K. A. (2004). Speak2Me: Using synchronous audio for ESL teaching in Taiwan. *The International Review of Research in Open and Distributed Learning, 5*(1). https://doi.org/10.19173/irrodl.v5i1.166

Lawley, J. (2016). Spelling: Computerised feedback for self-correction. *Computer Assisted Language Learning, 29*(5), 868–880. https://doi.org/10.1080/09588221.2015.1069746

Le, H., Janssen, J., & Wubbels, T. (2018). Collaborative learning practices: Teacher and student perceived obstacles to effective student collaboration. *Cambridge Journal of Education, 48*(1), 103–122. https://doi.org/10.1080/0305764X.2016.1259389

Lee, J. S., & Chen Hsieh, J. (2019). Affective variables and willingness to communicate of EFL learners in in-class, out-of-class, and digital contexts. *System, 82*, 63–73. https://doi.org/10.1016/j.system.2019.03.002

Lee, L. (2002). Enhancing learners' communication skills through synchronous electronic interaction and task-based instruction. *Foreign Language Annals, 35*(1), 16–24. https://doi.org/10.1111/j.1944-9720.2002.tb01829.x

Lee, L. (2010). Exploring wiki-mediated collaborative writing: A case study in an elementary Spanish course. *CALICO Journal, 27*(2), 260–276. https://doi.org/10.11139/cj.27.2.260-276

Lewis, S. (2011). Are communication strategies teachable? *Encuentro, 20*, 46–54.

Li, J. T., & Tong, F. (2019). Multimedia-assisted self-learning materials: The benefits of E-flashcards for vocabulary learning in Chinese as a foreign language. *Reading and Writing, 32*(2019), 1175–1195.

Lineweaver, T. T., Crumley-Branyon, J. J., Horhota, M., & Wright, M. K. (2019). Easy or effective? Explaining young adults' and older adults' likelihood of using various strategies to improve their memory. *Aging, Neuropsychology, and Cognition*, 1–17. https://doi.org/10.1080/13825585.2019.1566432

Liu, X. Q., Zheng, D. P., & Chen, Y. S. (2019). Latent classes of smartphone dictionary users among Chinese EFL learners: A mixed-method inquiry into motivation for mobile assisted language learning. *International Journal of Lexicography, 32*(2), 242–243. https://doi.org/10.1093/ijl/ecz006

Loach, J. C., & Wang, J. Z. (2016). Optimizing the learning order of Chinese characters using a novel topological sort algorithm. *PLOS ONE, 11*(10), e0163623. https://doi.org/10.1371/journal.pone.0163623

Lyu, L., & Xu, Z. (2019). A case study on L2 learning strategies of middle-aged learners. *English Language Teaching, 12*(3), 214–219. https://doi.org/10.5539/elt.v12n3p214

Mahfouz, S. M., & Ihmeideh, F. M. (2009). Attitudes of Jordanian university students towards using online chat discourse with native speakers of English for improving their language proficiency. *Computer Assisted Language Learning, 22*(3), 207–227. https://doi.org/10.1080/09588220902920151

Maranto, G., & Barton, M. (2010). Paradox and promise: MySpace, Facebook, and the sociopolitics of social networking in the writing classroom. *Computers and Composition, 27*(1), 36–47. https://doi.org/10.1016/j.compcom.2009.11.003

McAlpine, J., & Myles, J. (2003). Capturing phraseology in an online dictionary for advanced users of English as a second language: A response to user needs. *System, 31*(1), 71–84. https://doi.org/10.1016/S0346-251X(02)00074-X

McNally, B. (2017). Flipped classroom experiences: Student preferences and flip strategy in a higher education context. *Higher Education, 73*(2), 281–298. https://doi.org/10.1007/s10734-016-0014-z

Murday, K., Ushida, E., & Ann Chenoweth, N. (2008). Learners' and teachers' perspectives on language online. *Computer Assisted Language Learning*, *21*(2), 125–142. https://doi.org/10.1080/09588220801943718

Nation, I. S. P. (2001). *Learning vocabulary in another language*. Cambridge, UK: Cambridge University Press.

Oxford, R. (1990). *Language learning strategies: What every teacher should know*. Boston, UK: Newbury House.

Oxford, R. (2011). *Teaching and researching: Language learning strategies*. London, UK: Routledge.

Oxford, R. (2017). *Teaching and researching language learning strategies: Self-regulation in context* (2nd ed.). New York, NY: Routledge.

Pappas, C. (2015). Ten netiquette tips for online discussions. *eLearning Industry*. Retrieved from https://elearningindustry.com/10-netiquette-tips-online-discussions

Park, H.-R., & Kim, D. (2011). Reading-strategy use by English as a second language learners in online reading tasks. *Computers & Education*, *57*(3), 2156–2166. https://doi.org/10.1016/j.compedu.2011.05.014

Perveen, A. (2016). Synchronous and asynchronous e-language learning: A case study of Virtual University of Pakistan. *Open Praxis*, *8*(1), 21–39. https://doi.org/10.5944/openpraxis.8.1.212

Politis, J., & Politis, D. (2016). The relationship between an online synchronous learning environment and knowledge acquisition skills and traits: The Blackboard Collaborate experience, *14*(3), 204.

Quick guide to good netiquette. (2019). Griffith University. Retrieved from https://www.griffith.edu.au/__data/assets/pdf_file/0024/464055/Netiquette_v2d.pdf

Regan, V. (1998). Sociolinguistics and language learning in a study abroad context. *Frontiers: The Interdisciplinary Journal of Study Abroad*, *4*(2), 61.

Regan, V., Howard, M., & Lemée, I. (2009). *The acquisition of sociolinguistic competence in a study abroad context*. Bristol, UK; Buffalo, NY: Multilingual Matters.

Reio, T. G., & Crim, S. J. (2013). Social presence and student satisfaction as predictors of online enrollment intent. *American Journal of Distance Education*, *27*(2), 122–133. doi:https://doi.org/10.1080/08923647.2013.775801

Rodrigues, D., Rodrigues, D., Prada, M., Prada, M., Gaspar, R., Gaspar, R., . . . Lopes, D. (2018). Lisbon emoji and emoticon database (LEED): Norms for emoji and emoticons in seven evaluative dimensions. *Behavior Research Methods*, *50*(1), 392–405. doi:https://doi.org/10.3758/s13428-017-0878-6

Rokoszewska, K. (2012). The influence of pronunciation learning strategies on mastering English vowels. *Studies in Second Language Learning and Teaching*, *2*(3), 391–413. doi:https://doi.org/10.14746/ssllt.2012.2.3.7

Scott, D., & Beadle, S. (2016). Improving the effectiveness of language learning: CLIL and computer assisted language learning. *European Journal of Language Policy*, *8*(2), 272–275.

Sepasdar, M., & Soori, A. (2014). The impact of age on using language learning strategies. *International Journal of Education and Literacy Studies*, *2*(3), 26–31. doi:https://doi.org/10.7575/aiac.ijels.v.2n.3p.26

Shakarami, A., Hajhashemi, K., & Caltabiano, N. J. (2017). Compensation still matters: Language learning strategies in third millennium ESL learners. *Online Learning Journal*, *21*(3), 235–250. doi:https://doi.org/10.24059/olj.v21i3.1055

Shen, H. H. (2005). An investigation of Chinese-character learning strategies among non-native speakers of chineseChinese. *System*, *33*(1), 49–68. doi:https://doi.org/10.1016/j.system.2004.11.001

Shen, H. H., & Xu, W. (2015). Active learning: Qualitative inquiries into vocabulary instruction in Chinese L2 classrooms. *Foreign Language Annals, 48*(1), 82–99. doi:https://doi.org/10.1111/flan.12137

Shi, L., & Stickler, U. (2019). Using technology to learn to speak Chinese. In C. Shei, M. M. Zikpi, & D.-L. Chao (Eds.), *The Routledge Handbook of Chinese Language Teaching* (1st ed., pp. 509–525). New York, NY: Routledge.

Shih, H.-C. J., & Huang, S.-H. C. (2019). College students' metacognitive strategy use in an EFL flipped classroom. *Computer Assisted Language Learning*, 1–30. doi:https://doi.org/10.1080/09588221.2019.1590420

Short, J., Williams, E., & Christie, B. (1976). *The social psychology of telecommunications*. London, UK: Wiley.

Skehan, P. (2009). Modelling second language performance: Integrating complexity, accuracy, fluency, and lexis. *Applied Linguistics, 30*(4), 510–532.

So, H.-J., & Brush, T. A. (2008). Student perceptions of collaborative learning, social presence and satisfaction in a blended learning environment: Relationships and critical factors. *Computers & Education, 51*(1), 318–336. doi:https://doi.org/10.1016/j.compedu.2007.05.009

Solak, E., & Cakir, R. (2015). Language learning strategies of language e-learners in Turkey. *E-Learning and Digital Media, 12*(1), 107–120. doi:https://doi.org/10.1177/2042753014558384

Stickler, U., & Lewis, T. (2008). Collaborative language learning strategies in an email tandem exchange. In S. Hurd & T. Lewis (Eds.), *Language learning strategies in independent settings* (pp. 237–261). Bristol, UK: Multilingual Matters.

Storch, N. (2002). Patterns of interaction in ESL pair work. *Language Learning, 52*(1), 119–158. doi:https://doi.org/10.1111/1467-9922.00179

Suler, J. (2004). In class and online: Using discussion boards in teaching. *CyberPsychology & Behavior, 7*(4), 395–401. https://doi.org/10.1089/cpb.2004.7.395

Truman, M. (2008). Self-correction strategies in distance language learning. In S. Hurd & T. Lewis (Eds.), *Language learning strategies in independent settings* (pp. 262–282). Bristol, UK: Multilingual Matters.

Tudini, V. (2003). Using native speakers in chat. *Language Learning and Technology, 7*(3), 141–159.

Van Vliet, E. A., Winnips, J. C., & Brouwer, N. (2015). Flipped-class pedagogy enhances student metacognition and collaborative-learning strategies in higher education but effect does not persist. *CBE Life Sciences Education, 14*(3), 1–10.

Wang, J., Spencer, K., & Xing, M. (2009). Metacognitive beliefs and strategies in learning Chinese as a foreign language. *System, 37*(1), 46–56. https://doi.org/10.1016/j.system.2008.05.001

Wang, Q., & Woo, H. L. (2006). Comparing asynchronous online discussions and face-to-face discussions in a classroom setting. *British Journal of Educational Technology, 38*(2), 272–286. https://doi.org/10.1111/j.1467-8535.2006.00621.x

Wang, S. (2019). Project-based language learning: Email exchanges between non-native English speakers. *Theory and Practice in Language Studies, 9*(8), 941–945. https://doi.org/10.17507/tpls.0908.07

Wang, S., & Heffernan, N. (2010). Ethical issues in computer-assisted language learning: Perceptions of teachers and learners. *British Journal of Educational Technology, 41*(5), 796–813. https://doi.org/10.1111/j.1467-8535.2009.00983.x

Wang, Y., & Qi, G. Y. (2018). Mastery-based language learning outside class: Learning support in flipped classrooms. *Language Learning and Technology, 22*(2), 50–74. doi:https://doi.org/10.125/44641

White, C. (1995). Autonomy and strategy use in distance foreign language learning. *System*, *23*(2), 207–221.

White, C. (2006). Distance learning of foreign languages. *Language Teaching*, *39*(4), 247–264. https://doi.org/10.1017/S0261444806003727

White, C. (2014). The distance learning of foreign languages: A research agenda. *Language Teaching*, *47*(04), 538–553. https://doi.org/10.1017/s0261444814000196

Winne, P. H., & Hadwin, A. F. (1998). Studying as self-regulated engagement in learning. In D. J. Hacker, J. Dunlosky, & A. C. Graesser (Eds.), *Metacognition in educational theory and practice* (pp. 277–304). Hillsdale, NJ: Lawrence Erlbaum.

Woo, Y., & Reeves, T. C. (2008). Interaction in asynchronous web-based learning environments: Strategies supported by educational research. *Journal of Asynchronous Learning Networks*, *12*(3–4), 179–194.

Wu, J. G. (2018). Mobile collaborative learning in a Chinese tertiary EFL context. *TESL-EJ*, *22*(2), 1–15.

Xiao, J., & Hurd, S. (2007). Language learning strategies in distance English learning: A study of learners at Shantou Radio and Television University, China. *Journal of Asia TEFL*, *4*(2), 141–164.

Xu, Y. I., Chang, L.-Y., & Perfetti, C. A. (2014). The effect of radical-based grouping in character learning in Chinese as a foreign language. *The Modern Language Journal*, *98*(3), 773–793. https://doi.org/10.1111/j.1540-4781.2014.12122.x

Yantraprakorn, P., Darasawang, P., & Wiriyakarun, P. (2018). Self-efficacy and online language learning: Causes of failure. *Journal of Language Teaching and Research*, *9*(6). https://doi.org/10.17507/jltr.0906.22

Zhou, Y., & Wei, M. (2018). Strategies in technology-enhanced language learning. *Studies in Second Language Learning and Teaching*, *8*(2), 471–495. https://doi.org/10.14746/ssllt.2018.8.2.13

7 Conclusion

7.1 Introduction

This research project has focused on understanding students' language-learning-strategy (LLS) use in online Chinese learning. Whilst LLS research has demonstrated that LLS use is of significant assistance to learners and also makes their learning more effective and enjoyable, much of the early research in the field focused on LLS use in traditional classroom-based language learning. The picture of LLS use that has emerged in this research has clearly demonstrated some unique aspects of the participants' LLS use in online Chinese learning. These aspects reflect the fact that some of these strategies are supported by and are heavily reliant on technology, whilst some are specific to synchronous and asynchronous environments, or to Chinese-language learning.

Unfortunately, some of the earlier studies were lacking in terms of integrating these unique aspects with LLS research. In order to fill this gap, this research has investigated the types of LLSs that learners use in online Chinese learning, and how their LLS use is influenced by the characteristics of the specific learning contexts and individual learner characteristics.

7.2 Contributions of this book

The contributions of this book are related to the findings concerning LLS use in online language learning, both in general and specifically to the three learning contexts: Chinese-language learning, influencing factors, and the recommendations.

Previous studies of LLSs in online language learning are limited in number and mainly focused on LLS use in an asynchronous environment. These studies did not offer researchers additional insights on how strategies are used in synchronous environments in online language learning. In addition, there has been a general lack of research on Chinese-language learning. This research aimed to contribute to filling these gaps by investigating LLS adoption by students engaged in three learning contexts in both synchronous and asynchronous environments in online Chinese learning.

The findings of my research show that the mixed-methods approach is a powerful research methodology for revealing students' LLS use in online learning.

By combining self-reported data with observed data, this project gradually constructed a detailed picture of LLS use by the project participants. This research also confirmed the richness of the technological tools available for online language learning, both those specifically designed for language learning and those designed for other purposes, such as communication tools, and the important roles that technology plays in learners' LLS use in online language learning.

My research has explored LLS use in distinct learning contexts and revealed that students used LLSs and technologies differently in the three different learning contexts that it considered: self-directed language learning outside online classes (asynchronous environment); assessment-task completion (asynchronous environment); and online class participation (synchronous environment). These findings reinforce the recommendation of LLS scholars, such as Oxford (2017) and Huang (2018), that researchers should understand LLS use from a contextual perspective.

The findings of this research confirmed that online students strategically adjust their learning behaviours in line with the learning contexts. Their LLS use is also influenced by the categories of interactants and environmental factors. The analysis of the participants' LLS use suggested that, although they were able to use a wide repertoire of LLSs and technological tools to facilitate their independent learning and solve problems, the efficiency of their efforts could be further improved by practising LLSs consciously and systematically.

Most of the previous LLS studies in online language learning were not set within the context of a flipped-classroom approach. The few studies which have involved this approach have only focused on LLS use in an asynchronous environment. This research contributes to our understanding of the impact of the flipped classroom on students' LLS use in both the asynchronous and synchronous environments. The research has demonstrated that the LLSs used by the participants in the two learning environments were significantly influenced by the flipped-classroom method.

The findings on LLS use in collaborative learning confirmed Oxford's view (2017, p. 48) that: 'language learners often use strategies flexibly and creatively; combine them in various ways, such as strategy clusters or strategy chains; and orchestrate them to meet learning needs'. The participants in this study employed various LLSs and even created a cluster of social strategies in order to effectively collaborate with their language partners, peers, and teachers at a distance. This cluster, which was labelled 'Collaborating with others', contains four social strategies: '*Netiquette*'; '*Sharing with other students*'; '*Negotiating with other students*'; and '*Using tools available to improve communication and interaction*'. These strategies expand the social-strategy categories that have been identified in the literature and relate specifically to collaborative learning. In this respect, it will be noted that many studies in online language learning are still using Oxford's Strategy Inventory for Language Learning (SILL), which does not cover these social strategies, which are specific to collaborative learning.

The findings of this research also provided further evidence of a specific Chinese-character learning strategy, '*Creating stories for memorising Chinese-character writing*', and revealed that the linguistic features of the semantic-phonetic compounds in Chinese characters are factors in determining whether this memory strategy will be used. Given that more than 90% of Chinese characters are semantic-phonetic compounds, this strategy seems likely to be extremely important for mastering Chinese characters in self-directed learning.

The final contribution of this research is in examining relationships between online language learners' LLS use and individual learner characteristics. According to the literature, the influences of some individual learner characteristics (e.g., personality traits, motivation, language proficiency) have been well researched, but others have not received as much attention. The results of this research demonstrated that, although the participants shared certain similarities in using LLSs in online Chinese learning, their idiosyncratic selection of specific LLSs was important and had significant implications for both students and teachers. Four learner characteristics appeared to influence the participants' LLS use: the motive of desiring to become able to communicate with Chinese-speaking friends or family; the learning goal of attaining a very high level of proficiency and being able to work as a translator/ interpreter or teach Chinese; different age groups of adult language learners; and the length of prior Chinese learning experience.

7.3 Implications for online language teaching and learning

The findings of this research contain several important implications for practice in relation to online language teaching and learning and understanding the impacts of learning contexts and individual differences on online Chinese learning. One of the pedagogic implications of this research is that, as technology-enhanced language learning (TELL) options and online learning options increase, LLSs appropriate to TELL need to be taught explicitly in order to equip learners with the ability to adapt to online learning environments. Language learners need strategy training in how to use LLSs efficiently as a way to enhance learning performance.

This research echoes this notion and suggests that the explicit teaching of LLSs, and of their application in both self-directed learning and collaborative learning, may be necessary. This would help students to be more effective in using LLSs and to understand how to use technology to enhance their learning effectiveness. These recommendations and suggestions will provide learners with ideas about how to embed LLSs into online learning activities and assessment tasks, and how to positively reinforce the effective use of LLSs via learning resources and tools.

For language teachers, the findings on the types and the repertoire of LLSs, and on the different ways in which LLSs can be used within different learning contexts, provide a reference point for conducting LLS training for online students. Oxford (1990) suggested that strategy training could be made up of LLS-awareness training, one-time strategy training, and long-term strategy training. Through awareness training, teachers can introduce students to the repertoire and types of LLSs and the different ways of using them in different contexts to students. Teachers can also guide students in their practising of LLSs through specific learning activities by using one-time and long-term strategy training. As Graham (1997) proposed, LLS training 'needs to be integrated into students' regular classes if they are going to appreciate their relevance for language-learning tasks; students need to constantly monitor and evaluate the strategies they develop and use; and they need to be aware of the nature, function and importance of such strategies' (p. 169).

The insights into the individual students' strategy use obtained from this research suggest that it is necessary to integrate LLS instruction with online language-learning materials to suit individual student needs. To meet this challenge, teachers may need to provide explicit instructions regarding LLS use in coping with assessment tasks and learning activities. Such LLS instructions would inform learners of the value and the purpose of LLSs in a systematic way in both self-directed and collaborative learning.

Teachers could also play a pivotal role in helping individual learners develop their learning plans and assist them in achieving improved collaboration with others by identifying individual learners' needs and considering the individual differences which affect students' LLS use. For instance, teachers could provide suggestions on use of affective and memory strategies based on the findings regarding LLS use in different age groups. These suggestions could extend the teacher's role in supporting and facilitating self-directed learning.

Language learners may benefit from understanding the repertoire of LLSs that exist and the different ways in which LLSs can be used in the three learning contexts. Learners need to be aware of the LLSs they use and why they use them to cope with various learning activities or assessment tasks within different learning contexts. Through LLS training, learners may supplement their online-learning-related LLS use, and update their understanding of technology use accordingly. For example, if they are anxious, find online learning difficult, and are less motivated when learning independently, they may learn from LLS training to rely on a repertoire of affective strategies to reduce their learning anxiety, and to discuss learning difficulties with peers and teachers in an online platform. Training based on the findings may also help them make better LLS decisions by raising their awareness of LLSs and helping them select appropriate technological tools in different contexts, or by improving their existing LLS use.

The findings will also be of value in the training of students for collaborative online learning. Learners are likely to benefit from the use of particular strategy categories and technology in collaboration. Through such training, learners may be able to take on more responsibility when collaborating with others, seek more practice opportunities with their peers, and complete collaborative learning activities more effectively and efficiently. Learners need to be aware of the differences between the use of LLSs in a traditional collaboration context and online collaboration.

Language learners would also benefit from an in-depth understanding of their own LLS use and its influencing factors (characteristics of learning environments and individual learners). They would thus be able to decipher their own LLS use and fulfil their individual needs within their own language environments. The individual student reports and the decisions related to LLS and technology use presented in my research could be employed as a reference for language learners in determining their LLS adoption. When learners consciously choose LLSs that fit their needs, these LLSs become 'a useful toolkit for active, conscious, and purposeful self-regulation of learning' (Graham, 1997, p. 2).

7.4 Limitations of this research project

Like any study, this research project had a number of limitations which should be taken into consideration when interpreting the results. Firstly, this research was limited in terms of the relatively small number of participants. Hence, any generalisation of the findings to a larger population with different native languages or cultural backgrounds may be of limited helpfulness. However, as mentioned previously, this limitation has been mitigated somewhat by the mixed-methods approach adopted in this research project.

Secondly, although the participants consisted of beginning-, intermediate- and advanced-level learners, the small number of more advanced participants made it difficult to compare the LLS use of participants of different proficiency levels and its relationships with various potentially influencing factors.

Thirdly, the survey questionnaire was only sent to the students once, after they had completed the whole online Chinese course. Therefore, the results only reflect students' thinking about their LLS adoption at that moment. If the questionnaire had been sent at different times during the course, the results might have been different, as students' LLS use is dynamic.

Fourthly, the classroom observations undertaken for this research were limited by the duration of the observations, which affected both their validity and reliability. Longer-term observations of distance students' self-learning and collaborative learning would be preferable for future research. At the same time, it was not possible to observe the participants' off-screen behaviour in their physical environments whilst they were participating in online classes.

Fifthly, this research was conducted at a single university utilising online Chinese courses that included specific assessment tasks, resources and materials, technological tools, and a flipped-classroom approach. All these tasks, resources, and tools, as well as the delivery approach, can be seen as factors which could have had an impact on the students' LLS adoption, which thus limits the generalisation of the current results.

Finally, this research has clearly illustrated how most LLSs were employed, but data regarding the use of affective and memory strategies were not easy to obtain. This is because most affective and memory strategies could not be observed or tracked, and therefore my data analyses had to heavily rely on students' self-reported data.

7.5 Recommendations for future research

This research project has only been concerned with students' LLS adoption in a limited number of learning tasks and activities in Chinese-language courses. Further research should be undertaken to investigate which LLSs can be used, and how, for a greater variety of learning tasks and activities.

Some interesting questions have arisen from the interview data, concerning matters such as the relationships between online LLSs and language-learning styles, motivation, gender, cultural background, and multilingual background, which my research was not designed to investigate. These are all potential areas that future studies could consider.

This study has analysed data on LLSs that were collected using four research instruments. Future research could consider using other research instruments based on technological tools, such as student online learning diaries or learner portfolios, to gain a more comprehensive understanding of students' LLS use during the learning process. Such research instruments may help reduce the burden on research participants as well as administration costs, whilst improving data quality. In particular, data collection utilising a longitudinal approach would be a helpful way to explore how students develop LLSs whilst they gain language proficiency.

Finally, this project has only investigated the LLSs of online students. Researchers could consider conducting comparison studies between on-campus students and online students to investigate the differences in their LLS use.

References

Graham, S. (1997). *Effective language learning*. Clevedon, UK: Multilingual Matters.
Huang, S. C. (2018). Language learning strategies in context. *The Language Learning Journal, 46*(5), 647–659. https://doi.org/10.1080/09571736.2016.1186723
Oxford, R. (1990). *Language learning strategies: What every teacher should know*. Boston, UK: Newbury House.
Oxford, R. (2017). *Teaching and researching language learning strategies: Self-regulation in context* (2nd ed.). New York, NY: Routledge.

Appendix I
Survey questionnaire

This survey questionnaire consists of three parts. We would appreciate it if you could kindly complete all three parts and provide detailed responses to the open-ended questions in Part III. Thank you very much for your willingness to participate.

Please provide your name (Optional, for research purposes ONLY)

_____

I. Basic information

Please provide the following information by selecting a response.

1. Your age is

    18–20
    21–30
    30–40
    Over 40

2. Are you a Chinese heritage learner (Chinese heritage learners are raised in homes where any Chinese language varieties are spoken)?

    Yes
    No

3. At which level are you studying Chinese through OUA?

    Level 1 (CHN 11, CHN 12)
    Level 2 (CHN 222)
    Level 3 (CHN 31, CHN 32)

4. How long have you been studying Chinese?

    Less than 6 months
    From 6 months to 1 year
    From 1 year to 2 years
    More than 2 years

5. Why are you learning Chinese as a foreign language? (tick all answers that apply)

   For pleasure and interest
   As an intellectual challenge
   To assist me in my present or future work
   To improve my career prospects
   I hope to use it in my present or future work
   To be able to communicate with Chinese-speaking friends or family
   To be able to communicate when visiting a Chinese-speaking country
   It's a compulsory part of my degree
   Others _____

6. How many hours do you spend on learning Chinese each week, on average, including online class time?

   Up to 2 hours
   2–4 hours
   4–6 hours
   6–8 hours
   8–10 hours
   10–12 hours
   Over 12 hours

7. What level are you aiming at in your Chinese studies?

   I just want to get a taste of the language and culture
   I'd like to be able to use Chinese for simple conversations and obtaining information when travelling in a Chinese-speaking country
   I'd like to live and work in a Chinese-speaking country and be able to speak it in most everyday life situations
   I'd like to attain a very high level of proficiency and be able to work as a translator/interpreter or teach Chinese
   Others _____

II. Survey questionnaire incorporating SILL

We would like you to tell us how frequently you use the strategies by simply writing a number from 1 to 5, Please do not leave out any items.

Never or almost never true of me	Generally not true of me	Somewhat true of me	Generally true of me	Always or almost always true of me
1	2	3	4	5

Appendix I: Survey questionnaire 237

Never or almost never true of me means that the statement is very rarely true of you; that is, you do the behaviour which is described in the statement only in very rare instances.

Generally not true of me means that the statement is usually not true of you; that is, you do the behaviour which is described in the statement less than half the time, but more than in very rare instances.

Somewhat true of me means that the statement is true of you about half the time; that is, sometimes you do the behaviour which is described in the statement, and sometimes you don't, and these instances tend to occur with about equal frequency.

Generally true of me means that the statement is usually true of you; that is, you do the behaviour which is described in the statement more than half the time.

Always or almost always true of me means that the statement is true of you in almost all circumstances; that is, you almost always do the behaviour which is described in the statement.

Self-directed learning outside the online classes

	Questionnaire item	1	2	3	4	5
1.	I encourage myself to take risks in Chinese learning, such as guessing meanings or trying to speak, even though I might make some mistakes.					
2.	I encourage myself so that I will continue to try hard and do my best in Chinese learning.					
3.	I talk to someone I trust about my attitudes and feelings concerning the language-learning process.					
4.	I give myself a tangible reward when I have done something well in my Chinese learning.					
5.	I search online for the meaning of Chinese words I don't know (e.g. using an online dictionary site or Google Translate).					
6.	I search for background information on Chinese words online.					
7.	I imitate the tones that native Chinese speakers use.					
8.	I try to understand what I hear or read without translating it word-for-word into my own language.					
9.	I summarise Chinese grammar points in my head as a way to reinforce my understanding.					
10.	I respect my language partner's time when we work together.					
11.	I use character cards to help memorise new Chinese words.					
12.	When I am learning a new Chinese word, I put it in a sentence so I can remember it.					
13.	When I am learning a new Chinese word, I list words I know that are related to it and draw lines to show relationships.					
14.	When speaking with other students, I tend to steer the conversation onto a topic for which I know the words.					

15. I try to speak Chinese whenever I can.
16. I arrange a comfortable environment for studying, to promote learning.
17. I develop a routine so that I study Chinese regularly, not just when there is the pressure of tests.
18. I evaluate the progress I have made in learning Chinese.
19. I record myself speaking by using an audio or video recorder so that I can listen to myself and correct my pronunciation.
20. I review the resources that are recommended in the online Chinese courses.
21. I prepare questions in advance to ask in the online classes.
22. I try to notice my errors when speaking Chinese and to work out the reason for them.

Assessment-task completion outside the online classes (a speaking/writing assignment or an oral test)

Questionnaire item	1	2	3	4	5
23. I read aloud to practise for the speaking assignment.					
24. I read other students' wiki-writing assessments to learn from them.					
26. I put comments on other students' wiki-writing assignments to help them with my suggestions.					
26. I respond as soon as possible to my language partner's queries.					
27. I reply to other students' comments on my wiki page.					
28. I write the conversation scripts of the speaking assignment together with my language partner					
29. I discuss the wiki-writing assignment with my language partner.					
30. I ask my language partner to check my script.					
31. I ask my language partner to correct me whenever I make a mistake.					
32. I ask my teacher to provide feedback on my early drafts.					
33. I encourage other students to leave comments on my wiki page.					
34. I read the comments other students leave on my wiki page.					
35. I revise my wiki-writing assignment taking on board the other students' comments and suggestions on it.					

Online class participation

Questionnaire item	1	2	3	4	5
36. I search for the information online if I do not understand					
37. I take notes.					
38. I prefer keeping the webcam on to let the teacher and other students see me.					
39. I ask other students to correct me.					
40. I ask the teacher to correct me.					

41. If I do not understand, I ask the teacher to explain/repeat.
42. If I do not understand, I ask the other students to slow down, repeat, or clarify what was said
43. I ask the teacher to verify that I have understood or said something correctly
44. I type text messages for effective communication
45. I ask other students to tell me the right word if I cannot think of it.

III. Open-ended questions

1. What is the most difficult part in working with a language partner? How do you deal with it?

    _____
    _____

2. What are the most effective language-learning strategies that you have found so far in your Chinese learning in this course (e.g., strategies for time management; for establishing good study routines; for keeping yourself motivated; for using resources like online dictionaries; textbook, video lectures; for learning vocabulary; for improving your listening, speaking, reading and writing, etc.)?

    _____
    _____

3. Is there anything you do to support your Chinese learning (either during online classes or at other times) that hasn't been covered by the questions?

    _____
    _____

Thank you for your cooperation!

Appendix II
Interview questions

Thank you for letting me interview you about your learning experience in online Chinese courses. I really appreciate it.

Topic 1 Language-learning motives and learning goals

1. Could you please begin by telling me a little about yourself and your Chinese-learning experience? Why do you want to learn Chinese?
2. Why did you prefer to sign up for an online Chinese course rather than an on-campus course?
3. How will having some Chinese language influence your future?
4. Do you have a plan or a goal for your Chinese learning?

Topic 2 Survey questionnaire

5. When and how do you use the strategy of question x in the survey questionnaire?

Topic 3 Language-learning difficulties

6. What have you found most difficult about learning Chinese? How do you overcome these difficulties?
7. What types of software and equipment do you use for learning Chinese? Do you have any difficulties in using them?
8. Do you have any difficulties in completing assessment tasks? How do you overcome these difficulties?

Topic 4 LLSs in coping with various assessment tasks

9. What do you normally do before attending the online classes?
10. How do you memorise vocabulary or Chinese characters?
11. Do you study Chinese with others?
12. Do you reward yourself when you do well in Chinese?

13 How do you prepare for the tests?
14 Which LLSs have you found most useful for completing the assessment tasks?
15 Were there any LLSs in the survey questionnaire that you think might help you become a better language learner?
16 Do you have suggestions for other Chinese language learners who want to enrol in online Chinese courses?

Index

Note: Page locators in **bold** indicate a table. Terms in *italics* indicate a language learning strategy.

affective strategies 29, 37, 66–71, 91, 108, 109, 205–207, 212–214; identified in the interview data **70**; reported by the survey respondents **68**
age 133–138
asking for clarification or verification 156
asking for correction 101, 117, 120, 214–215
assessment tasks and modes of interaction for the courses at the three proficiency levels **9**
assessment-tasks design 8, 9
asynchronous 10, 22–23, 31, 53, 90–93, 103, 105, 108–115, 216, 230
audience 16

Chiang. T.H.-C. (2017) 213
Chinese as a particularly difficult language for English speakers to learn 24–25
Chinese-character-learning strategy use 38
Chinese language 2, 5
Chinese LLS use in TELL 40
Chinese orthography 25
cognitive strategies 30, 66, 71–76, 111, 192, 196, 205–207, 212–214; identified in the interview data **75**; reported by the survey respondents **72**
Cohen, A.D. (et al 2002) 25, 45
compensation strategies 33–34, 66, 85–86, 97–98, 210–211; reported by the survey respondents **85, 86**
creating stories for memorising Chinese character writing 84, 198–199

data collection 14, 15
data sources, their explanations and abbreviations used in this book **15**

definition of LLS 26
discussing your feelings with someone else 68–69, 91, 123, 188–189

Ellis, R. (2012) 3, 26

five-point Likert scale 14

Gao, X. (2010) 26
Griffiths, C. (2004) 4, 26–27
grouping of the 23; survey respondents by the **12**; learner characteristics under consideration **121**

Hauck, M. (et al 2008) 23, 29, 30
Hong-Nam, K. (et al 2006) 194
Hu, B. (2010) 38
Hurd, S. (2008) 42

in-depth individual student studies 14
Individual Difference (ID) 41

Kan, Q. (et al 2018) 5, 24, 38
key findings and recommendations in regard to LLS use in self-directed learning outside online classes 182, 205
key to understand the averages' for language-learning-strategy (LLS) use 14

language proficiency 42–43
learner autonomy 43–44
learning design 7, 8
learning goals 127–133
Lee, L. (2002) 31
length of prior learning of Chinese 138
LLS (language learning strategies) 25, 26; importance of technology in LLS

use 218–219; number of different LLSs used in the asynchronous and synchronous environments, by LLS category **108**; number of LLSs used when interacting with different interactants **116**; repertoire of LLSs in online Chinese learning 55–65
LLS adoption when using Board, WeChat, Google Drive, and email 96
LLS classification, complexity of 219
LLSs specific to online learning 35–36
LLS training 28
LLS use in Chinese speaking 39–40
LLS use in online classes obtained from the observed data **99**

making positive statements 67–68, 135, 187
massive open online courses (MOOCs) 21
mean scores of LLS use by category for the 23; survey respondents **66**
memory strategies 33, 66, 85–86, 97–98, 210–211; identified in the interview data and the open-ended questions from the survey questionnaire **83**; reported by the survey respondents **82**
metacognitive strategies 34–35, 66, 86–90, 95–97, 202–204; identified in the interview data and the open-ended questions from the survey questionnaire **90**; reported by the survey respondents **87**
metacognitive strategy adoption when using Board, WeChat, Google Drive, and email 96
motivation 41–42
motive 127–133

negotiating with other students 208
netiquette 24, 30–31, 77–78, 208–209

O'Malley, M. (et al 1990) 4, 25
online Chinese programme 7, 10
online learning 21, 22
organisation of this book 16
organising 87, 96, 202–203
overviewing and linking with known material 202
Oxford, R. (2017) 4, 26, 27

participant 12–13
Pearson's *r* correlation analysis 15
placing new words into a context 200
practising naturalistically 125
preparing questions for attending online classes 203

repeating 30, 72–73, 194–195
representing sounds in mind 199–200

seeking practice opportunities 132
self-monitoring 202
sharing with other students 94, 208–210
Shen, H. H. (2005) 5, 24, 38
social strategies 30–32, 66, 76–81, 92, 95, 113–114, 118–120, 196–198, 207–210, 214–218; identified in the interview, observed and additional data **80–81**; observed in participants' use of Discussion Board, Google Drive, and WeChat **92**; reported by the survey respondents **77–78**
social strategy use in the asynchronous and synchronous learning environments **113–114**
synchronous 10, 11, 22, 23, 31, 53, 90, 98, 105, 108–115
synchronous and asynchronous environments 10–13

taking risks wisely 187
taking steps to minimise anxiety when practising 189–190
TELL (technology-enhanced language learning) 22–24, 27, 40

using linguistic clues 86
using mechanical techniques 129, 199–120
using resources for receiving and sending messages 72, 192–194
using the tools available to improve communication and interaction 79–80, 95, 103–104, 133, 196–198, 215

WeChat moments 168
White, C. (2010) 29, 190

Xiao, J. (et al) 192

For Product Safety Concerns and Information please contact our EU representative GPSR@taylorandfrancis.com
Taylor & Francis Verlag GmbH, Kaufingerstraße 24, 80331 München, Germany